# Medicinal Plants of Uttarakhand

## Diversity, Livelihood and Conservation

# Medicinal Plants of Uttarakhand

## *Diversity, Livelihood and Conservation*

*by*

Chandra Prakash Kala

BIOTECH

2010

BIOTECH BOOKS

Delhi - 110 035

ISBN 81-7622-209-7
ISBN 978-81-7622-209-9



*The information contained in this book is meant to provide clues for clinical, laboratory or other research work. It is not a work for prescribing treatments for any ailment or disorder. No plant or plant parts or herbal formulations, as described in this book, should be tried by a layman for treatment of any kind of disease.*

*Published by* : **BIOTECH BOOKS**
1123/74, Deva Ram Park, Tri Nagar,
DELHI – 110 035
Phone: 27383999, (M) 09868812760
E-mail: biotechbooks@yahoo.co.in

*Showroom* : 4762-63/23, Ansari Road, Darya Ganj,
NEW DELHI - 110 002
Phone: 23245578

*Laser Typesetting* : **Classic Computer Services**
Delhi - 110 035

*Printed at* : **Chawla Offset Printers**
Delhi - 110 052

PRINTED IN INDIA

# Acknowledgements

The present document–'*Medicinal Plants of Uttarakhand: Diversity, Livelihood and Conservation*'–is an attempt to synthesize various information in order to assist the medicinal plants sector. A number of individuals and organizations have made this study possible, and I would like to express my sincere gratitude to them all. I thank Shri B.S. Sajwan, Chief Executive Officer, National Medicinal Plants Board, Government of India, New Delhi for continuous guidance and support. I thank Dr. R.B.S. Rawat, Principal Chief Conservator of Forests, Uttarakhand and former CEO of the National Medicinal Plants Board, New Delhi.

I thank Dr. R.B. Lal, Director, Indian Institute of Forest Management for intellectual support. I acknowledge the support extended by the Director, scientists, technicians, and researchers of the G.B. Pant Institute of Himalayan Environment & Development (GBPIHED), especially Dr. P.P. Dhyani, Dr. R.K. Maikhuri, Dr. P.K. Samal, Dr. N.A. Farooquee and Dr. B.S. Majila for helping in various ways. It gives me immense pleasure to express deep sense of gratitude to all traditional herbal healers of Uttarakhand, especially *Vaidyas* for their co-operation and support during the course of this study.

I extend my thanks to Prof. D.K. Bandopadhyay, Vice Chancellor, Indraprastha University, New Delhi, Prof. A.N. Purohit, former Vice Chancellor, H.N.B. Garhwal University, Prof. R.D. Gaur, Prof. A.B. Bhatt, Dr. Subhash Nautiyal, Forest Research Institute, Dr. K.S. Negi, Principal Scientist National Bureau of Plant Genetic Resources, Bhowali, Dr. R.C. Sundriyal, Director, Herbal Research and Development Institute, Prof. A.R. Nautiyal and Prof. M.C. Nautiyal, High Altitude Plant Physiology Research Center, Dr. Ghayur Alam Center for Sustainable Development, Dr. E.L. Berlow, University of California, Dr. Frederick Pank, Germany, and Prof. Dea Bericevic, University of Ljubljana, Slovenia for helping in various ways.

I am indebted to my father S.M. Kala and mother K.D. Kala for inculcating the sanctity of nature in my mind. I thank my brother M.P. Kala for continuous encouragements. Richa, I thank you and Shaurya for your patient and support during the preparation of this document.

**Chandra Prakash Kala**

*E-mail: cpkala@yahoo.co.uk*

बी० एस० सजवाण, आई०एफ०एस०
मुख्य कार्यकारी अधिकारी
B.S. SAJWAN, I.F.S.
Chief Executive Officer

भारत सरकार
स्वास्थ्य और परिवार कल्याण मंत्रालय
आयुष विभाग
राष्ट्रीय औषधीय पादप बोर्ड
Government of India
Ministry of Health & Family Welfare
Department of AYUSH
National Medicinal Plants Board

# *Foreword*

The plant based health care practices are common to most civilisations in the world. Years of experimentation and subsequent evolution of various health care systems, such as, Ayurveda, Unani, Siddha, and Homeopathy has led to the present level of the knowledge on medicinal plant species. The importance of medicinal plants today is restricted not only to the health care but also for livelihood and income generation.

The characteristics of the medicinal plants vary with the geographical locations and climatic variations. The Himalayas are regarded as the rich repository of valuable medicinal plants since time immemorial. Being a part of the Himalayas, the Uttarakhand state of India harbours a rich diversity of medicinal plants. The availability of this resource has increased manifold in terms of species diversity, population density and productivity in Uttarakhand due to the diverse climatic, geographical and altitudinal variations. Mythologically, the most popular and peculiar life saving medicinal plant - Sanjeevani, as mentioned in the Ramayana – is known to occur in the higher reaches of Uttarakhand state.

Over past three decades a number of explorations have been made in the state, especially on the use of medicinal plants by different community

चन्द्रलोक बिल्डिंग, 36, जनपथ, नई दिल्ली-110001 • Chandralok Building, 36, Janpath, New Delhi-110001
फोन/Tel. 011-23319360, फैक्स/Fax: 011-23319356 • ई-मेल/E-mail : info-nmpb@nic.in • वेबसाइट/Web Site: www.nmpb.nic.in

groups. However, the outcomes of such explorations are generally presented in bits and pieces. The absence of a comprehensive database on the Himalayan plants, has been a felt need requiring further investigations in view of the need for screening the existing resource for its quality, efficacy and safety. Compilations of the scattered information including 240 herbal formulations prepared by traditional herbal healers and 964 plant species used for curing of various ailments is the timely effort of the author.

In order to ensure that the resource is available in perpetuity for health care, it is important to conserve this resource by using various *ex-situ* and *in-situ* conservation measures. It has been realized through generations that there is a tremendous pressure on high value medicinal plants of the Himalayan region due to escalating demand across the world. The various recommendations as given in this book on the conservation, cultivation and commercialization will help to improve the medicinal plants sector.

I am confident that the book *'Medicinal Plants of Uttarakhand: Diversity, Livelihood and Conservation'* will be useful for different stakeholders of medicinal plants sector within and outside of the state. The information as given in the book will also be useful for further research and development on medicinal plants and screening of these plants for the discovery of plant based drugs in future.

14/1-2010

**B.S. Sajwan**

*Chief Executive Officer*

# Preface

For past couple of decades, medicinal plants have been increasingly recognized for their role as not only for health care but also contributing to livelihood. Also, increasing commercialization has led to the overharvesting of some economically important medicinal plant species, many of which have become rare, endangered and threatened. Since medicinal plants form an important health commodity and livelihood option, sustainable utilization and conservation of this valuable bio-resource is an urgent need of the hour. At the same time, there has been continuous erosion in the traditional knowledge on the use of medicinal plants due to several reasons including lack of proper documentation. Realizing the loss of valuable traditional knowledge on plants use for health care in the past and the increasing interest in herbal therapy at present, there was a need to compile information on medicinal plants.

Medicinal plants are distributed across diverse habitat types, landscapes and altitudinal ranges. Information is urgently required on the source and availability of raw material for herbal industry, especially on the aspects of present production, if cultivated, or range and pattern of natural distribution and areas with rich population, if originating from the wild. The present book mainly deals with the traditional knowledge of plants use for therapy, availability of medicinal plants resources and their conservation along with constraints in medicinal plants enterprise development and initiatives taken up by the Government of India to mitigate the constraints and strengthen the medicinal plants sector.

The present compilation deals primarily with the state of Uttarakhand, as this newly created state is endowed with rich medicinal plants diversity on account of its distinct geographical, ecological and climatic conditions. Such rich resource availability is an asset for developing and promoting the state as the "Herbal State". *Medicinal plants of Uttarakhand: Diversity, Livelihood and Conservation* is an endeavour to compile the existing information as well as to gather information by carrying out primary surveys in various parts of the state. A total of 964 medicinal plant species growing in various habitat types across the state from sub-tropical to temperate and alpine regions were documented and placed in the book. This pool of identified species for raw material may be further screened for their efficacy, quality and safety for establishing the herbal-based medical industries as well as to promote the medicinal plants knowledge among the various user groups.

Apart from compiling over 240 herbal formulations prepared by traditional *Vaidyas* for curing 73 types of ailments, the book also portrays the challenges faced by different stakeholders, especially the growers and collectors and the available opportunities in developing the medicinal plants sector. The preferences of local people towards cultivation and conservation of specific medicinal plants are also discussed in the book. Several livelihood and conservation-oriented issues along with ecological significance, cultural values, cultivation, and role of institutions in medicinal plants sector are discussed.

The book is, therefore, concerned with understanding medicinal plants values, diversity, conservation measures, prospects and constraints, and enterprise development. The information compiled in this book will be useful to the different stakeholders of the medicinal plants.

**Chandra Prakash Kala**

# Contents

# Chapter 1

# Medicinal Plants of Uttarakhand: An Overview

Uttarakhand, the 27th state of Indian republic, was carved out of existing state of Uttar Pradesh in November 2000 to facilitate the rapid development of this hilly region, is well known for its rich biological, spiritual and cultural values. The state lies between $28^0 43'$ to $31^0 8'$ N and $77^0 35'$ to $81^0 2'$ E and comprises of 13 districts. Himachal Pradesh bounds Uttarakhand on northwest, Tibet (China) on north, Nepal on east, and Uttar Pradesh on south (Figure 1.1). The average rainfall recorded in this state is 1000 to 2000 mm per year. The total geographical area of the state is 53,485 $km^2$ that falls between the elevation ranges of 210 m to 7,817 m.

The total human population of the state is around 84,79,562, of which 78 per cent fall under rural category. About 20 per cent of the state population has been classified under the categories of Schedule Castes and Schedule Tribes, which draw the associated benefits marked separately for the backward communities by the Government of India. The socio-cultural fabric in the state is characterized by diverse ethnic groups, which have developed their own cultures based on available natural resources, giving rise to a cultural diversity (Kandari and Gusain, 2001). Uttarakhand covers about 12.18 per cent of the total Indian Himalaya, and about 40

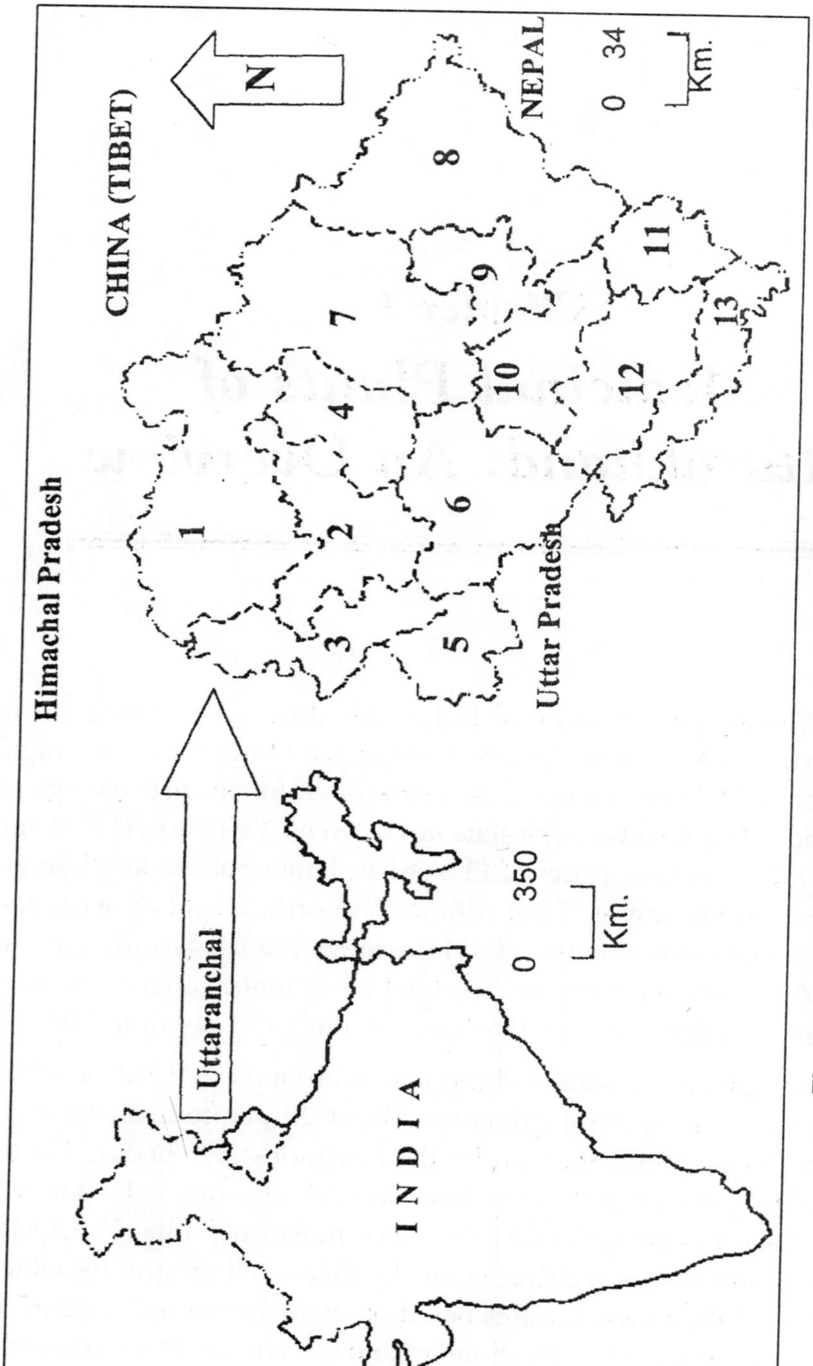


Figure 1.1: Location of Study Area (Indian State of Uttarakhand)
The numerical values indicate the localities of districts in the state.
1: Uttarkashi; 2: Tehri; 3: Dehradun; 4: Rudraprayag; 5: Haridwar; 6: Pauri; 7: Chamoli;
8: Pithoragarh; 9: Bageshwar; 10: Almora; 11: Champawat; 12: Nainital; 13: Udham Singh Nagar

per cent of its total area falls under different forest types. Some of the major vegetation types classified along the altitudinal gradient are tropical, sub-tropical, temperate, sub-alpine and alpine.

For time immemorial plants have been playing an important role in the health care of a vast majority of people all over the world. In India, approximately two million traditional health practitioners use medicinal plants for curing various ailments (Venkatesh, 2002), of these a sizeable number of herbal practitioners regard the Himalaya as a storehouse of varieties of herbal medicines. Located in the Himalaya, the vegetation wealth of Uttarakhand has received a significant attention throughout the ages in curing various chronic human ailments (Gaur, 1999). Unfortunately, the centuries old traditional knowledge on therapy developed over the years of experiments and experiences has declined sharply since the spread of allopathic drugs (Kala, 1998). This decline has resulted in the loss of knowledge on the use of many important plant species and techniques of making various indigenous medical formulations (Kala *et al.*, 2004).

Moreover, with the growing problems of bio-piracy there is a need to document the various uses of these valuable bio-resources with a view to reduce the possibility of bio-piracy and protect the rights of traditional herbal healers. The patent drama on turmeric highlights that the centuries old traditional knowledge on medicinal plants can not be protected fully within the patent system as it stands today (Udgaonkar, 2002). Thus, there is an urgent need to document the therapeutic uses of various ingredients used by the traditional healers to avoid the misuse of their intellectual property. Plants being the major ingredients in traditional medical system need a special care for their long term sustainable utilization so that the raw material can be made available for preparing medicine to the herbal healers as well as to the herbal industries.

In the present document, attempts have been made to compile the existing relevant literature apart from the collection of primary data by carrying out the field surveys in the various parts of the state. Structured and semi-structured questionnaire surveys were conducted among various knowledgeable herbal healers including traditional *Vaidyas* (practitioners of Ayurvedic medical system) of Uttarakhand basically to generate information on the various uses of medicinal plants. One of the aims of this study was to document the medicinal plants and their uses in order to explore the availability of bio-resources for establishing the herbal-based medical industries as well as to promote the traditional knowledge among various user groups on the use of medicinal plants. Attempts were also made to examine the problems and prospects in the development of medicinal plants sector. Apart from this, several conservation-oriented issues have also been addressed in the present document.

The existing literature used for compilation of medicinal plants includes Uniyal (1968), Shah and Joshi (1971), Shah and Gupta (1976), Mehrotra (1979), Nautiyal (1981), Shah (1982), Kritikar and Basu (1984), Malhotra and Bashu (1984), Malhotra and Balodi (1984), Maheshwari and Singh (1984, 1990), Sundriyal *et al.* (1985), Singh *et al.* (1987), Pangtey and Rawat (1987), Kaushik (1988), CSIR (1989), Pangtey *et al.* (1989), Badoni (1990), Mamgain and Rao (1990), Paliwal and Badoni (1990), Negi and Gaur (1991), Jain (1991), Negi and Pant (1992), Bhatt and Gaur (1992), Negi *et al.* (1993), Pandey (1995), Samant *et al.* (1996; 1998), Farooquee and Saxena (1996), Purohit (1997), Kala (1998a; 1998b; 2002a; 2002b; 2003), Maikhuri *et al.* (1998), Gaur (1999), Pandey and Pande (1999), Arya *et al.* (1999), Nautiyal *et al.* (2000), Dhar *et al.* (2000), Maikhuri *et al.* (2000), Silori and Badola (2000), Badoni and Badoni (2001) and Anon (2002). Although, the majority of information was collected from the secondary sources, field surveys were also undertaken for several years for gathering data on the availability and uses of medicinal plant species across various localities in the state varying from tropical to alpine zone. The primary information was gathered from various traditional *Vaidyas* located across the various parts of the state. The nomenclature as given in Bennet (1987), Polunin and Stainton (1984) and Gaur (1999) was followed.

## Availability and Uses of Medicinal Plants

During the present course of investigation, a total of 964 species of medicinal plants have been compiled for Uttarakhand, of these about 45 per cent were documented through interviews with traditional *Vaidyas* during the field surveys. Attempts have been made to document the local name of medicinal plant species both with the help of literature (*e.g.* Jain, 1991; Kala, 1998a; and Gaur, 1999) and field surveys (Appendix). It has been observed that the local name of a medicinal plant sometime varies with locality and in some cases two or more than two different plant species have common local name that create confusion in identification. Besides, each medicinal plant species has been described and placed in Appendix with family name, life form, plant part used, and the various therapeutic uses of plant species.

**Profile of Medicinal Plants in Uttarakhand**

| | |
|---|---|
| Total number of species | 964 |
| ✰ Number of families | 158 |
| ✰ Number of tree species | 160 |
| ✰ Number of shrub species | 190 |
| ✰ Number of herb species | 614 |
| Use of plant species in curing number of ailments | 135 |

Among the various life forms of medicinal plant species of Uttarakhand herbaceous species are most dominant as out of 964 medicinal plant species, 614 are herbs, 190 are shrubs and 160 are trees. These plant species are distributed over 158 families. In terms of number of species occupied, Asteraceae is the most dominant family (87 species) of medicinal plants in Uttarakhand, followed by Fabaceae (58 species), Lamiaceae (49 species), Rosaceae (30 species), Liliaceae (29 species), Apiaceae (28 species), Euphorbiaceae (26 species), Ranunculaceae (26 species), Orchidaceae (23 species), Gentianaceae (18 species), Poaceae (18 species), Rubiaceae (18 species) and Verbenaceae (18 species) (Table 1.1). Of the 158 families, 61 families have single medicinal plant species, 27 families have 2 medicinal plant species and 11 families have 3 medicinal plant species.

In preparing various medical formulations and drugs different parts of these plant species such as flower, fruit, root, tuber, bark, stem, and leaf are used. The analysis of medicinal plants of Uttarakhand indicates that underground plant parts (root, rhizome, and tuber) are used alone in the majority of cases (205 species), followed by leaf (154 species). The whole plant of 112 medicinal plant species is used in preparing medicine. Of about 270 species more than one plant part is used. (Figure 1.2).

These 964 plant species are used in curing about 135 ailments, of which the highest numbers of plant species alone (80 species) are used in healing cut and wounds, followed by fever (75 species), diarrhea and dysentery

(57 species), skin ailments (52 species), asthma and bronchitis (46 species), cough and cold (37 species) and snake bite (35 species). Based on the number of species used in curing, the top 12 ailments have given in Table 1.2. Generally, most of the plant species are used to cure more than one ailment as evident from the checklist of medicinal plants (Appendix). An analysis made by Kala *et al.* (2004) revealed that there are about 48 uses of *Vitex nigundo*, 40 uses of *Azadirachta indica* and 35 uses of *Woodfordia fruticosa* across the various districts of Uttarakhand state.

**Table 1.1: Based on the Number of Medicinal Plants, Top 30 Families of Medicinal Plants in Uttarakhand**

| *Family* | *No. of Species* | *Family* | *No. of Species* | *Family* | *No. of Species* |
|---|---|---|---|---|---|
| Asteraceae | 87 | Poaceae | 18 | Convolvulaceae | 14 |
| Fabaceae | 57 | Rubiaceae | 18 | Caesalpiniaceae | 13 |
| Lamiaceae | 49 | Verbenaceae | 18 | Scrophulariaceae | 13 |
| Rosaceae | 30 | Cucurbitaceae | 17 | Brassicaceae | 12 |
| Liliaceae | 29 | Malvaceae | 17 | Araceae | 11 |
| Apiaceae | 26 | Rutaceae | 17 | Boraginaceae | 11 |
| Euphorbiaceae | 26 | Solanaceae | 17 | Moraceae | 11 |
| Ranunculaceae | 26 | Polygonaceae | 16 | Amaranthaceae | 10 |
| Orchidaceae | 23 | Asclepiadaceae | 15 | Caryophyllaceae | 10 |
| Gentianaceae | [illegible] | Apocynaceae | 14 | Berberidaceae | 9 |

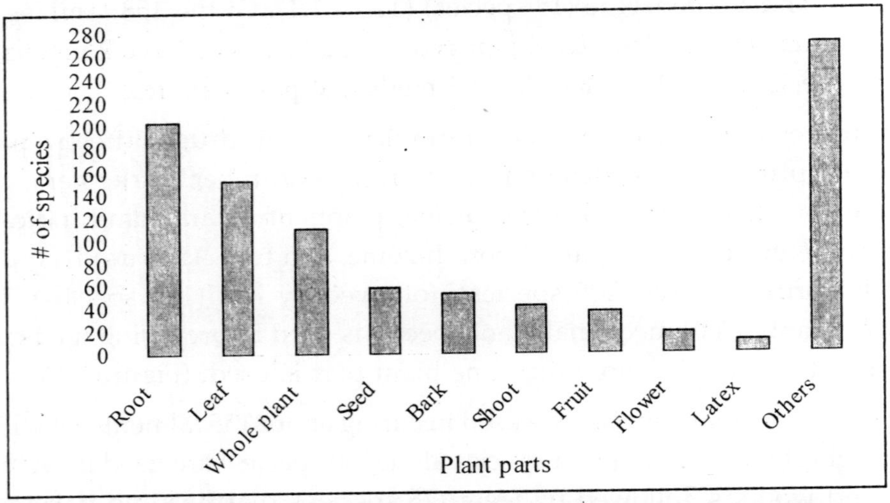


**Figure 1.2: Plant Parts Used (in number) for Preparation of Medicine**

**Table 1.2: Important Ailments Ranked on the Basis of Number of Species Used in Curing**

| Sl.No. | Ailments | No. of Plant Species Used |
|---|---|---|
| 1. | Cut and wounds | 80 |
| 2. | Fever | 75 |
| 3. | Diarrhoea and dysentery | 57 |
| 4. | Skin ailments | 52 |
| 5. | Asthma and bronchitis | 46 |
| 6. | Cough and cold | 37 |
| 7. | Snake bite | 35 |
| 8. | General tonic | 29 |
| 9. | Bodyache | 24 |
| 10. | Rheumatism | 18 |
| 11. | Antiseptic | 18 |
| 12. | Bone fracture | 18 |

In the present analysis, I selected one most common use of a plant species rather then summing up all the uses of a plant species. For the better presentation and inclusion of all 135 ailments in the analysis, the medicinal plants have been arranged into 12 classes of diseases such as dermatological problem, gastrointestinal disorder, generalized bodyache, respiratory disorder, urogenital disorder, bone diseases, blood related disorder, general health and hair tonic, eye diseases, mental/psychological disorder, anti poison and others. Medical practitioners were consulted in classifying the ailments into 12 broad classes of diseases. The data were quantified by counting the number of species used in curing the various ailments falling in each broad class of disease.

Among the various classes of diseases, the highest numbers of plant species are used in curing the dermatological problems (212 species), followed by gastrointestinal disorders (192 species), generalized bodyache (170 species) and respiratory disorders (102 species; Table 1.3).

## Opportunities for Economic Development

Since Uttarakhand is a newly created Himalayan state, the efforts are being made within government and outside to promote the medicinal plant based industries and develop the state as "Herbal State". Different programs such as workshops, seminars, discussions and policy level changes are being carried out in the state to strengthen the medicinal plant sector as one of the leading economic development sectors within the state. Government, non-government and people's forum have organized more than two dozens major workshops in the state. Such workshops have largely focused on developing the technological knowledge to grow medicinal plants, maximizing the benefits to the farmers and reducing the role of middlemen in the trade of medicinal plants by promoting large-scale cultivation so that industries can come forward and make contacts directly with the farmers. The state Government has augmented huge funds and allocated about US$ 2192000 in the year 2004 to Herbal Research and Development Institute at Gopeshwar, the state Nodal Agency for the large-scale cultivation of medicinal plants and related infra-structural development in the state. Further, to minimize the role of middlemen and the contractors, the village community organizations, called 'samooh' are being promoted. In addition, at the policy level, attempts are being made to strengthen the traditional Ayurvedic system of medicine by making it a mandatory curriculum in the schools and colleges, prescribing Ayurvedic medicine compulsory at least in some rural and urban hospitals, and also to register the *Vaidyas* (Ayurvedic practitioners) and local healers.

**Table 1.3: Various Classes of Diseases Ranked According to Number of Species Used in Curing Diseases**

| *Sl.No.* | *Ailments* | *No. of Plant Species Used* |
|---|---|---|
| 1. | Dermatological problem | 212 |
| 2. | Gastrointestinal disorder | 192 |
| 3. | Generalized bodyache | 170 |
| 4. | Respiratory disorder | 102 |
| 5. | Urogenital disorder | 56 |
| 6. | Bone diseases | 49 |
| 7. | Blood related disorder | 47 |
| 8. | General health and hair tonic | 41 |
| 9. | Anti poison | 38 |
| 10. | Eye diseases | 27 |
| 11. | Mental/psychological disorder | 19 |
| 12. | Others | 6 |

The availability of 964 medicinal plant species indicates the potential of medicinal plant based economic development in the state. However, with a view to conserve the wild resource for long term and also to procure the raw material for industries, cultivation of these valuable species has realized the need of hour. For the successful farming of the medicinal plants, identification of suitable areas, species and agro-techniques need to be developed on the basis of habitat, altitudinal range and other climatic and edaphic factors. Further the prioritization of species needs to be done for cultivation, based on the ecological and economic needs. For instance, *Acorus calamus, Piper longum, Withania somnifera, Cinnamomum tamala* and *Gloriosa superba* grow naturally in tropical areas, *Swertia* sp., *Hedychium spicatum* and *Berberis aristata* grow in temperate areas and *Podophyllum hexendrum, Picrorhiza kurrooa, Dactylorhiza hatagirea, Nardostachys grandiflora* etc grow in the alpine areas, and accordingly they should be cultivated across their natural distribution range for successful farming and better economic return due to their high demand.

Though there have been preliminary attempts by the state Government and other stakeholders in developing medicinal plants sector, there are several constraints in streamlining the entire sector, especially for the collection of medicinal plants from wild, easy and cost effective techniques of cultivation, large scale cultivation, long gestation period for their crop production, unstable prices, and lack of assured regular market for sale. In view of these constraints the economic viability of the medicinal plant sector has been negatively affected and therefore cultivation, at present, is restricted to small plots and kitchen gardens. Moreover, the economic benefits generated by medicinal plants farming are not percolating properly to the farmers as there are enormous variations in the prices of the medicinal plants at the different market levels and middlemen use to share a large part of economic benefit (Table 1.4). They generally sell the product at about double of its purchase cost from the gatherers or farmers.

The income-expenditure analysis reveals that the medicinal plants farming is a profitable business, and also the potential average income from cultivating medicinal plants is greater than from cultivating traditional crops (Silori and Badola, 2000; Maikhuri *et al.*, 2000). The projected productivity figures by Maikhuri *et al.* (2003) further elucidate the potential for greater economic returns from the cultivation of medicinal plants.

Migration from hills to plains in Uttarakhand has led to the large extent of agriculture fallow that can be used for medicinal plants cultivation. The possible steps to mitigate the various problems related with medicinal plants sector have been highlighted in table 1.5. One of the potential steps could be the direct linkage of industries with the farmers to promote buy-back scheme and pricing policy as an incentive to promote large-scale cultivation.

**Table 1.4: Total Income of per ha Production and Prices of Some Medicinal Plants**

| *Species, Local Name* | *Prices at Three Different Market Level (US $ / kg)* | | |
|---|---|---|---|
| | *Villagers* | *Middlemen* | *Wholesaler* |
| *Aconitum heterophyllum*, Atis | 15.78 | 23.58 | 36.73 |
| *Allium humile*, Faran | 1.39 | 1.90 | 2.91 |
| *Angelica glauca*, Choru | 0.63 | 2.03 | 3.42 |
| *Carum carvii*, Kala jira | 2.03 | 6.33 | 10.13 |
| *Dactylorhiza hatagirea*, Hathajari | 3.80 | 7.59 | 11.39 |
| *Nardostachys grandiflora*, Jatamansi | 1.10 | 1.62 | 1.90 |
| *Picrorhiza kurrooa*, Katuki | 0.71 | 1.22 | 1.87 |

*Source*: Maikhuri *et al.*, 2003.

For the sustainable utilization of these valuable natural resources, the Government of India has created a National Medicinal Plants Board under the Ministry of Health and Family Welfare. The National Medicinal Plants Board also promotes the various schemes including survey and inventory of medicinal plants and their *in-situ* and *ex-situ* conservation. Similarly, the Government of Uttarakhand has set up the State Medicinal Plants Board chaired by the Chief Minister of the state with the major objectives to assess the medicinal plants wealth of the state, their demand and supply, advise concerned departments, promotion of *ex-situ* and *in-situ* conservation, setting up of databases and building liaison among different stakeholders in medicinal plants sector. The present documentation of the medicinal plants of Uttarakhand and various ailments cured by these plant species would be helpful for further research on exploring their medical efficacy, value addition and use in curing for various old and new diseases.

**Table 1.5: Assessment of Activities, Initiatives, Problems and Remedies for Medicinal Plant Based Economic Venture in Uttarakhand**

| *Activity* | *Initiatives* | *Problems* | *Possible remedy* |
|---|---|---|---|
| Collection | Regulate wild collection and reduced role of middlemen by forming 'samooh' (Village committee) | Middlemen have also formed their own 'samooh' to maintain their control over collection. | Implementation of existing Acts on wild collection. |
| | | Continued illegal collection from wild has led to depletion of many important species. | |
| Cultivation | Few organizations such as Herbal Research and Development Institute, High Altitude Plant Physiology Research Centre, Society for Himalayan Environmental Research, G.B. Pant Institute of Himalayan Environment and Development, Forest Research Institute etc. have been trying to develop techniques to promote cultivation in the state. | Agro-technology is not available for many valuable medicinal plant species. | Development of agro-technology and promotion of rural biotechnology for large scale cultivation. |
| | | Cultivation is restricted to small plots near the farmer's houses. | Capacity building programmes for farmers. |
| | | Issuing license or permit to farmers for growing medicinal plants is a time consuming process, and farmers are sometime not aware of the process. | Process of issuing permits should be made easier and faster. |
| | | Lack of linkages among the different stakeholders. awareness on the latest | Farmers should be encouraged by providing incentives, training and develop- ments and policies related to the medicinal plants. |
| | | The other economic factors discouraging farmers in adopting the medicinal plants farming are high risk, long gestation period, and low prices of medicinal plants. | Selection of planting material for cultivation should be based on their habitats, locality, climate and altitudes. |
| | | Research is mostly focused on the low productive and high cost rare and endangered medicinal plant species. | |

*Contd...*

**Table 1.5–Contd...**

| *Activity* | *Initiatives* | *Problems* | *Possible remedy* |
|---|---|---|---|
| Marketing | State Government is attempting to promote herbal industries. | The supply chain of medicinal plants is quite large and primary producers are dependent on the middlemen and still they face difficulty in selling the product. | Direct selling to industry by producers should be encouraged. |
| | About two dozens major workshops have been conducted in the state on the promotion of medicinal plants sector and economic development of the state. | Reliable information on demand and prices is not available. | Buy-back arrangements between farmers and pharmaceutical companies can be useful for strengthening the medicinal plants sector. |
| | | Lacking of research on understanding and developing the well-planned marketing mechanism for medicinal plants. | |

Based on the results it is concluded that Uttarakhand state of India is endowed with a rich diversity of medicinal plant species right from the tropical areas to the high altitude alpine pastures. The compilation of 964 medicinal plant species indicates that the state sustains a rich raw material for establishing pharmaceutical industries. The wasteland and barren agriculture areas across the habitats, elevations and eco-climatic zones in the state can be made useful through medicinal plants farming. The values of these known medicinal plants may be further enhanced with the help of research and repeated clinical trials. The herbal products are generally user-friendly and don't inflict harmful effects on the human body. The state has a high literacy rate and also harbors rich biodiversity but the per capita income is lower (US$ 158) than the national average (US$ 235), therefore there is a need to explore and exploit the economic viable resources for the prosperity of its inhabitants.

## References

Anon (2002). *Flora of Himalaya Database.* http://www.llsh.univ-savoie.fr/sc/infos.html

Arya, K.R., P.C. Pande, and V.P. Tiwari (1999). Ethnobotanical study on tribal areas of Almora district. *Ethnobotany,* 11: 100-104.

Badoni, A.K. (1990). An ethnobotanical study of Pinswari community: A preliminary survey. *Bulletin of Botanical Survey of India,* 32: 103-115.

Badoni A.K. and K. Badoni (2001). Ethnobotanical heritage. In: *Garhwal Himalaya: Nature, Culture and Society* (Eds. O.P. Kandari and O.P. Gusain). TransMedia, Srinagar Garhwal, India. pp 127-147.

Bhatt, K.C. and R.D. Gaur (1992). A contribution to ethnobotany of Rajis in Pithoragarh district. *Acta Botanica Indica,* 20: 76-83.

Bennet, S.S.R. (1987). *Name Changes in Flowering Plants of India and Adjacent Regions.* Triseas Publishers, Dehradun, India.

CSIR (1989). *The Wealth of India: Raw Materials.* New Delhi: Publications and Information Directorate, Council of Scientific and Industrial Research.

Dhar, U., R.S. Rawal and J. Upreti (2000). Setting priorities for conservation of medicinal plants –a case study in the Indian Himalaya. *Biological Conservation,* 95: 57-65.

Farooquee, N.A. and K.G. Saxena (1996). Conservation and utilization of medicinal plants in high hills of central Himalaya. *Environmental Conservation,* 23: 75-80.

Gaur, R.D. (1999). *Flora of the district Garhwal northwest Himalaya (with ethnobotanical notes).* TransMedia, Srinagar Garhwal, India.

Jain, S.K. (1991). *Dictionary of Indian folk medicine and ethnobotany.* Deep Publications, New Delhi.

Kala, C.P. (1998a). *Ethnobotanical survey and propagation of rare medicinal herbs for small farmers in the buffer zone of the Valley of Flowers National Park, Garhwal Himalaya.* A Report, ICIMOD, Kathmandu, Nepal.

Kala, C.P. (1998b). *Ecology and Conservation of Alpine Meadows in the Valley of Flowers National Park, Garhwal Himalaya.* Ph.D. Thesis, Forest Research Institute, Dehradun, India.

Kala, C.P. (2002a). Indigenous knowledge of Bhotiya tribal community on wool dying and its present status in the Garhwal Himalaya, India. *Current Science,* 83: 814-817.

Kala, C.P. (2002b). *Medicinal Plants of Indian Trans-Himalaya.* Bishen Singh Mahendra Pal Singh, Dehradun, India.

Kala, C.P. (2003). Commercial exploitation and conservation status of high value medicinal plants across the borderline of India and Nepal in Pithoragarh. *The Indian Forester,* 129: 80-84.

Kala, C.P., N.A. Farooquee and U. Dhar (2004). Prioritization of medicinal plants on the basis of available knowledge, existing practices and use value status in Uttarakhand, India. *Biodiversity and Conservation,* 13: 453-469.

Kandari, O.P. and O.P. Gusain (2001). *Garhwal Himalaya: Nature, Culture and Society.* TransMedia, Srinagar Garhwal, India.

Kaushik, P (Ed.) (1988). *Indigenous Medicinal Plants.* Today and Tomorrow Printers and Publisher, New Delhi.

Kritikar, K.R. and B.D. Basu (1984). *Indian Medicinal Plants.* Bishen Singh Mahendra Pal Singh, Dehra Dun, Vol: I-IV.

Maheshwari, J.K. and J.P. Singh (1984). Contribution to the ethnobotany of Bhoxa tribe of Bijnor and Pauri Garhwal district, U.P. *Journal of Economic and Taxonomic Botany,* 5: 253-259.

Maheshwari, J.K. and H. Singh (1990). Herbal remedies of Boxas of Nainital district, U.P. *Ayurvaidan*, 4: 251-259.

Maikhuri, R.K., S. Nautiyal, K.S. Rao and K.G. Saxena (1998). Medicinal plants cultivation and biosphere reserve management: a case study from Nanda Devi Biosphere Reserve, Himalaya. *Current Science*, 74: 157-163.

Maikhuri, R.K., S. Nautiyal, K.S. Rao and R.L. Semwal (2000). Indigenous knowledge of medicinal plants and wild edibles among three tribal sub-communities of the Central Himalayas, India. *Indigenous Knowledge and Development Monitor*, 8: 7-13.

Maikhuri, R.K., K.S Rao, K. Chauhan, L.S. Kandari, P. Prasad and Rajasekaran (2003). Development of marketing of medicinal plants and other forest products–can it be a path way for effective management and conservation ? *The Indian Forester*, 129: 169-178.

Malhotra, C.L. and B. Balodi (1984). Wild medicinal plants in the use of Johari tribals. *Journal of Economic and Taxonomic Botany*, 5: 881-883.

Malhotra, C.L. and D. Bashu (1984). A preliminary survey of plants resources of medicinal and aromatic value from Almora. *Journal of Economic and Taxonomic Botany*, 5: 859-864.

Mehrotra, B.N. (1979). Survey of medicinal plants around Kedarnath Shrine of Garhwal Himalaya. *The Indian Forester*, 105: 788-801.

Mumgain, S.K. and R.R. Rao (1990). Some medicinal plants of Pauri Garhwal. *Journal of Economic and Taxonomic Botany*, 14: 633-640.

Nautiyal, S. (1981). Some medicinal plants of Garhwal hills: a traditional use. *J. of Scientific Research in Plants and Medicines*, 2: 12-18.

Nautiyal, S., K.S. Rao, R.K. Maikhuri, R.L. Semwal and K.G. Saxena (2000). Traditional knowledge related to medicinal and aromatic plants in tribal societies in a part of Himalaya. *Journal of Medicinal and Aromatic Plant Sciences*, 22/4A and 23/1A: 528-441.

Negi, K.S. and R.D. Gaur (1991). Little known endemic wild Allium species in the Uttar Pradesh hills. *Mountain Research and Development*, 11: 162-164.

Negi, K.S. and K.C. Pant (1992). Less known wild species of *Allium* Linn (Amaryllidaceae) form mountainous region of India. *Economic Botany*, 46: 112-116.

Negi, K.S., J.K. Tiwari, R.D. Gaur and K.C. Pant (1993). Notes on ethnobotany of five districts of Garhwal Himalaya, U.P., India. *Ethnobotany*, 5: 73-81.

Paliwal GS and Badoni AK (1990). Ethnobotany of the hill tribes of Uttarkashi; medicinal plants. *Journal of Economic and Taxonomic Botany* 14: 421-442.

Pandey, B. and P.C. Pande (1999). Ethnobotanical studies on Gymnospermic plants of Kumaun Himalaya. *Journal of Economic and Taxonomic Botany*, 23: 253-255.

Pandey, G. (1995). *Medicinal Plants of Himalaya.* Vol. I-II. Sri Satguru Publications, Delhi, India.

Pangtey, Y.P.S. and G.S. Rawat (1987). A contribution to the ethnobotany of alpine region of Kumaun. *Journal of Economic and Taxonomic Botany*, 11: 139-148.

Pangtey, Y.P.S., S.S. Samant and G.S. Rawat (1989). Ethnobotanical notes on Bhotia tribes of Kumaun Himalaya. *Indian Journal Forestry*, 12: 191-196.

Polunin, O. and A. Stainton (1984). *Flowers of Himalaya*. Oxford University Press: New Delhi.

Purohit, A.N. (1997). Medicinal plants–need for upgrading technology for trading the traditions. In: *Harvesting Herbs–2000*. (Eds. A.R. Nautiyal, M.C. Nautiyal and A.N. Purohit). Bishen Singh and Mahendra Pal Singh, Dehradun, India. pp. 46-76.

Samant, S.S., U. Dhar and L.M.S. Palni (1998). *Medicinal Plants of Indian Himalaya: Diversity Distribution Potential Values*. G.B. Pant Institute of Himalayan Environment and Development, Almora, India.

Samant, S.S., U. Dhar and R.S. Rawal (1996). Natural resource use by some natives within Nanda Devi Biosphere Reserve in west Himalaya. *Ethnobotany*, 8: 40-50.

Shah, N.C. (1982). Herbal folk medicines in Northern India. *Journal of Ethnopharmacology*, 6: 293-301.

Shah, N.C. and L.K. Gupta (1976). Useful medicinal plants of Ranikhet-I. *Indian Drugs*, 14: 47-52.

Shah, N.C. and M.C. Joshi (1971). An ethnobotanical study of Kumaun region of India. *Economic Botany*, 25: 414-422.

Silori, C.S. and R. Badola (2000). Medicinal plant cultivation and sustainable development: a case study in the buffer zone of the Nanda Devi Biosphere Reserve, Western Himalaya, India. *Mountain Research and Development*, 20: 72-279.

Singh, K.K., S. Saha, and J.K. Maheswari (1987). Observation on the ethnobotany of Boxa tribe of Bajpur block of Nainital district, Uttar Pradesh. *Himalayan Research and Development*, 6: 25-29.

Sundriyal, R.C., S.C. Negi, A.P. Joshi and R. Dhasmana (1985). Some important medicinal trees of Kotdwara, lansdowne and vicinity. *Himalayan Chem. Pharm. Bull.*, 2: 45-48.

Uniyal, M.R. (1968). Medicinal plants of Bhagirathi valley laying in Uttarkashi Forest Division. *The Indian Forester*, 94: 407-420.

# Chapter 2
# Use of Plants by Traditional Vaidyas

## Introduction

In Asia, Ayurveda, Unani and Chinese medical systems have developed and perfected the knowledge related to different forms of treatments purely based on the extracts of available natural resources. Of these, Ayurveda was developed much earlier, and the oldest existing literature on this form of treatment is mentioned in Rigveda around 4500-1600 B.C., Charak Samhita (1000-800 B.C.) and Susruta Samhita (800-700 B.C.). The Unani system of medical treatment developed much later and attained popularity in India during medieval period. Muslim rulers are known to introduce the Greco-Arabic system of medicine in India and later it was mixed up with native Ayurvedic system; this mixture is today known as Unani system. Alexander the Great could be the person who first got mixed up both these system in 327 B.C. Likewise the Chinese Medical System developed in China and came to India through their association with Buddhism and trade and migration. In all these historical monumental work the Himalaya has been repeatedly regarded as a rich repository of valuable medicinal plants.

During past few decades, the advent of allopathic drugs had given a way to decline the traditional medical systems all over the world including Ayurveda. By bringing both systems together and their adoption and rejection by the user groups without any prejudice may be useful in finding ways to establish the concerned system of medicines. Since the traditional herbal medical systems have always been integrated with communities and their cultures, these systems are much closure to the communities compared to modern medical system. This thoughtful reality might be used in making the traditional medical systems more popular than the modern medicines.

The traditional medicinal industry and those of its raw material, particularly medicinal plants, could mean for India in the world market. The global herbal market is worth $120 billion a year and Ayurveda represents $60 billion (Stock, 2002), which can be enhanced many fold if more organized attempts are made to convey its miraculous healing properties. Moreover, to recognize the historical herbal traditions officially and also to deploy the effective services of herbal healers, it is necessary to collect information on such traditions. Attempts have been made to document the use of medicinal plants and about 3500 formulations in Ayurveda, followed by Siddha and Unani have been documented (Banerjee, 2002). However, a large amount of knowledge occupied by various traditional herbal healers on the medicinal plants is not yet documented. The present work has envisaged the documentation of various herbal formulations prepared by traditional herbal healers and *Vaidyas* of Uttarakhand.

## Methods

Field surveys were undertaken across the various districts of Uttarakhand during 2001-2006. Semi-structured questionnaire survey was conducted among selected knowledgeable traditional *Vaidyas* with a view to document the knowledge on the use of medicinal plants and the preparation of various medical formulations. Information was also gathered on the local name of medicinal plants, plant part used in treatment and number of ailments being cured by the use of medicinal plants. A total of 60 traditional *Vaidyas* were interviewed to collect such information. These *Vaidyas* belonged to different districts and localities of Uttarakhand, such as Rishikesh, Maletha, Srinagar, Sumari, Balori, Pauri, Khirsu, Rudraprayag, Karnprayag, Gopeshwar, Tehri, Lambgaun, Ginouti, Naugaun, Uttarkashi, Dunda, Dhontri, Joshimath, Bhyundar, Nauti, Gwaldam, Tharali, Narayanbagad, Garur, Someshwar, Bageshwar, Pithoragarh and Almora. Field visits were made with *Vaidyas* for the identification of medicinal plants. Interviewing more than three *Vaidyas* on the use of specific plant and preparation of medical formulation made crosschecking of data. Participant observation method was employed to understand the methods and techniques adopted by *Vaidyas* in preparation of formulations. Besides, workshops were organized and various groups of indigenous people including *Vaidyas* were invited to generate and help in documenting the indigenous knowledge on such parameters. Qualitative information so gathered was verified by cross-examination with different traditional *Vaidyas*.

Since the list of ailments was quite long therefore these ailments were classified into 12 broad groups of diseases and the documented medicinal plant species were arranged accordingly. The classified groups of diseases are generalized bodyache, gastrointestinal disorder, uro-genital disorder, dermatological problem, bone diseases/fractures, eye diseases, blood related disorder, mental/psychological disorder, anti-venum/scorpion bite/dog bite, respiratory disorder, heart diseases and general health tonic. Medical practitioners were consulted in classifying the locally named ailments into the above-mentioned group of diseases.

## Results

During the present study 243 formulations, prepared by different traditional *Vaidyas*, were documented. These formulations were used in curing 73 different ailments (Table 2.1). Plants were the major ingredients in these medical formulations as 156 medicinal plants were documented those were used in preparing medical formulations by various traditional *Vaidyas* (Table 2.2). The highest numbers of formulations were documented for curing cough and cold, followed by headache, indigestion, dysentery and toothache. Of the 60 *Vaidyas* interviewed, 9 were young (16-25 years), 22 were adult (26-45 years) and 29 were old (>46 years). There was a sharp decline in the number of recognized *Vaidyas*, however, there were number of women and men in the villages who know the healing properties

**Table 2.1: Ailments Cured by Traditional Vaidyas with the help of Various Indigenous Herbal Formulations**

| Sl.No. | Ailment | Methods of Preparation and Prescription for Using the Indigenous Formulations |
|---|---|---|
| 1. | Fever, cold | Immature inside part of Bel (*Aegle marmelos*) fruit is crushed to powder and eat it twice in a day (morning and evening). |
| | | About 100 gm Bel (*Aegle marmelos*) root decoction is made with 1 glass of water and to eat it twice in a day (morning and evening). |
| | | Decoction of about 100 gm of Mehandi (*Lawsonia inermis*) leaf and one glass milk is given to patient. |
| | | Mix up salt and Pudina (*Mentha longifolia*) in tea and have it 4-5 times in a day. |
| | | 50 gm tuber of Hathajari (*Dactylorhiza hatagirea*), 1 spoon sugar, 10 gm seeds of Dhaniya (*Coriandrum sativum*) are boiled with 250 ml water and eat 10 gm of this mixture three times in a day. |
| | | 3 gm root powder of Chippi (*Pleurospermum angelicoides*), 50 ml leaf juice of Ban Tulsi (*Origanum vulgare*) are mixed up with 1 spoon honey and eat 10 gm of this mixture 2 times in a day. |
| 2. | Stomachache | About ½ spoon of Ajwain (*Trachyspermum ammi*) and ¼ of salt are taken with hot water three times in a day at a regular interval. |
| | | 5 ml Pudina (*Mentha longifolia*) juice and 5 ml Adrak (*Zingiber officinale*) juice is mixed up with 2 gm salt and eat it two times in a day. |
| | | 10 gm Neem (*Azadirachta indica*) seeds, 10 gm Tulsi (*Ocimum sanctum*) leaves, 10 gm Sonth and 10 Kali-Mirch (*Piper nigrum*) are crushed and use the paste twice in a day. |
| | | 50 gm root of Katuki (*Picrorhiza kurrooa*) is dipped into 200 ml water for 3 hours. Mix up 2 spoons of honey in this water and use 2 spoons of this decoction in the morning. |
| | | 10 gm bark powder of Thuner (*Taxus baccata*) and 100 gm leaf powder of Badamula (*Megacarpaea polyandra*) are heated on fire with 2½ spoon of butter and eat 20 gm of this medicine three times in a day. |
| 3. | Eye pain | The milk of Aak (*Calotropis* sp) is applied on the opposite site of toe. In case of pain in both the eyes then applied the Aak milk in both the legs toe and wash the leg in the morning. |

Contd...

**Table 2.1–Contd...**

| Sl.No. | Ailment | Methods of Preparation and Prescription for Using the Indigenous Formulations |
|---|---|---|
| 4. | Kidney stones | After removing leaves from the twigs of Muli (*Raphanus sativus*) juice is extracted. About 10 gm juice is taken 2-3 times in a day. This technique melts the stones, which come out with urine. |
| | | Muli (*Raphanus sativus*) is given for three times till the stones melt completely. |
| | | Juice of Palak (*Spinacea oleracea*) is given everyday in the morning. |
| | | Awala (*Phyllanthus emblica*) powder is mixed up with Muli (*Raphanus sativus*) and use it two times in a day. |
| | | 6 gm root of Papita (*Carica papaya*) is dissolved in 50 ml water and use it two times in a day for 21 days. |
| | | 20 gm seeds of Gajar (*Daucus carota*) and 20 gm seeds of Shaljam (*Brassica rapa*) are filled inside a Muli (*Raphanus sativus*) and roast it in fire. Take out the seeds of Gajar and Shaljam from Muli and crush them to powder. Eat 5 gm of this powder with water for a month. |
| | | Decoction of Pasanbhed (*Bergenia ligulata*) root is used. |
| 5. | High blood pressure | Honey and juice of Pyaz (*Allium cepa*) is taken twice in a day (morning and evening) after the meals. |
| | | Muli (*Raphanus sativus*) is given regularly. |
| | | Equal quantity of Shilajeet and Sarpgandha (*Rauvolfia serpentina*) is crushed to powder and prepare its pills. Have a pill after every 6 hour in a day. |
| | | Equal quantity of Sarpgandha (*Rauvolfia serpentine*), Awala (*Phyllanthus emblica*), Giloe (*Tinospora cordifolia*), bark of Arjun (*Terminalia arjuna*), Ashgandh (*Withania somnifera*) and Punarnawa (*Boerhaavia diffusa*) are crushed to powder. Eat 5 gm of this powder two times in a day. |
| 6. | Vomiting | Adrak (*Zingiber officinale*) and Pyaz (*Allium cepa*) juice is given in equal quantity. |
| | | 6 gm Pudina (*Mentha longifolia*) and 2 gm salt is dissolved with 150 ml water and drink it three times in a day. |
| | | Crushed Rai (*Brassica rugosa*) to powder and mix up with water. Apply the paste on the belly. |

Contd...

**Table 2.1–Contd...**

| Sl.No. | Ailment | Methods of Preparation and Prescription for Using the Indigenous Formulations |
|---|---|---|
| 7. | Epilepsy/hysteria | 4-5 Leaves of Bichu (*Martynia annua*) are crushed to powder and given to patient. |
| | | Leaf and bulb of Pyaz (*Allium cepa*) is taken. |
| | | 10 gm of Mulethi (Liquorice) powder is mixed up with ½ spoon cow butter and eat it. |
| | | About 5 gm powder of Bach (*Acorus calamus*) is taken with ½ spoon of honey once in a day. |
| | | 10 gm leaves of Anar (*Punica granatum*) and 10 gm leaves of Gulab (*Rosa* sp) are boiled with ½ liter of water till the solution is reduced to ½ of its volume. Sieve the solution, mix up 25 gm refined butter in the solution and drink it for 25 days. |
| 8 | Cough, cold, and throat-ache | Have 2 spoons Adrak (*Zingiber officinale*) juice and jaggary, 4-5 times in a day. Child should have ½ of this dose. |
| | | About 10 gm juice of Adrak (*Zingiber officinale*) and 10 gm honey is heated up and eats twice in a day. |
| | | Fresh leaves of Tulsi (*Ocimum sanctum*) and juice of Adrak (*Zingiber officinale*) is mixed up with honey. |
| | | 5 gm of Choru (*Angelica glauca*) is mixed up with Gahath (*Macrotyloma uniflorum*) to use. |
| | | Choru (*Angelica glauca*) is mixed up in tea. |
| | | Chew 2-4 leaves of pan (*Piper betle*). |
| | | The decoction of Ajwain (*Trachyspermum ammi*) made with the juice of Pyaz (*Allium cepa*) is massaged on the chest. |
| | | Juice is extracted from the leaves of Basinga (*Adhatoda vasica*) and about ½ kg juice is mixed up with ½ spoon Haldi (*Curcuma domestica*), Zeera (*Cuminum cyminum*), ghee and eggs. Have it before meals in the morning. |
| | | 59 ml juice of Launki (*Lagineria siceraria*) is mixed up with 1 spoon honey and 1 spoon sugar. Drink it 2 times a day to cure burning sensation in throat. |
| | | Drink fruit juice of Shahtoot (*Morus alba*). |

*Contd...*

**Table 2.1–Contd...**

| *Sl.No.* | *Ailment* | *Methods of Preparation and Prescription for Using the Indigenous Formulations* |
|---|---|---|
| | | 10 leaves of Tulsi (*Ocimum sanctum*), 5 Kali-Mirch (*Piper nigrum*), 2 Long, 5 gm Adrak (*Zingiber officinale*) and 1 Elayachi (Comfit) are cooked with water and milk. Drink it three times in a day. |
| | | Equal quantity of Long (Clove), Kali-Mirch (*Piper nigrum*), Kattha (*Acacia catechu*) and Baheda (*Terminalia bellirica*) are crushed to powder. Dissolve the powder with a solution of Babool (*Acacia nilotica*) bark and make pills. Eat a pill at every 2 hours interval. |
| 9. | Boils | 2-3 leaves of Seesam (*Delbergia sesoo*) is crushed and heated up with 10 gm of sugar. The paste is applied on the infected part. |
| | | Fresh leaf of Bel (*Aegle marmelos*) crushed without water and the paste is kept on the infected part and tied with bandage. |
| | | Pindalu (*Colocasia esculenta*) leaves are burnt to ashes and the ash mixed up with Sarson (*Brassica campestris*) oil and is applied on the infected part. |
| | | Apply the crushed roots of Karela (*Momordica charantia*) on the infected part. |
| 10. | Black spots around eyes | Kheera (*Cucumis melo*) is crushed and 5-6 drops of extracted juice is applied around the eyes with the help of cotton, and then the eyes are cleaned with cold water. |
| 11. | Acidity and gastric disorders | Half piece of Neebu (*Citrus* sp) is squeezed in a glass of water and dissolves 5 gm salt and 5 gm soda in it with 4-5-spoon sugar. Drink this decoction one hour before meal. |
| 12. | In removing glass piece, spine and needle from flesh | One spoon Ajwain (*Trachyspermum ammi*) and 1 spoon tobacco is mixed up with jaggary. This paste is applied and tied on the infected organ. In the morning the desired thing comes out. |

*Contd...*

**Table 2.1–Contd...**

| Sl.No. | Ailment | Methods of Preparation and Prescription for Using the Indigenous Formulations |
|---|---|---|
| 13. | Earache and secretion from ears | 3-4 drops of half boiled Tulsi (*Ocimum sanctum*) leaf extract pour in the ears. |
| | | About 100 gm inside part of unripe Bel (*Aegle marmelos*) is mixed up with ½ liter of Sarson (*Brassica campestris*) oil, 2 liters water, 2 liters goat milk and 100 ml cow urine. The cow urine is mixed up with inside part of unripe Bel and cooks in iron pot on slow heat. Once the paste becomes red, it is taken out and sieved. The sieved oil is dropped into the ear with dropper and closes the ear with cotton so that oil cannot flow out. |
| | | New leaves of mango (*Mangifera indica*) are crushed and the extracted juice is heated up and dropped 2-3 drops into ear. |
| | | Green stem of Sullu (*Euphorbia royleana*) is heated on direct fire till its outer surface becomes brown. Later it is squeezed and its juice is kept into a vessel. Pour the juice in the ear and after 5 minutes take the water out. |
| | | Pyaz (*Allium cepa*), root of Bel (*Aegle marmelos*) and Haldi (*Curcuma domestica*) are mixed up in equal proportion and put it inside the ear. |
| | | Til (*Sesamum orientale)* oil is heated with Lahsun *(Allium sativum)* and 4 drops of this oil is poured in ears before going to bed. |
| | | Juice extract from the stem of Kela (*Musa* sp) after heating on fire is poured in ears before going to bed in night. |
| 14. | Toothache | About 5-6 Lahsun (*Allium sativum*) are rapped in a clean square cloth after washing and crushing to pieces. This put close to the nose and inhales deeply almost 5-6 times in a day. |
| | | Have 3 gm sonth with water once in a day. |
| | | Chew leaves of Tulsi (*Ocimum sanctum)* |
| | | Mix up with equal quantity of milk in the Bel (*Aegle marmelos*) fruits juice and have it ½ cup twice a day (morning and evening). |
| | | Root and latex of Arandi (*Ricinus communis*) is kept at the spot of pain. |

*Contd...*

**Table 2.1–Contd...**

| Sl.No. | Ailment | Methods of Preparation and Prescription for Using the Indigenous Formulations |
|---|---|---|
| | | Boiled the Mehndi (*Lawsonia inermis*) *leaf* with water and wash the teeth and mouth. |
| | | Press Kapoor (Camphor) between upper and lower teeth. |
| | | Roasted piece of Haldi (*Curcuma domestica*) is pressed between the upper and lower teeth and suck the juice oozes out of it. |
| 15. | Scorpion bite | 1-2 fruit cover of Ritha (*Sapindus mukorosii*) are kept in the Chilam of Hukka (A traditional instrument for smoking) and burnt. To smoke this Hukka relives the pain. |
| | | Scratch the heated seed of Imli (*Terminalia indica*) till its internal white cotyledon is appeared. Place the scratched part of Imli on the affected part. |
| | | Eat Pudina (*Mentha longifolia*) leaves. |
| 16. | Bad smell in mouth | Sarson (*Brassica campestris*) oil with paste of Haldi (*Curcuma domestica*) and alam is used to wash the teeth twice in a day. |
| 17. | Unconscious | 5-10 drops of Ritha (*Sapindus mukorosii*) fogs are poured in the nostrils. |
| 18. | Food poisoning | Drink the decoction of Ritha (*Sapindus mukorosii*), which make to do vomiting. |
| 19. | To reduce fat | Eat seeds of Methi (*Trigonella foenum-graecum*) with water in morning and evening. |
| | | Muli (*Raphanus sativus*) juice with salt and Neebu (*Citrus* sp) juice should be taken regularly. |
| 20. | Joint pains | Eat Methi (*Trigonella foenum-graecum*) seeds with water two times in a day (morning and evening). |
| | | 10 gm Ajwain (*Trachyspermum ammi*) and 10 gm Lahsun (*Allium sativum*) is heated with 50 ml Sarson oil. Massage the oil on the affected organs in the evening. |
| 21. | Piles | Collect the fresh leaves of Bod (*Ficus benghalensis*) before sunrise and drops the oozing latex on Batasha and eat it. |
| | | 20 gm of Kali-Mirch (*Piper nigrum*) is mixed up with 10 gm Jira (*Cuminum cyminum*) and 15 gm mishri (sugar candy). The prepared powder after crushing is eaten with water. |

*Contd...*

**Table 2.1–Contd...**

| *Sl.No.* | *Ailment* | *Methods of Preparation and Prescription for Using the Indigenous Formulations* |
|---|---|---|
| | | 200 gm Muli (*Raphanus sativus*) is given everyday in the meals. |
| | | Hardi (*Terminalia chebula*) is roasted and crushed to powder. One spoon of powder is taken with 250 gm juice of Muli (*Raphanus sativus*) before having meals two times in a day. |
| | | Fruit cover of Nariyal (*Cocus nucifera*) is burnt to ashes. Sieve the ashes by a thin cotton piece and mix it with milk, and drink the decoction in the evening. |
| | | Use Awala (*Phyllanthus emblica*) powder with curd. |
| | | 50 gm Ritha (*Sapindus mukorosii*) is placed on the iron plate that is heated on fire for ½ an hour and closes the Ritha by a bowl. After cooling down remove the bowl and collect the ashes of Ritha. Mix up 20 gm Kattha (*Acacia catechu*) with 20 gm of Ritha ashes and eat this powder with 20 gm butter two times in a day. Also drink 250 gm cow milk and continue this exercise for 15 days. |
| 22. | Indigestion | Eat Methi (*Trigonella foenum-graecum*) seeds with water in morning and evening. |
| | | Adrak (*Zingiber officinale*) and jaggary is given. |
| | | Eat 2-3 fruits of Amrood (*Psidium guava*) along with seeds. |
| | | 10 gm Mulethi is mixed up with 20 gm sugar and eat it with milk. |
| | | Have juice of wheat (*Triticum aestivum*) plant. |
| | | 15 gm Dalchini (*Cinnamomum verum*), 100 gm Saunf (*Foeniculum vulgare*) and 10 chhoti Elayachi (Comfit) are crushed to powder and use ½ spoon of this powder in the evening with water. |
| | | Green Dhaniya (*Coriandrum sativum*), Kali-Mirch (*Piper nigrum*), salt and Jira (*Cuminum cyminum*) are crushed together and eat this powder with water. |
| | | Juice of ½ Neebu (*Citrus* sp), ½ spoon of Kali-Mirch (*Piper nigrum*) powder and ½ spoon of salt are dissolved with 150 ml water. Drink it two times in a day. |
| | | Equal quantity of Haida (*Terminalia chebula*), Baida (*Terminalia bellirica*) and Awala (*Phyllanthus emblica*) is crushed to powder and eat it with 200 gm cow milk. |

*Contd...*

**Table 2.1–Contd...**

| Sl.No. | Ailment | Methods of Preparation and Prescription for Using the Indigenous Formulations |
|---|---|---|
| 23. | Reproductive disorder | Bod (*Ficus benghalensis*) bark is cleaned and decoction is prepared with water, which is given to the person feeling burning sensations during release of urine. |
| | | The apical parts of the aerial roots of Bod (*Ficus benghalensis*) are crushed and the powder is used with milk. |
| | | About 100 gm bark of Semal (*Bombax ceiva*) and 13 Munakka (Raisin) are mixed up with 200 ml milk. |
| 24. | Dysentery | About 100 gm green leaves of Doob (*Cynodon dactylon*), half spoon soth and ½ spoon Saunf (*Foeniculum vulgare*) is boiled with 1 glass of water. The boiled water is cooled down and then drinks 3 times a day (morning, noon and evening). |
| | | Immature inside part of Bel (*Aegle marmelos*) fruits is half roasted and mixed up with equal quantity of sugar. It is taken twice in a day. |
| | | Bel is mixed up with fruit coat of Anar (*Punicum granatum*) and uses it with honey. |
| | | 10 gm cotyledons of mango (*Mangifera indica*) are mixed up with 100 gm curd. |
| | | About 10 gm cotyledons of mango are mixed up with 10 gm honey and use it three times in a day. |
| | | About 12 gm Methi (*Trigonella foenum-graecum*) powder is mixed up with 50 gm curd and eats the decoction two times a day. |
| | | Two spoon of Dhaniya (*Coriandrum sativum*) is boiled in water for 5 minutes and then use the cooked dhaniya two times a day. |
| | | One unripe fruit of Kela (*Musa* sp) boiled with water is mixed up with ½ spoon of butter, one Long (Clove), 100 gm curd and ¼ spoon of Haldi (*Curcuma domestica*), and eats the decoction two times a day. |
| 25. | Skin diseases | Doob (*Cynodon dactylon*) is mixed up with Haldi (*Curcuma domestica*) and the paste is applied on the infected organ. |
| | | Fresh leaves of Tulsi (*Ocimum sanctum*) are crushed and mixed up with equal amount of Neebu (*Citrus* sp) juice and applied on the infected skin. |

Contd...

**Table 2.1–Contd...**

| Sl.No. | Ailment | Methods of Preparation and Prescription for Using the Indigenous Formulations |
|---|---|---|
| | | The latex oozes out from plucking mango (*Mengifera indica*) fruits is applied on the skin spots. |
| | | Cow urine is applied on the body and also used to drink. |
| | | The paste of Neem (*Azadirachta indica*) leaves is applied on the allergic part or drinks the decoction of Neem. |
| | | About 250 gm of Sarson (*Brassica campestris*) oil is boiled with 250 gm of Neem leaves and then fried with 25 gm Haldi (*Curcuma domestica*). Once the Haldi is cooked it is taken out to be cooled down for 2 minutes and is sieved. It is stored in a bottle and is used on the allergic part whenever required. |
| 26. | Uro-genital disorders | The roots of Doob (*Cynodon dactylon*) are washed with tap water and then crushed to paste. A spoon of this paste is eaten with fresh 50 gm of curd before taking the meal in the morning. |
| | | The immature inside part of Bel (*Aegle marmelos*) fruits is crushed and mixed up with sugar. The half-cup of it should be taken with milk two times (morning and evening). |
| | | Have a Muli (*Raphanus sativus*) everyday. |
| | | A Karela (*Momordica charantia*) is crushed and mix up with 200 ml water. After sieving drink the water for 10 days. |
| | | Eat roasted cauliflower and boiled Bhindi (*Abelmoschus esculentus*). |
| | | Equal quantity of Haida (*Terminalia chebula*), Baheda (*Terminalia bellirica*) and Awala (*Phyllanthus emblica*) is crushed and use it with the juice of Khas-Khas (*Vetiveria zizanioides*) for 10 days. |
| 27. | Anaemia | About 250 gm green Doob (*Cynodon dactylon*) is washed and crushed with water to prepare the paste. The paste is kept inside clean cloth and pressed to get the extract or juice, which is taken in the morning before meal for 45 days. This treatment enhances the hemoglobin. |

Contd...

**Table 2.1–Contd...**

| Sl.No. | Ailment | Methods of Preparation and Prescription for Using the Indigenous Formulations |
|---|---|---|
| 28. | Improving eyesight | Half spoon powder of Kali-Mirch (*Piper nigrum*) is mixed up with butter and eats it. |
| | | Eat one Muli (*Raphanus sativus*) everyday in the morning. |
| | | The mixture of 10 gm Saunf (*Foeniculum vulgare*) and 10 gm sugar is mixed up with 7 Badam (*Terminalia catappa*) and takes it with one glass of hot milk before going to bed every night. Don't take water after having this mixture. |
| | | The powder of equal quantity of Elayachi (Comfit) and sugar is mixed up with Arandi oil (*Ricinus communis*). Use 4 gm mixture per day for 40 days. |
| 29. | Tuberculosis | Half spoon Kali-Mirch (*Piper nigrum*) powder with honey is given 3-4 times in a day. |
| | | The leaves of Basinga (*Adhatoda vasica*) is dried and crushed to powder and eat one small spoon of this powder before going to bed in night. |
| | | The milk and meet of goat is given to patient. |
| | | 15 leaves of Tulsi (*Ocimum sanctum*), ½ spoon salt, ½ spoon Jira (*Cuminum cyminum*) and juice of a Neebu (*Citrus* sp.) are mixed up and have it two times a day for 2 months. |
| | | Dry bark of Pipal (*Ficus religiosa*) is crushed to powder and eat it with hot water three times in a day. |
| | | Mango cotyledons are crushed to powder and eat 5 gm of this powder with water everyday in the morning. |
| 30. | Nose bleeding | Green leaves of Doob (*Cynodon dactylon*) are washed with water and crushed to extract the juice. 3-4 drops of juice is poured inside both the nostrils. |
| 31. | Vomiting in pregnancy | The inside part of the unripe Bel (*Aegle marmelos*) fruit is mixed up with the boiled rice water and have ½ cup twice in a day (morning and evening) |
| 32. | Worms in stomach | About 5-6 Bel (*Aegle marmelos*) leaf is mixed up with 1 glass of water and eat it twice in a day (morning and evening). |
| | | Have one Muli (*Raphanus sativus*) everyday. |
| | | Soaked 25 gm Channa (*Cicer arietinum*) in the extract of Ganna (*Saccharum officinarum*) over night and eat the soaked channa in morning. Don't eat anything for about 6-7 hours after having these channa. |

Contd...

**Table 2.1–Contd...**

| Sl.No. | Ailment | Methods of Preparation and Prescription for Using the Indigenous Formulations |
|---|---|---|
| 33. | Excess heat | An unripe mango (*Mengifera indica*) fruit is roasted in direct fire and sieved after mixing with one glass of water. The sieved extract is mixed up with one spoon sugar to drink. |
| | | 20 gm leaf of Imli (*Terminalia indica*) boiled with 100 ml water, and drink it two times a day. |
| 34. | Pimples | Eat Muli (*Raphanus sativus*) every day in the morning. |
| | | Massage Anar (*Punica granatum*) juice. |
| | | ½ spoon Haldi (*Curcuma domestica*) and ½ spoon salt is heated with 10 ml Neebu (*Citrus* sp) juice and paste it on the face once in a week. Wash the face with cold water after 20 minutes. |
| | | Paste of Neem (*Citrus* sp) root prepared with water applies on the face. |
| 35. | Jaundice | About 250 gm Muli (*Raphanus sativus*) with leaves is given three times in a day. |
| | | Keep the Anar (*Punica granatum*) juice in the iron vessels over night and drink it in the morning. |
| | | Eat cooked unripe Papita (*Carica papaya*) two times a day. |
| | | 300 gm of Awala (*Phyllanthus emblica*) is mixed up with 100 gm honey and eat it three times in a day. |
| | | 5 leaves of Pipal (*Ficus religiosa*) and 5 leaves of Lisoda are crushed and after mixing it with salt use two times in a day. |
| | | 100 gm root powder of Kut (*Saussurea costus*) is mixed up with 2 spoon honey and take this dose with 100 ml milk two times in a day. |
| 36 | Diabetes | Eat 150 gm Muli (*Raphanus sativus*) everyday. |
| | | Crush Tejpatta (*Cinnamomum tamala*) leaves to powder and have 5 gm powder everyday with water. |
| | | 4 green and mild leaves of Jamun (*Syzygium cuminii*) are crushed to powder and mix up with 60 gm water. After sieving drink it in the morning for 10 days. |

*Contd...*

**Table 2.1–Contd...**

| *Sl.No.* | *Ailment* | *Methods of Preparation and Prescription for Using the Indigenous Formulations* |
|---|---|---|
| 37. | Pyria | 2-3 mild leaf of Neem (*Azadirachta indica*) with Kali-Mirch (*Piper nigrum*) and Kala salt is given everyday in the morning. |
| | | Use Long (Clove). |
| | | Wash the mouth and teeth by bark juice of Akhrot (*Juglans regia*) twice in a day (morning and after dinner). |
| | | Massage the juice of Neebu (*Citrus* sp.) on the jaws and teeth. |
| | | Massage on teeth the paste of 200 ml Arandi (*Ricinus communis*) oil, 5 gm powder of Bans Kapoor and 100 ml of honey. |
| | | Powder of roasted Awala (*Phyllanthus emblica*) and salt is mixed up with 2-3 drops of Sarson (*Brassica campestris*) oil and wash teeth everyday by this paste. |
| 38. | Blood purification | The mild leaf of Neem (*Azadirachta indica*) with Kali-Mirch (*Piper nigrum*) and Kala-salt is given everyday in the morning. |
| | | The juice of Anar (*Punica granatum*) has three times in a day. |
| | | Cow urine is used. |
| | | 100 gm mild leaves of Neem (*Azadirachta indica*) are boiled with 100 ml water and ½ kg cow butter and cook it till the whole water evaporates. Eat 5 gm of this medicine with 250 ml of milk per day in the morning. |
| | | Leaves and twigs of Chirayata (*Swertia chiraiyta*) are crushed to powder. Mix up 4 gm of this powder in 600 gm water and use it upto 4 days. Keep on doing this exercise for 40 days. |
| 39. | Headache | Eat Long (Clove) twice a day (morning and evening). |
| | | Paste of Moru seeds is applied on the forehead. |
| | | Paste of Surajmuki (*Helianthus annus*) seeds is pasted on the forehead. |
| | | Paste of Karela (*Momordica charantia*) leaf and Pyaz (*Allium cepa*) is poured in the ear. |
| | | Drink fruit juice of Awala (*Phyllanthus emblica*) during the headache in summer. |

*Contd...*

**Table 2.1 Contd...**

| Sl.No. | Ailment | Methods of Preparation and Prescription for Using the Indigenous Formulations |
|---|---|---|
| | | Juice of Mulethi (Liquorice) leaves is boiled with Sarson oil and massages the paste on the forehead. |
| | | 5 Tejpatta (*Cinnamomum tamala*) are crushed with water and apply the paste on the forehead. |
| | | Crush Neebu (*Citrus* sp) leaves and extract its juice. Pour this juice inside the nostrils. |
| | | Eat 5 gm roots of Katuki (*Picrorhiza kurrooa*) two times in a day. |
| | | Apply root paste of Atis (*Aconitum heterophyllum*) on the forehead. |
| 40. | Brain tonic | Mixture of 10 gm Saunf (*Foeniculum vulgare*) and 10 gm sugar is mixed up with 7 Badam (*Terminalia catappa*). This is taken with a glass of hot milk before going to bed every night. Don't take water after having this medicine. |
| | | About 100 gm juice of Gajar (*Daucus carota*) root mixed up with 7 Badam (*Terminalia catappa*) and ½ kg milk and drink it early in the morning. |
| | | Eat an apple 10 minutes before taking meals. |
| | | Drink leaf juice of Brahmi (*Centella asiatica*). |
| 41. | Backache, Bodyache | Massage the Badam (*Terminalia catappa*) oil every day and eat 5 Badams each day after soaking in water with a glass of milk. |
| | | 10 gm of dry Pudina (*Mentha longifolia*), 10 gm Awala (*Phyllanthus emblica*), 10 gm Haida (*Terminalia chebula*), 10 gm Sonth and 10 gm Mehandi (*Lawsonia inermis*) are mixed up and crushed to powder. Make its pills with juice of Lahsun (*Allium sativum*) and have a pill each time with water twice in a day (morning and evening). |
| | | 3 gm Heeng (*Ferula narthex*), 3 gm Kali-Mirch (*Piper nigrum*), 10 gm Pipal (*Ficus religiosa*) roots and 10 gm Narangi (*Citrus* sp) are crushed together and sieve. Mix-up 10 gm Brahmi (*Centella asiatica*) and 50 gm oil of roasted Til (*Sesamum orientale*) and use the decoction. |
| 42. | Paralysis | Pour the 4-5 drops of Akhrot (*Juglans regia*) oil in nostrils many times. |
| | | Adrak (*Zingiber officinale*) mixed up with honey and eat it two times in a day. |

Contd...

**Table 2.1–Contd...**

| *Sl.No.* | *Ailment* | *Methods of Preparation and Prescription for Using the Indigenous Formulations* |
|---|---|---|
| 43. | Madness | Keep the Amrood (*Psidium guava*) overnight in the water and eat it in the morning. |
| 44. | Blisters in mouth | Eat a ripened Kela (*Musa* sp) with 50 gm curd. |
| | | Chew 2-3 leaves of Amrood (*Psidium guava*) with Katha (*Acacia catechu*). |
| | | 20 gm Haldi (*Curcuma domestica*) mix-up with 200 ml water sieve it to wash the mouth. |
| 45. | Eye diseases | Mix up the honey and Santra (*Citrus* sp) juice in equal quantity and drop it in the eyes. |
| | | Eating roasted fruits of Amrood (*Psidium guava*) if water comes out frequently from eyes. |
| | | Equal quantity of Haldi (*Curcuma domestica*) and Arhar (*Cajanus cajan*) is cooked on fire and let it dries. Mix up water with this hard paste and applied on the eye lids. |
| | | 100 gm root powder of Kingod (*Berberis aristata*) is mixed up with 200 ml water and pour 2-3 drops of this medicine in the infected eye. |
| | | Bark of Kathbhoj (*Betula alnoides*) is burnt to ashes and 100 gm of this ash is mixed up with 2 spoon of butter and apply 5 gm of this paste on the eyelids three times in a day. |
| 46. | Internal injuries | Have 10 gm of Haldi (*Curcuma domestica*) with 1 glass of milk |
| | | About 10 gm root of Archa (*Rheum moorcroftianum*) is crushed and mixed up with a little salt. |
| 47. | Cut and wounds | Put the paste of Pudina (*Mentha longifolia*) leaves on the infected part. |
| | | 100 gm dried leaf of Brahmakamal (*Saussurea obvallata*) is mixed up with 10 gm salt and this paste is applied on the wounded areas. |
| | | 10 gm tuber of Hathajari (*Dactylorhiza hatagirea*) and 50 gm root of Dholu (*Rheum australe*) is heated on fire for 2-3 minutes and apply on the wounded portion. |
| 48. | Sciatica | The cow ghee is massaged on the infected parts. |
| | | About 150 gm juice of Singoli (*Vitex negundo*) is cooked on light fire with 2.50 gm of Sarson (*Brassica campestris*) oil till the all water is evaporated. |

*Contd...*

**Table 2.1–Contd...**

| *Sl.No.* | *Ailment* | *Methods of Preparation and Prescription for Using the Indigenous Formulations* |
|---|---|---|
| | | Paste of potato (*Solanum tuberosum*) is applied on the painful part. |
| | | Eat small roasted pieces of Adrak (*Zingiber officinale*), and also massage the paste of Adrak roasted in Til (*Sesamum orientale*) oil on the painful part. |
| | | 5 gm Methi (*Trigonella foenum-graecum*) and 5 gm Sonth are crushed to powder and eat it with jaggary. |
| | | Equal quantity of Asgandh (*Withania somnifera*) root and Khand are crushed to powder and eat 5 gm of this powder with milk two times in a day. |
| | | Root of Mitha (*Aconitum balfourii*) is boiled with Sarson (*Brassica campestris*) oil. A special instrument of iron (U shaped trident) is dipped into this boiled oil and then touch on the painful portion of the body. |
| 49. | Tonsils | About 20 gm bark of Quiral (*Bahunia variegata*) is boiled with 200 gm water and then it is rolled inside the mouth. |
| 50. | Child dysentery | About 4-5 mild twigs of Amrood (*Psidium guava*) are crushed and are cooked with 10 gm Kali-Mirch (*Piper nigrum*) and 100 gm water. Give 1-2 spoons to child. |
| 51. | Cholera | About 5 gm Heeng (*Ferula narthex*), 10 gm Kapoor (Camphor), 10 gm Kattha (*Acacia catechu*), 10 mild twigs of Neem (*Azadirachta indica*) is mixed up with 10 gm leaves of Tulsi (*Ocimum sanctum*) and the paste is rolled to make the pills. Eat one pill four times a day. |
| | | 10 gm Kali-Mirch (*Piper nigrum*), 10 gm Heeng (*Ferula narthex*) and 20 gm camphor are crushed to powder and make the pills. Eat a pill at every 30 minute interval. |
| | | Drink Pudina (*Mentha longifolia*) juice. |
| 52. | Cataract | 5 Badams (*Terminalia catappa*), 7 Kali-Mirch (*Piper nigrum*) and 20 gm sugar are grinned to powder and then dissolve in 100 ml water. Use it two times in a day. |
| | | Mix up Saunf (*Foeniculum vulgare*) and Dhaniya (*Coriandrum sativum*) in equal proportion with sugar and eat 10 gm of it per day. |
| | | Paste of Supari (*Areca catechu*) is applied on eyelids. |

Contd...

**Table 2.1–Contd...**

| *Sl.No.* | *Ailment* | *Methods of Preparation and Prescription for Using the Indigenous Formulations* |
|---|---|---|
| 53. | Conjunctivitis | The powder of 10 gm Bel (*Aegle marmelos*) leaf, 6 Kali-Mirch (*Piper nigrum*) and 25 gm sugar are mixed up and have it two times in a day. |
| | | Drink Tamatar (*Lycopersicon esculentum*) juice in every morning and evening. |
| 54. | Jaws swelling | Arandi (*Ricinus communis*) oil mixed up with camphor is massaged slowly on the jaws. |
| 55. | Eczema | 250 gm root bark of Kaner (*Nerium indicum*) is cooked with 1 liter Sarson (*Brassica campestris*) oil and sieve it. Apply 4-5 drops of oil everyday on the affected part. |
| | | Fruit cover of Tarbooj (*Citrullus lanatus*) after drying is burnt to ashes and the ashes are mixed up with Nariyal (*Cocus nucifera*) oil to apply on the eczema. |
| 56. | Snake bite | 30 ml juice of Pyaz (*Allium cepa*) is mixed up with 30 ml Sarson (*Brassica campestris*) oil and use this liquid. |
| | | Root of Tulsi (*Ocimum sanctum*) is crushed to powder and apply it on the snake bitten portion of the body. |
| 57. | Dog bite | Pastes of red chilies (*Capsicum anum*) apply on the wounded part. |
| | | 10 ml juice of Pyaz (*Allium cepa*) is mixed up with 15 gm honey and this paste is applied on the wounded part. |
| 58. | Spermatorrhoea | Eat mixed powder of 5 gm Badam (*Terminalia catappa*), 5 gm Kali-Mirch (*Piper nigrum*), 2 gm Sonth (dried ginger) and 5 gm mishri (candy sugar) with 250 ml cow milk everyday for a month. |
| | | 25 gm juice of Semal (*Syzygium cuminii*) bark and 25 gm of mishri is given with 250 gm milk two times in a day (morning and evening) before having meals. |
| | | Eat 50 gm water soaked Channa (*Cicer arietinum*) and 5 Badam (*Terminalia catappa*) with milk for a month. |
| 59. | Leucorrhoea | ½ spoon juice of Satawari (*Asparagus racemosus*) root, ½ spoon juice of Giloe (*Tinospora cordifolia*) and 10 gm refined sugar is mixed up with 250 gm cow milk. Use it 2 times in a day (morning and evening). |
| | | After eating Kela (*Musa* sp) drink 100 ml milk mixed up with 1 spoon of honey for a month. |
| | | 10 ml leaf juice of Tulsi (*Ocimum sanctum*) is mixed up with 1 spoon of honey and 200 ml cow milk. Drink it in the evening before going to bed. |

*Contd...*

**Table 2.1–Contd...**

| Sl.No. | Ailment | Methods of Preparation and Prescription for Using the Indigenous Formulations |
|---|---|---|
| 60. | Child stomachache | ½ spoon juice of Adrak (*Zingiber officinale*), ½ spoon of Haldi (*Curcuma domestica*), and a spoon of Kala-jira (*Bunicum persicum*) is given to child two times in a day. |
| 61. | Migraine | Drink 100 ml juice of Angoor (*Vitis vinifera*) before sunrise. |
| | | 10 ml juice of Tulsi (*Ocimum sanctum*) leaf is mixed up with 1 spoon of honey and uses it two times in a day. |
| 62. | Heart diseases | 10 leaves of Tulsi (*Ocimum sanctum*), 6 Kali-Mirch (*Piper nigrum*) and 6 Badam (*Terminalia catappa*) are crushed and eat it with 100 ml water. |
| 63. | Sprains | 1 spoon of Haldi (*Curcuma domestica*) and ½ spoon Pyaz (*Allium cepa*) juice is mixed up with 1 spoon of Sarson (*Brassica campestris*) oil and apply on the affected organ. |
| | | Paste of Gular (*Ficus racemosa*) leaves is applied on the injured part of the body. |
| 64. | Malaria | 6 leaves of Tulsi (*Ocimum sanctum*), 2 Kali-Mirch (*Piper nigrum*) and Pipali (*Piper longum*) are mixed up with ½ spoon of sugar and eat with water three times a day. |
| | | Soaked aerial parts of Chirayiata (*Swertia* sp.) overnight in water and drink this water in the morning. |
| | | 5 gm Lahsun (*Allium sativum*) and 10 gm Til (*Sesamum orientale*) oil are mixed up with 5 gm salt and eat it in the early morning. |
| 65. | Typhoid | Eat 5-6 leaves of Tulsi (*Ocimum sanctum*) with tea. |
| | | Mix up 5 gm sugar with the juice of Pudina (*Mentha longifolia*) and Tulsi (*Ocimum sanctum*) and drink it three times in a day. |
| 66. | Leucoderma | Drink juice of Bathuwa (*Chenopodium album*) two times in a day. |
| | | Haida (*Terminalia chebula*) mixed up with Lahsun (*Allium sativum*) juice and applied on the white spots. |
| 67. | Irregular menstruation | 10 gm seeds of Tulsi (*Ocimum sanctum*) are boiled with water and drink it two times a day. |
| | | Mild twigs of Neem (*Azadirachta indica*) are boiled with water. Sieve it and drink three times in a day. |

Contd...

**Table 2.1–Contd...**

| Sl.No. | Ailment | Methods of Preparation and Prescription for Using the Indigenous Formulations |
|---|---|---|
| 68. | Burn | Mild leaves of Bod (*Ficus benghalensis*) are crushed with cow butter and paste it on the affected part of the body. |
| | | Apply juice of Karela (*Momordica charantia*) on the burning part. |
| 69. | Cancer in uterus | 30-40 leaves of Tulsi (*Ocimum sanctum*) are stirred with 250 gm curd and drink the decoction two times in a day. |
| 70. | Low blood pressure | 30 gm Kishmish (*Vitis vinifera*) is soaked in 150 ml water. Eat these Kishmish per day in the morning. |
| 71. | Pneumonia | Mix up honey with Pudina (*Mentha longifolia*) juice and drink it at every 2 hours interval. |
| 72. | Rheumatism | 10 gm root of Jatamansi (*Nardostachys jatamansi*) is heated on fire with 50 gm cow butter for 5 minute and then rubbed on the painful portion of the body. |
| | | 50 gm root bark of Bidaru (*Juniperus communis*) is heated on fire with 200 ml seed oil of Aru (*Prunus persica*) and then 4 drops of this oil is rubbed on the painful area. |
| 73. | Bone fracture | Resin of Kail (*Pinus wallichiana*) is heated on fire and then applies on the fractured portion. |
| | | Root and leaves of Brahmakamal (*Saussurea obvallata*) are crushed to powder and 200 gm of this powder is mixed up with 20 ml oil of Devdar (*Cedrus deodara*) and applies on the painful portion. |
| | | 100 gm leaves of Semru (*Rhododendron campanulatum*) and 10 gm ash of cow dung are heated on fire with 25 ml Sarson (*Brassica campestris*) oil and paste it on the fractured portion. |

of some of the medicinal plants. The loss of knowledge on preparing medicine is due to the decline in number of *Vaidyas* coming forward to adopt this traditional healing practice professionally. At present, the knowledge is scattered among the local inhabitants.

**Table 2.2: General Profile of the Various Components of the Study**

| | |
|---|---|
| *Vaidya* interviewed | 60 |
| Age group in *Vaidyas* | |
| ✰ Young (16-25 years) | 9 |
| ✰ Adult (26-45 years) | 22 |
| ✰ Old (>46 years) | 29 |
| *Vaidyas* having disciples | 24 |
| Number of plants documented | 156 |
| Number of formulations documented | 243 |
| Number of diseases treated | 73 |

While grouping the diseases highest numbers of ailments were found in the generalized bodyache and colic, followed by gastrointestinal disorders (Table 2.3). The analysis of collected information reveals that the highest numbers of medical formulations were developed by using highest number of plant species for the treatment of generalized bodyache and colic, followed by gastrointestinal disorders, uro-genital problems and dermatological problems. The least number of plant species and medical formulations were recorded for general health tonic and heart diseases. The analysis depicts that the traditional herbal healers, on the basis of the commonality of the diseases, have developed the number of formulations (Table 2.4). There was a correlation between the number of formulations developed by *Vaidyas* and number of diseases cured (Figure 2.1). Besides, a pattern has given in Figure 2.2 between the number of species and occurrences of number of diseases.

Most of the species are used in curing a single disease, which depicts the uniqueness of species for curing the particular type of disease. Of the 156 medicinal plants documented 66 species are used in preparation of one formulation and each formulation is used in curing a single ailment only. Seventeen species are used in preparation of 2 formulations and each formulation is used in curing two ailments. Since there is a ban on collection of many plant species from wild, the *Vaidyas* admit for facing tremendous difficulty in making the specific formulation. Inspite of this difficulty, *Vaidyas* are determined to keep the tradition alive. These *Vaidyas* have focused their experiments for making herbal medicine on those plant species, which are available in nearby areas including kitchen and kitchen gardens.

**Table 2.3: Number of Formulations and Number of Species Used in Curing the Number of Ailments and Different Groupings of Diseases**

| *Sl.No.* | *Groups of Diseases* | *No. of Ailments* | *No. of Formulations* | *No. of Species* |
|---|---|---|---|---|
| 1. | Generalized bodyache | 16 | 59 | 49 |
| 2. | Gastrointestinal disorder | 14 | 55 | 45 |
| 3. | Uro-genital disorder | 8 | 26 | 25 |
| 4. | Dermatological problem | 8 | 22 | 23 |
| 5. | Bone diseases/fractures | 5 | 20 | 24 |
| 6. | Eye diseases | 5 | 15 | 16 |
| 7. | Blood related disorder | 3 | 12 | 10 |
| 8. | Mental/psychological disorder | 4 | 9 | 10 |
| 9. | Antivenum/scorpion bite/dog bite | 3 | 7 | 8 |
| 10. | Respiratory disorder | 2 | 7 | 7 |
| 11. | Heart diseases | 3 | 6 | 11 |
| 12. | General health tonic | 2 | 5 | 6 |

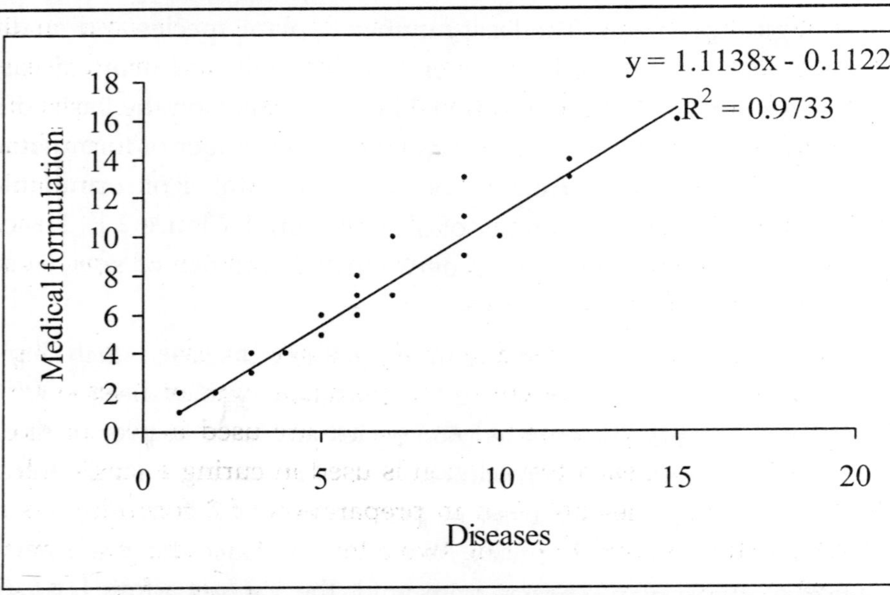


**Figure 2.1: Correlations Between Number of Formulations Developed by Vaidyas and the Number of Diseases Cured**

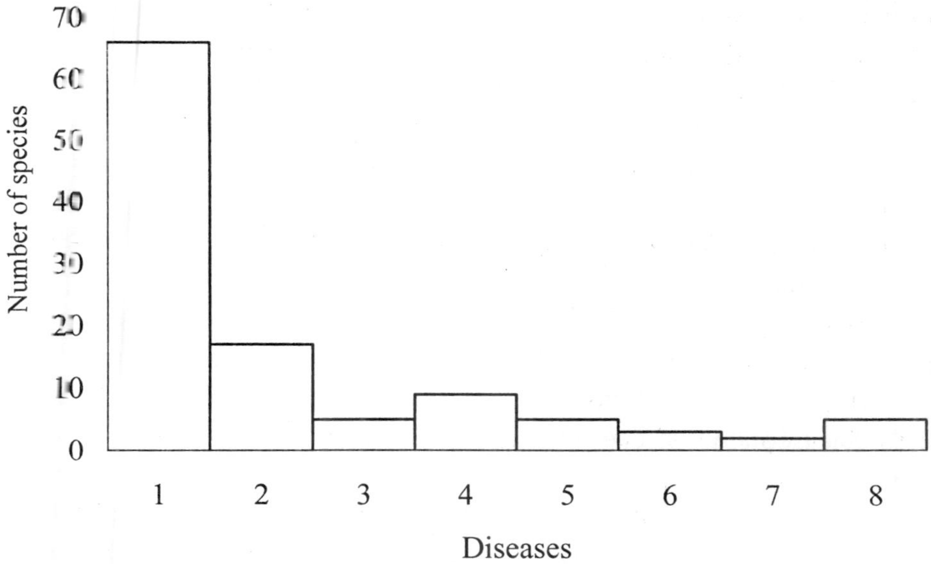


**Figure 2.2: Pattern Between Number of Species and Number of Diseases Cured by Vaidyas**

**Table 2.4: Major Diseases as per the Availability of Formulations and Species for Therapy**

| *S.No.* | *Disease* | *No. of Formulations Used* | *No. of Species Used* |
|---|---|---|---|
| 1. | Cough and cold | 12 | 16 |
| 2. | Headache | 10 | 12 |
| 3. | Indigestion | 8 | 12 |
| 4. | Dysentery | 8 | 9 |
| 5. | Toothache | 8 | 7 |
| 6. | Kidney stones | 7 | 6 |
| 7. | Earache | 7 | 10 |
| 8. | Piles | 7 | 9 |
| 9. | Sciatica | 7 | 8 |
| 10. | Tuberculosis | 6 | 6 |
| 11. | Jaundice | 6 | 6 |
| 12. | Fever | 6 | 7 |

The findings of this study indicate that most of the common species, which used to grow in the gardens and adjacent to the village areas in cultivated or forested lands, were used by traditional *Vaidyas* in majorities of the cases for preparation of herbal medical formulations. *Ocimum sanctum* locally known as Tulsi and also a religious plant was reported to cure 15 types of diseases and *Vaidyas* used to prepare 16 medical formulations by using this plant species. The other species that were frequently used by *Vaidyas* for making medical formulations were *Piper nigrum, Curcuma domestica, Brassica compestris* and *Raphanus sativus* (Table 2.5). The analysis of data further reveals that of the 156 plant species used, at present, by *Vaidyas* for preparing medicine 55 per cent are cultivated and 45 per cent are wild species. Of the cultivated species 80 per cent grow in the kitchen garden and 20 per cent in the agricultural fields. The frequency of use of kitchen garden species is highest in preparing the medical formulations as in 243 formulations the relative frequency of use of such species is 87 per cent, which goes upto 92 per cent if agricultural species are also taken into account. The relative frequency of use of the medicinal plants growing in wild is 55 per cent in preparing herbal medical formulations.

**Table 2.5: Medicinal Plants Used in Curing Number of Ailments and Number of Herbal Medical Formulations**

| *Latin Name* | *Sanskrit/Hindi Name and English Name in Bracket* | *Used in Curing No. of Ailments* | *Used in Preparation of No. of Formulations* |
|---|---|---|---|
| *Abelmoschus esculentus* | Bhindi (Lady finger) | 1 | 1 |
| *Acacia catechu* | Kattha (Catechu) | 4 | 4 |
| *Acacia nilotica* | Babool (Acacia) | 1 | 1 |
| *Aconitum balfourii* | Mitha (Aconite) | 1 | 1 |
| *Aconitum heterophyllum* | Atis (Aconite) | 1 | 1 |
| *Acorus calamus* | Bach | 1 | 1 |
| *Adhatoda vasica* | Basinga | 2 | 2 |
| *Aegle marmelos* | Bel | 9 | 11 |
| *Ajuga bracteosa* | Neel kanthi | | |
| *Allium cepa* | Pyaz (Onion) | 9 | 9 |
| *Allium sativum* | Lahsun (Garlic) | 6 | 6 |
| *Angelica glauca* | Choru | 1 | 2 |
| *Malus* sp. | Apple | 1 | 1 |

*Contd...*

**Table 2.5–Contd...**

| Latin Name | Sanskrit/Hindi Name and English Name in Bracket | Used in Curing No. of Ailments | Used in Preparation of No. of Formulations |
|---|---|---|---|
| *Areca catechu* | Supari (Betel nut) | 1 | 1 |
| *Asparagus racemosus* | Satawari | 1 | 1 |
| *Azadirachta indica* | Neem | 6 | 7 |
| *Bahunia variegata* | Quiral | 1 | 1 |
| *Berberis aristata* | Kingod | 1 | 1 |
| *Bergenia ligulata* | Pasanbhed | 1 | 1 |
| *Betula alnoides* | Kathbhoj (Birch) | 1 | 1 |
| *Bombax ceiva* | Semal (Silk cotton) | 1 | 1 |
| *Brassica campestris* | Sarson (Mustard) | 10 | 10 |
| *Brassica olerecia* | Fulgobhi (Cauliflower) | 1 | 1 |
| *Bunicum persicum* | Kala-jira (Black cumin) | 1 | 1 |
| *Cajanus cajan* | Arhar (Pigeon pea) | 1 | 1 |
| *Calotropis* sp. | Aak | 1 | 1 |
| *Capsicum anum* | Mirch (Chilly) | 1 | 1 |
| *Carica papaya* | Papita (Papaya) | 2 | 2 |
| *Cedrus deodara* | Devdar | 1 | 1 |
| *Centella asiatica* | Brahmi | 2 | 2 |
| *Chenopodium album* | Bathuwa | 1 | 1 |
| *Cicer arietinum* | Channa (Gram) | 2 | 2 |
| *Cinnamomum tamala* | Tejpat (Cassia) | 2 | 2 |
| *Cinnamomum verum* | Dalchini (Cinnamon) | 1 | 1 |
| *Citrullus lanatus* | Tarbuj (Water melon) | 1 | 1 |
| *Citrus* sp. | Neebu (Lemon) | 7 | 7 |
| *Citrus* sp. | Santra (Orange) | | |
| *Cocus nucifera* | Nariyal (Coconut) | 2 | 2 |
| *Colocasia esculenta* | Pindalu | 1 | 1 |
| *Coriandrum sativum* | Dhaniya (Coriander) | 4 | 4 |
| *Cucumis melo* | Kheera (Cucumber) | 1 | 1 |
| *Cuminum cyminum* | Jira (Cumin) | 2 | 2 |
| *Curcuma domestica* | Haldi (Turmeric) | 12 | 13 |
| *Cynodon dactylon* | Doob | 4 | 4 |

*Contd...*

**Table 2.5–Contd...**

| Latin Name | Sanskrit/Hindi Name and English Name in Bracket | Used in Curing No. of Ailments | Used in Preparation of No. of Formulations |
|---|---|---|---|
| *Dactylorhiza hatagirea* | Hathajari | 2 | 2 |
| *Daucus carota* | Gajar (Carrot) | 2 | 2 |
| *Delbergia sesoo* | Seesam | 1 | 1 |
| - | Elayachi (Comfit) | 1 | 1 |
| *Ephedra gerardiana* | Somlata | | |
| *Euphorbia royleana* | Sullu | 1 | 1 |
| *Ferula narthex* | Heeng (Asafoetida) | 1 | 2 |
| *Ficus benghalensis* | Bod (Banyan) | 3 | 4 |
| *Ficus racemosa* | Gular | 1 | 1 |
| *Ficus religiosa* | Pipal | 3 | 3 |
| *Foeniculum vulgare* | Saunf (Aniseed) | 5 | 5 |
| *Helianthus annuus* | Surajmukhi | 1 | 1 |
| *Juglans regia* | Akhrot (Chestnut) | 1 | 1 |
| *Juniperus communis* | Bidaru | 1 | 1 |
| *Lagineria siceraria* | Launki (Bottle gourd) | 1 | 1 |
| *Lawsonia inermis* | Mehandi (Myrtle) | 3 | 3 |
| – | Long (Clove) | 1 | 1 |
| *Lycopersicon esculentum* | Tamatar (Tomato) | 1 | 1 |
| *Macrotyloma uniflorum* | Gahath | 1 | 1 |
| *Mangifera indica* | Aam (Mango) | 5 | 6 |
| *Martynia annua* | Bichu | 1 | 1 |
| *Megacarpaea polyandra* | Badmula | 1 | 1 |
| *Mentha longifolia* | Pudina (Mint) | 9 | 9 |
| *Momordica charantia* | Karela (Bitter gourd) | 4 | 4 |
| – | Moru | 1 | 1 |
| *Morus alva* | Shahtoot (Mulberry) | 1 | 1 |
| *Glycyrrhiza glabra* | Mulethi (Liquorice) | 2 | 2 |
| – | Munakka (Raisin) | 1 | 1 |
| *Musa* sp | Kela (Banana) | 4 | 4 |
| *Nardostachys grandiflora* | Jatamansi | 1 | 1 |
| *Nerium indicum* | Kaner (Oleander) | 1 | 1 |

*Contd...*

**Table 2.5–Contd...**

| *Latin Name* | *Sanskrit/Hindi Name and English Name in Bracket* | *Used in Curing No. of Ailments* | *Used in Preparation of No. of Formulations* |
|---|---|---|---|
| *Ocimum sanctum* | Tulsi (Sacred basil) | 15 | 16 |
| *Origanum vulgare* | Ban tulsi | 1 | 1 |
| *Phyllanthus emblica* | Awala | 9 | 9 |
| *Picrorhiza kurrooa* | Katuki | 2 | 2 |
| *Pinus wallichiana* | Kail | 1 | 1 |
| *Piper betle* | Pan (Betel) | 1 | 1 |
| *Piper longum* | Pipali | 1 | 1 |
| *Piper nigrum* | Kali-Mirch (Black pepper) | 12 | 14 |
| *Pleurospermum angelicoides* | Chippi | 1 | 1 |
| *Prunus persica* | Aru (Peach) | 1 | 1 |
| *Psidium guava* | Amrood (Guava) | 5 | 5 |
| *Punicum granatum* | Anar (Pomegranate) | 5 | 5 |
| *Brassica rugosa* | Rai (Mustard) | 1 | 1 |
| *Raphanus sativus* | Muli (Radish) | 9 | 13 |
| *Rauvolfia serpentina* | Sarpgandha | 1 | 2 |
| *Rheum australe* | Dholu | 1 | 1 |
| *Rheum moorcroftianum* | Archa | 1 | 1 |
| *Rhododendron campanulatum* | Semru | 1 | 1 |
| *Ricinus communis* | Arandi | 4 | 4 |
| *Rosa* sp | Gulab (Rose) | 1 | 1 |
| *Saccharum officinarum* | Ganna (Sugar cane) | 1 | 1 |
| *Brassica rapa* | Shaljam (Turnip) | 1 | 1 |
| *Sapindus mukorosii* | Ritha | 4 | 4 |
| *Saussurea costus* | Kut | 1 | 1 |
| *Saussurea obvallata* | Brahmakamal | 2 | 2 |
| *Sesamum orientale* | Til (Sesamum) | 3 | 3 |
| *Solanum tuberosum* | Alu (Potato) | 1 | 1 |
| *Spinacea oleracea* | Palak (Spinach) | 1 | 1 |
| *Swertia chiraiyta* | Chiraita | 2 | 2 |
| *Syzygium cuminii* | Jamun (Black berry) | 2 | 2 |
| *Taxus baccata* | Thuner (Himalayan yew) | 1 | 1 |

*Contd...*

**Table 2.5–Contd...**

| Latin Name | Sanskrit/Hindi Name and English Name in Bracket | Used in Curing No. of Ailments | Used in Preparation of No. of Formulations |
|---|---|---|---|
| *Terminalia arjuna* | Arjun | 1 | 1 |
| *Terminalia bellirica* | Baheda | 3 | 3 |
| *Terminalia catappa* | Badam (Almond) | 6 | 8 |
| *Terminalia chebula* | Haida | 5 | 5 |
| *Terminalia indica* | Imli (Tamarind) | 2 | 2 |
| *Tinospora cordifolia* | Giloe | 2 | 2 |
| *Trachyspermum ammi* | Ajwain (Caraway) | 4 | 4 |
| *Trigonella foenum-graecum* | Methi | 4 | 4 |
| *Triticum aestivum* | Gehun (Wheat) | 1 | 1 |
| *Vetiveria zizanioides* | Khas-Khas | 1 | 1 |
| *Vinis venifera* | Angoor (Grape) | 1 | 1 |
| *Vitex negundo* | Singoli | 1 | 1 |
| *Withania somnifera* | Ashgand | 2 | 2 |
| *Zingiber officinale* | Adrak (Ginger) | 7 | 10 |

The fundamental principles of preparing herbal medical formulations by *Vaidyas* are often combined with philosophy, religion and various ingredients. On the basis of nature and origin, the drugs are classified into three groups such as (1) vegetable, (2) animal and (3) metals/minerals. Drugs of vegetable origin are again divided into four groups based on the use of plant parts. These are: (1) prepared by fruits, (2) prepared by flowers and fruits, (3) prepared by creepers and (4) prepared by annuals. The drugs are developed and given to the patient in the form of juice, powder, decoction, paste, jam and pills. The Ayurvedic system of medicine pursues a holistic approach and does not aim to cure only the affected organs alone but aims to find out the origin and the causal factor of the disease in order to eradicate the disease from its root.

The interviews reflect that the traditional *Vaidyas* follow some specific guidelines while collecting these medicinal plants. They don't collect that medicinal plant which is infected by diseases, insects and any pest. *Vaidyas* avoid collecting plants for any medicinal use if the plants are affected by any toxicity, sunstroke, high velocity of winds, hailstorm, fire and flood.

They also avoid collecting medicinal plants from cemeteries, cremation grounds, sacred places, temples, public places, slaughter houses, areas affected by sewer discharge or polluted water, termite infected areas, road sides, landslides prone areas, and areas furrowed by rodents.

For preparing herbal medicine, *Vaidyas* collect plants when plants attain maturity that is judged by height of plants, patterns of branching, colour and other morphological characters including right fragrance and potency. All these judgments are mainly based on the experiences and knowledge of the collectors. There are also some guidelines for collection of different parts of a medicinal plant species. The branches are collected when they are fully-grown during spring and rains. Young leaves are collected mainly between flowering and ripening of fruits. If the roots of a tree are required for medicinal purpose, then only the bark of hard and woody roots are collected. Roots and rhizomes of annuals are collected in summer and winter after the leaf fall or when the new leaves are just emerging. Milk, sap, gum, resin, latex and other liquid exudes from plants are collected in autumn, yet the collection of these products depends on their availability. Similarly, as per the seasonality and availability the flowers and fruits are collected (Ajay Rastogi, pers. comm.).

The study further reveals that the traditional system of herbal use in Uttarakhand is not much popular in the younger generation. In past, the indigenous communities had a self-regulating system that was interwoven in such a way so that each individual could have got certain benefits with his profession. Mostly the traditional *Vaidyas* were marginal farmers and they used to provide their services free of cost. In return, the villagers helped *Vaidyas* in his agricultural land and also offered some donation in the form of cereals, pulses and vegetables. Traditionally, the *Vaidya* profession was valued as a matter of virtue and therefore the introduction of fee for any kind of treatment was highly discouraged. Realizing the good health being a necessity of society there was a thought if fee was introduced in the profession then the poor could be deprived from the treatment. This notion still persists in some localities of the state for some specific treatments, for example some traditional healers do not accept anything from the person who has undergone for treatment for snakebite under their supervision.

The current state of traditional *Vaidyas* tradition in Uttarakhand with respect to the use of medicinal plants reveals that the practitioners of this tradition, at present, mostly depend on the species growing in kitchen garden and agricultural fields. Due to ban on collection of many plant species from wild, the traditional healers purchase the required plant material from any prospective seller. In most of the cases the purchased material is not of good quality due to use of faulty methods for harvesting and storage of the medicinal plant material. On some occasions, due to unavailability of the required plant material, the *Vaidyas* either unable to prepare the formulation or they are forced to use their substitutes. All these problems have ultimately reduced the efficacy of the herbal medical formulation and at long run the tradition as a whole. Besides, changes in socio-economic pattern and less income in tradition are some of the causes leading to decline in tradition according to the interviewees.

## Discussion

The science of herbal formulations is one of the most significant contributions of Ayurveda to the health care however the knowledge of traditional Ayurvedic practitioners has not so far been adequately utilized. Many of the traditional *Vaidyas* enjoy high local acceptance and respect and thus put forth considerable influence on health belief and practice. According to them, some Ayurvedic formulations contain about 15 or more plant species to enhance the potency and support the primary plant species for effective use. The use of other plant species, mixed up in preparing the formulation, is sometime to counter any possible side effects from the actions of the primary plants. There are many Ayurvedic herbs such as Katuki (*Picrorhiza kurrooa*), Hardi (*Terminalia chebula*), Haida (*Terminalia bellarica*), Brahmi (*Centella asiatica*), Pudina (*Mentha longifolia*), Haldi (*Curcuma domestica*) and Ashwagandha (*Withania somnifera*) those are given alone to cure the ailments. *Vaidyas* use the whole herb instead of extracting the active ingredient from the plant. The notion of using the whole herb rather than the isolated ingredient may also contribute to a balanced formula less likely to have side effects.

Besides prescribing herbal medicine, in traditional Ayurvedic system a proper importance is given to the lifestyle, diet, sleep, daily and seasonal routines and internal cleaning. Eradicating diseases from its root and treatment of chronic problems are some of the main forces leading to the acceptance of Ayurvedic treatment all over the world in spite of the heavy consumption of allopathic drugs. During the last few years the research work in Vedic medicine has allotted around $18 million. There are over 600 scientifically evaluated studies happening in 27 countries at 220 institutions. Ayurveda has a record of curing some chronic disorders such as eczema, cystitis or migraines that do not respond well to western medicine (Banerjee, 2002).

Unfortunately, the practice of individual healer identifying plants and preparing various formulations himself for the use of his patients has been declining rapidly. Today due to rapid socio-economic changes and urbanization most of the *Vaidyas* largely depend on the products supplied by the pharmaceutical industry. For the future development of the country Ayurveda should be treated as a valuable traditional system. The various formulations provided by traditional *Vaidyas* must be documented systematically so that the patent drama played with regard to turmeric is not repeated. The present shifting social pattern in the west can be useful to popularize the Ayurveda across the globe. Its Vedic connection can make Ayurveda a highly saleable concept, and medical exporters could simply reap the benefits of west's disillusionment with allopathy. The high profile formulations can be developed if the measures are taken to organize all the traditional *Vaidyas*. Earlier, the reputation of the respective *Vaidya* and that of the formulations developed by him itself were criteria sufficient for people to believe in its value. Today, the absence of these recognized *Vaidyas* shows a major gap in the exercise.

Likewise other rural areas of India, the Uttarakhand state is served by state sponsored medical system in which Primary Health Centers are the key units for curing different diseases. However, these centers are not adequate in the state, and each Primary Health Center caters more than 31,000 populations against the stipulated norms of 20,000 for the hilly region. Apart from this inappropriateness in availability of Primary Health Center in Uttarakhand state, the cost of modern medicine is twenty times higher than the cost of indigenous medicine (Samal *et al.*, 2004). The low cost of herbal medicine is one of the reasons that discourage younger generation to adopt the *Vaidya* as a profession.

Establishing protected areas across the country has restricted the areas of medicinal plant collection. Plants being the major ingredient in Ayurveda for preparing medicine, the short supply of such important ingredients influence the existence of this age-old traditional medical system. Recently, it has been realized that even in India, most people, most practitioners of modern medicine and most scientists also do not take Ayurveda seriously (Parasnis, 2004). The lack of standardized medicines is one of the shortcomings in Ayurveda. The faulty processes in growing, harvesting and storing of herbs have also declined the potency of Ayurvedic medicines. Adulteration of herbal products and their crude processing are some of the causes of altered efficacy of Ayurvedic medicines. Science always demands for continual expansion of unknown boundaries and transformability. It discards, generally, unworkable, old and unconfirmed concepts and develops novel thoughts whenever required by experimentations and clarifications. However, Ayurveda does not accept transformability of principles.

Besides, there are several other reasons, which made to decline the tradition including lesser promotion of Ayurvedic medicine compared to the western medicine in the Indian education system inspite of the common belief that the pure vegetable drugs are more powerful in their efficacy than those which have undergone several laboratory processes (Nadkarni and Nadkarni, 1908). Moreover, the extraction of alkaloids by the use of alcohol is known to destroy the intrinsic therapeutic properties of the herbal drugs. To the indigenous communities of Uttarakhand who brought and grown up in their specific environment and enjoy the specific food, culture, habits of life and temperament, Ayurvedic drugs naturally may suit better and may be safer than western medicines. There is a need to adopt the natural therapeutic system such as Ayurveda for better health and also to avoid the side affects evolved due to continuous use of allopathic medicines. Research and development programs may include four basic parameters, for example, resource requirements, medical needs, innovative potential and economic gains while framing and prioritizing the research projects. To meet the aim of developing Ayurvedic medicines, high profile herbal drugs should be developed and the traditional claimed properties of the herbal drugs should be clinically tested in order to strengthen their validity.

## References

Banerjee M. (2002). Public policy and Ayurveda. *Economic and Political Weekly*, 37: 1136-1146.

Nadkarni, K.M. and A.K. Nadkarni (1908). *Indian Materia Medica.* Popular Prakashan, Bombay, India. 1319 pp.

Parasnis, A.S. (2004). Perceived bias against Ayurveda. *Current Science*, 87 (10): 1329-1333.

Samal, P.K., A. Shah, S.C. Tiwari and D.K. Agrawal (2004). Indigenous health care practices and their linkages with bio-resource conservation and socio-economic development in central Himalayan region of India. *Indian Journal of Traditional Knowledge*, 3 (1): 12-26.

Stock, J. (2002). Ayurveda goes global. *The Week*, 20 (34): 16-21.

# Chapter 3
# Medicinal Plants: Livelihood and Sustainable Development

## Introduction

Globally, about 85 per cent of the traditional medicines used in primary health care are derived from plants. Generally, most of the countries in Asia, Africa and Latin America use traditional medicine to meet primary health care needs. The industrialized countries have started realizing the potential of traditional medicine and they denote and use it as a complementary or alternative medicine. In China, traditional herbal preparations account for 30-50 per cent of the total medicinal consumption. In Africa, about 80 per cent population use traditional medicine for primary health care. At least once, about 50 per cent population in Europe and North America, 70 per cent population in Canada, and 90 per cent population in Germany use complementary medicine. Besides, in San Francisco, London and South Africa, 75 per cent of people infected with HIV/AIDS use traditional medicine (Bagozzi, 2003). Since the overall biodiversity and indigenous knowledge on herbal therapy are the major assets of developing countries, there is a need to add values in such a green gold for gaining the economic benefits as Arab countries getting from their oil resources.

People in the mountainous areas are dependent highly on the plant resources for food and medicine due to several reasons including isolation, and relatively poor access to arable lands. Over centuries of trial and errors they have developed knowledge about the utilization of diverse forest resources. The age-old traditional values attached with various forest types, meadows and with the varieties of forest products including the medicinal plants have gained a wide acceptance across the world at present (Stein, 2004; Kala, 2004a). Today, in developed countries like USA a majority of people (55 per cent) combine alternative treatments with conventional medicine, and 13 per cent try them as they think conventional medicine is too expensive (Stein, 2004). In addition, the cosmetic industries are increasingly using the natural ingredients, including extracts of medicinal plants, in their products (KIT, 2003, 2004; Awasthi and Uniyal, 2003). Different human societies have developed a diverse set of knowledge of using available plants for treatment of diseases. Different types of diseases are prevalent in different cultural groups and ethnic communities. As such, the variations exist in traditional system of health care among different geographical regions (Kala *et al.*, 2004).

Asia represents one of the important centers of knowledge base particularly with reference to the use of plant species for curing various types of diseases. Ayurveda, Unani and Chinese systems of medical care are some of the examples. In this context, it is interesting to note that the Himalayan medicinal plants are the major contributors to maintain the aforementioned systems of medicine (Kala *et al.*, 2004). In Asia, India and China are the two biggest giants that have the richest arrays of registered and relatively well-understood medicinal plants (Raven, 1998). Since the Indian subcontinent is well known for its diversity of forest products and age-old traditions associated with health care, there is an urgent need to establish these traditional values in both the national and international perspectives realizing the ongoing developmental trends in traditional knowledge.

Medicinal plants are mainly an alternate income-generating source of underprivileged communities (Myers, 1991; Lacuna-Richman, 2002); hence strengthening this sector may benefit and improve the living standard of poor people, too. A great deal of traditional knowledge on the use of various plant species is still intact with the indigenous people and this fact is more relevant with the mountainous areas, such as the Himalaya due to less accessibility of terrain, poor communication system and comparatively slow rate of development (Kala, 2002; Farooquee *et al.*, 2004). Various indigenous communities living in remote and far-flung areas are the witness of these facts as the knowledge prevalent with these communities, especially on the use of plants, reflects their wide-ranging awareness and intimate dependence on the surrounding bio-resources.

The growing faith in medicinal plants sector is due to several reasons including escalating demand of herbal medicine with a view of its less side-effects compared to allopathic medicine, and also to meet the demand of increasing population and their growing requirements for health care. Although, allopathic medicine can cure a wide range of diseases, its high prices and side effects are now making many people to return to herbal medicines that have fewer side effects. This thoughtful reality is making the medicinal plants as a commodity with high added values. The instant rising demand of plant-based drugs is however causing the heavy pressure on some selected high value medicinal plants population in wild due to over-harvesting. Many of these medicinal plant species have slow growth rates, low population densities and narrow geographic ranges (Kala, 1998; Nautiyal *et al.*, 2002); hence they are more prone to extinction (Jablonkski, 2004). The loss of biodiversity and increase in poverty in biodiversity rich areas has certain linkages, and thus both these important aspects need to be wisely tackled together.

As researchers started investigating the social, economic and ecological aspects of the medicinal plants harvest and sustainable development, it has been increasingly realized that the goal may be more difficult to achieve than initially envisioned. Since the information on the uses of plant species for therapeutic purpose has passed on through generations by word of mouth, with due course of time, in recent past, this knowledge started phasing out due to lack of recognition by younger generation as a result of shift in attitude and ongoing socio-economic changes (Kala, 2000; 2002). The indigenous knowledge on the use of lesser-known medicinal plants has also declined rapidly. Realizing the continuous erosion in traditional knowledge on many valuable plants for medicine in past and its renewed worldwide interest at present, a need was felt to study such a valuable knowledge with a larger perceptive in developing the medicinal plants sector for the development of underprivileged communities and ultimately the country.

Since there are many linkages and aspects in developing the medicinal plant sector, right from medicinal plants collection to their conversion into drugs, which go beyond the state boundaries and controls, a need was felt to study the medicinal plant sector as a whole in the broader perspective. This chapter deals with (1) to find out the wealth and potential in medicinal plants resources, (2) to assess the present state of knowledge on medicinal plants, (3) to discuss various parameters of medicinal plants sector including cultivation, conservation, commercialization, bio-prospects and bio-piracy, and (4) to suggest some recommendations based on the present state of knowledge for the benefit and development of medicinal plants sector.

## Medicinal Plant's Wealth

Globally, the estimated number of plant species used in curing therapy is about 52,885 and the proportion of medicinal plants to the total documented plant species in different countries varies from 4.4 per cent to 20 per cent (Schippmann *et al.*, 2002; Hamilton, 2004). In India, of the 17000 species of higher plants 7500 are known for medicinal uses (Shiva, 1996) that is the highest proportion of plants known medicinally to any country of the world out of the existing flora of the respective country (Table 3.1). Ayurveda, the oldest medical system in Indian sub-continent, has reported alone about 2000 medicinal plant species, followed by Siddha (Table 3.2), and the Charak Samhita recorded the uses of 340 herbal drugs (Prajapati *et al.*, 2003).

**Table 3.1: Distribution of Medicinal Plants**

| *Country or Region* | *Total Number of Native Species in Flora* | *No. of Medicinal Plant Species* | *Per cent of Medicinal plants* | *Source* |
|---|---|---|---|---|
| World | 2,97,000 | 52,885 | 10 | Schippmann *et al.*, 2002 |
| India | 17,000 | 7,500 | 44 | Shiva, 1996 |
| Indian Himalaya | 8,000 | 1,748 | 22 | Samant *et al.*, 1998 |
| Uttarakhand | – | 964 | – | Present study |

**Table 3.2: The Status of Various Medical Systems in India**

| Characteristics | Medical Systems | | | | |
|---|---|---|---|---|---|
| | *Ayurveda* | *Siddha* | *Unani* | *Tibetan* | *Homeopathy* |
| Medicinal plants known | 2000 | 1121 | 751 | 337 | 482 |
| Licensed pharmacies | 8533 | 384 | 462 | - | 613 |
| Hospitals | 3000 | 236 | 308 | - | 294 |
| Dispensaries | 14793 | 356 | 963 | - | 7397 |
| Registered practitioners | 427504 | 16599 | 42445 | - | 194147 |
| Under graduate college | 196 | 5 | 39 | - | 166 |
| Post graduate college | 53 | 2 | 5 | - | 17 |

Modified after Anonymous, 2004.

The Himalaya harbors a great diversity of medicinal plant species. The northeast Himalaya due to rich array of biodiversity has placed with eighteen-biodiversity hotspots of the world. So far about 8000 species of angiosperms, 44 species of gymnosperms and 600 species of pteridophytes have been reported from the Indian Himalaya (Singh and Hajra, 1996), of these 1748 are known as medicinal (Samant *et al.*, 1998). The maximum medicinal plants (1717 species) have been reported around 1800 m elevation range. At regional scale, the maximum species of medicinal plants have been reported from Uttarakhand Himalaya (Kala, 2004b), followed by Sikkim and North Bengal (Samant *et al.*, 1998). The trans-Himalaya harbors about 337 species of medicinal plants (Kala, 2002), which is low compared to other parts of the Himalaya, due to distinct geography and ecological marginal conditions (Kala and Mathur, 2002).

Of the total medicinal plant species 62 species are endemic to the Himalaya and 208 species extend their distribution to adjacent areas, hence classified as near endemic. More than 200 Himalayan medicinal plants are consumed raw, roasted, boiled, fried, cooked or in the form of oil, spices, jams and pickles (Samant *et al.*, 1998). About 81 species of the Himalayan medicinal plants are known to exploit for extraction of oil, *Aegle marmelos, Ricinus communis* and *Myrica esculenta*, for example. Of the total 675 species of wild edibles, 171 are used as medicine (Samant *et al.*, 2001). The importance of medicinal plants is not only restricted to the human use but animal husbandry also employs many plant species as a primary source of healthcare (Samal *et al.*, 2004). According to 'Kamarupi pharmacopoeia', which is a unique traditional medical system of Assam, a total of 52 plant species with 18 recipes have been documented to cure 14 types of ailments in elephant (Borthakur *et al.*, 2001).

## Ecological Significance

The ecological role of medicinal plants in maintaining the ecosystem may not be underestimated. Many medicinal plant species are known as major food items of several birds and animal species, and thus they play a major role in the food web (Dhyani and Kala, 2005). Monal pheasant has been observed during fieldwork feeding tubers of endangered medicinal plant species such as *Dactylorhiza hatagirea* and *Polygonatum verticillatum*. The Himalayan musk deer feeds *Skimmia laureola*, a medicinal and aromatic plant species and *Saussurea gossypiphora*, an endangered medicinal and religious plant species (Table 3.3). *Ferula jaeschkeana, Arnebia euchroma* and *Ephedra gerardiana* are among the rare and endangered medicinal plant species preferred for feeding by Asiatic ibex in trans-Himalayan region of India.

**Table 3.3: Rare and Endangered Medicinal Plant Species Preferred for Feeding by Wild Animal and Bird Species**

| *Rare Medicinal Plant, Local Name* | *Plant Part Preferred for Feeding* | *Wild Herbivores* |
|---|---|---|
| *Dactylorhiza hatagirea*, Hathajari | Tuber | Monal pheasant |
| *Polygonatum verticillatum*, Salam mishri | Tuber | Monal pheasant |
| *Saussurea gossypiphora*, Fenkamal | Flower | Musk deer |
| *Ferula jaeschkeana*, Thunak | Leaf | Ibex |
| *Arnebia euchroma*, Laljadi or Demok | Leaf | Ibex |
| *Ephedra gerardiana*, Tse | Shoot | Ibex |
| *Artimisia maritima*, Khamchu | Leaf | Ibex |
| *Bergenia ligulata*, Pattharchatta | Leaf | Goral |

The presence of some medicinal plants itself indicates the specific habitat or microhabitats due to their habitat specificity thus they also act as the indicator species. *Bergenia stracheyi* is one such endangered medicinal plant, known locally as "patharchatta" (literally meaning rock lickers) due to its habitat specificity that is either rocky or bouldery. The presence of many rare medicinal plants is the potential indicator of species richness and the level of anthropogenic pressures. There are many protected areas where ban on livestock grazing is mandatory, and a high density of many rare medicinal plants in such protected areas with high species richness is an indicator of removal of livestock grazing and its subsequent effects on some valuable medicinal plant species (Kala, 2004b; 2004c).

Selective removal of some valuable and ecologically important medicinal plant species may negatively impact the ecosystem functioning. The ecological effect of harvesting medicinal plants can be varied, and the impact can range from the level of genes to individual, populations, communities and ecosystems, all of which have important consequences (Hall and Bawa, 1993). Repeated and selective harvest of most productive and suitable individuals of certain medicinal plants can alter their genetic make up in wild populations and can deplete the vigor of wild gene pool. All this affects the natural survival and selection mechanism for establishing the healthy population of medicinal plant species in the wild. It can also affect the vigor of domesticated and cultivated populations of species drawn from such depleted wild stocks (Hall and Bawa, 1993; Rao *et al.*, 2004). Continuous and over-harvesting of certain medicinal plant species that help to stabilize soil can lead to degradation of ecosystem. Different harvesting regimes may result in different ecological effects on medicinal plant species.

## Cultural Values

The uses and values attached with medicinal plants reflect distinct cultural preferences across the world, and the centuries old reliability on medicinal plants is also due to their cultural significance. The utility level of herbal medicine in most developing countries is higher than the developed countries. The majorities of people in the Asia and Africa use traditional medicine as a primary source of health care whereas in United State of America a limited number of people use herbal medicines (Cunningham, 1998). Even in sub-Saharan Africa, rural people are increasingly turning to medicinal plants to cope with HIV/AIDS (Barany *et al.*, 2001). The ethics and the mythology of native communities have strong linkages with their immediate environments and biodiversity.

The medicinal plants component of biodiversity possesses a reputed place in the socio-economic and religious activities of native communities, who worship them in the form of various gods, goddesses and minor deities (Silori and Badola, 2000). Since the Ayurveda is rooted in Hindu culture, there are many medicinal plants, which are at the same time used for religious purposes by Hindus (Dhyani, 2000). *Origanum vulgare, Saussurea obvallata, Ocimum sanctum, Cedrus deodara, Nardostachys jatamansi, Cynodon dactylon, Aegle marmelos, Cannabis sativa, Juniperus communis, Musa paradissica* and *Zanthoxylum armatum* are some of the medicinal plants used highly for medicinal as well as religious point of view (Table 3.4). For Vedic era the Hindus have worshiped many medicinal plants like *Ficus benghalensis, Ficus religiosa, Zanthoxylum armatum* and *Aegle marmelos* as a symbolic of different deities. The traditional herbal practitioners of Ayurveda have a strong belief that without worshipping medicinal plants properly they cannot be effective as they suppose to be.

The concept of sacred groves has also some strong linkages with culture, values, health care and conservation. In Uttarakhand state, the lower caste Hindus or the Scheduled Castes worship *Prunus cerasoides*, a sacred medicinal plant species, during some special religious ceremonies and without the use of this species the ceremony cannot be accomplished. The Buddhist community across the world regards the fruit of *Terminalia chebula* as a most important medicine as well as a sacred fruit. It has been stated long back that the therapeutic potency of medicinal plants is more effective and suited to the person of that particular region or culture in which the plant is growing (Nadkarni and Nadkarni, 1908). This notion has made to prepare a new drug for the heart patient of a specific ethnic group of African countries (Pearson, 2004).

## Trade in Tradition and Escalating Rarity

About 25 per cent of modern medicines prepared today by using plant species were first used traditionally (Bagozzi, 2003). The World Health Organization has estimated the present demand for medicinal plants is about US $ 14 billion a year. Medicinal plants are a part of the US $36.89 billion global market for organic food. The annual demand of medicinal plant-based raw materials is growing at the rate of 15-25 per cent, and according to an estimate of the World Health Organization, the demand for medicinal plants is likely to increase from the current US $14 billion a year to US $5 trillion in 2050 (Kala, 2004b; Sharma, 2004).

**Table 3.4: Some Important Medico-Religious Plant Species of Uttarakhand Region**

| *Species* | *Religious Uses* | *Medicinal Uses* |
|---|---|---|
| *Aegle marmelos* | To worship the Lord Siva and the Goddess Laxmi | Digestive disorder, fever |
| *Artemisia nilagirica* | Sacred plant used in worshipping local deities | Asthma, skin ailment, headache, antiseptic |
| *Betula utilis* | Sacred plant | Cut, wounds, hysteria |
| *Cannabis sativa* | Associated with Lord Shiva | Delirium, eye disorder |
| *Cedrus deodara* | Associated with Gods and Goddesses | Ulcer, rheumatic pain |
| *Datura stramonium* | Associated with Lord Shiva | Asthma, joint pain |
| *Dendrocalamus strictus* | Used at various religious ceremonies performed right from the birth to death | Tonic, fever |
| *Ficus benghalensis* | Worship as symbol of Lord Shiva | Dysentery, scabies, tonic |
| *Ficus religiosa* | Worship as Lord Vishnu | Dysentery, cholera, scabies |
| *Hedychium spicatum* | Used on the marriage ceremony | Stomachache, liver disorder |
| *Juniperus communis* | Its incense used for worshipping Gods and Goddesses | Kidney trouble |
| *Musa paradissica* | Used on the marriage ceremony | Indigestion |
| *Nardostachys jatamansi* | Its incense used for worshipping Gods and Goddesses | Blood purification, cough |
| *Ocimum sanctum* | Worship as Goddess | Bronchitis, constipation |
| *Origanum vulgare* | Used in worshipping the Lord Badri Vishal or Vishnu | Diarrhoea, bronchitis |
| *Pinus roxburghii* | Used on the marriage ceremony | Cut, wounds, bone fracture |
| *Prunus cerasoides* | Used in some special religious occasion | Body swelling |
| *Saussurea obvallata* | Worship as Lord Brahma | Cuts, aphrodisiac |
| *Sesamum orientale* | Worship as Lord Saturn | Aphrodisiac, bodyache |
| *Zanthoxylum armatum* | Used in worshipping as Lord Shiva, Narsingh, Vairoun | Toothache |

In India, the medicinal plant related trade is estimated to be around US $ 1087 million a year (Joshi *et al.*, 2004). According to an estimate the quantity of export in Ayurvedic products of India has increased over recent past, and between last two financial years (2001-2002 and 2002-2003) this increase in export has become triple fold (Figure 3.1). The major market for Indian medicinal plants is North America, which deals with 50 per cent of total trade in Indian medicinal plants. The highly traded medicinal plants of India include *Emblica officinalis, Asparagus racemosus, Withania somnifera, Terminalia chebula, Saraca ashoka, Aegle marmelos, Cassia angustifolia, Adhatoda vasica, Piper longum* and *Bacopa monnieri* (Prahalathan, 2004).

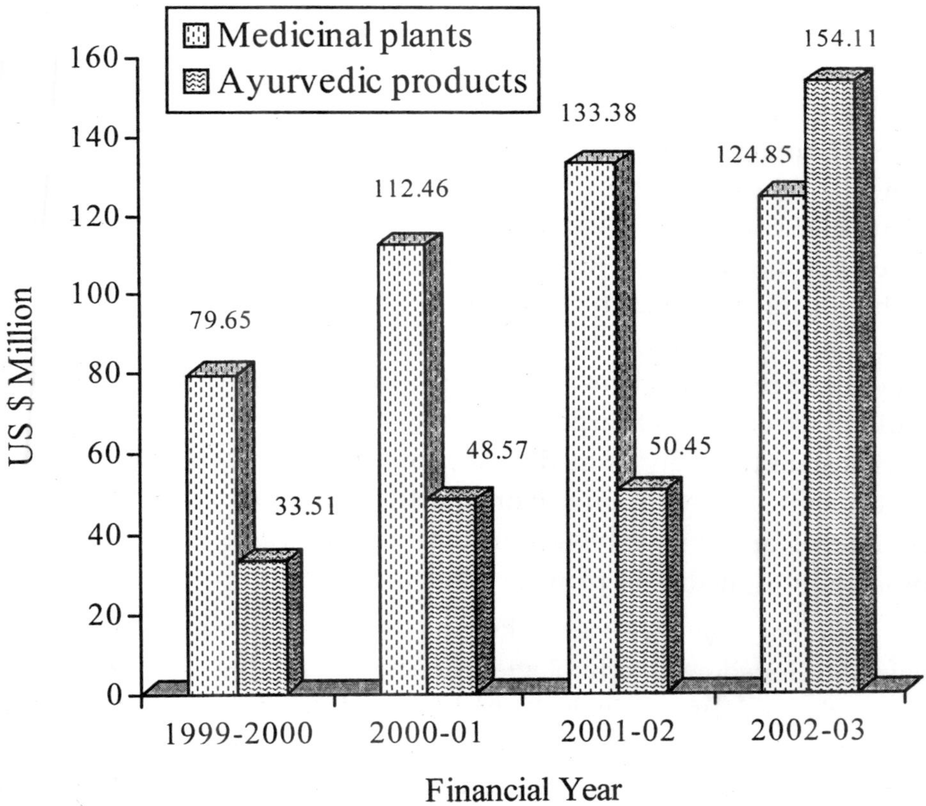


**Figure 3.1: Export Trends in Medicinal Plants and Ayurvedic Products of India Over Past Four Financial Years**
**(*Source*: Prahalathan, 2004)**

According to Hamilton (2004), about 4,000 to 10,000 species of medicinal plants face possible local, national, regional or global extinction, with serious consequences for livelihoods, economies and health care systems. The prime threats to the medicinal plants are those that affect any kind of biodiversity used by humans (Rao *et al.*, 2004; Kala, 2004d; 2005). For India, Nayar and Sastry (1987) have reported 621 rare and endangered species, of these 17 species were found in the Himalayan region and obtain medicinal properties. In 2003, 71 rare and endangered medicinal plant species have been assessed inhabiting the northwest Himalaya. Of the total rare medicinal plants of the Himalaya 92 per cent are in active trade; 74 per cent are traded nationally and 35 per cent are internationally (Anonymous, 2003).

## Domestication of Herbals

National Bank for Agriculture and Rural Development of India has estimated about 7-lakh acre of lands under the medicinal and aromatic plants farming (Kumar, 2004). The per hectare cost of cultivation, total annual production and cost benefit ratio fluctuate with different medicinal plant species. Out of 10-selected rare and endangered medicinal plant species of the Himalaya *Rheum emodi* was calculated as a most beneficial cash crop of medicinal plant in terms of net income generation (Table 3.5). However, at present, the farming of most of the medicinal plant species is poor and restricted to few hectares of land in different Himalayan states. India, in general, has a large variation in climatic and soil conditions and thus sustain a variety of medicinal plant species those can be cultivated according to their niche. Contract farming with pharmaceutical companies and with buyback arrangements may be a step forward in promotion of medicinal plant's cultivation.

Different organizations working on the cultivation of medicinal plants have developed agro-technologies for about more than 20 species of rare and endangered medicinal plants. Most of these rare species are herbs, *Rheum australe, Arnebia benthamii, Aconitum heterophyllum, Aconitum balfourii, Saussurea costus, Angelica glauca, Saussurea obvallata, Picrorhiza kurrooa, Valeriana wallichii, Podophyllum hexandrum* and *Dactylorhiza hatagirea*, for example. Besides, agro-biotechniques have also been developed for some shrub and under-shrub such as *Taxus baccata* and

*Rauvolfia serpentina* respectively. Since most of the medicinal plant species growing in diverse natural climates, which may obtain mycorrhizae as an important component to grow, establish and survive, the research work should also be carried out on the effects of such mycorrhizae while developing agro-biotechniques for such species.

**Table 3.5: Seedling Survival, Total Cost of Cultivation, and Net Income by Cultivation of 10 Important Species of the Rare and Endangered Medicinal Plants**

| *Species* | *Seedling Survival (Per cent)* | *Seed Required ha (gm)* | *Total Cost of Cultivation (US $)* | *Total Production (kg/ha)* | *Income (US $)* | *Net Income (US $)* |
|---|---|---|---|---|---|---|
| *Aconitum balfourii* | 60-70 | 614 | 2117 | 495 | 2692 | 575 |
| *Aconitum heterophyllum* | 60-70 | 614 | 2258 | 83 | 4528 | 2270 |
| *Angelica glauca* | 70-80 | 800 | 1630 | 1000 | 2174 | 544 |
| *Carum carvi* | >90 | 500 | 1652 | 650 | 2826 | 1826 |
| *Nardostachys jatamansi* | 50-60 | 600 | 2723 | 1129 | 6135 | 1412 |
| *Picrorhiza kurrooa* | 50-60 | 64 | 1117 | 612 | 1663 | 546 |
| *Podophyllum hexandrum* | 50-60 | 32,125 | 2718 | 4000 | 5218 | 2500 |
| *Rheum emodi* | 60-70 | 600 | 3044 | 9880 | 17183 | 14140 |
| *Rhem moorcroftianum* | 50-60 | 600 | 3044 | 4100 | 7130 | 4087 |
| *Saussurea costus* | 80-90 | 500 | 1783 | 3500 | 2283 | 500 |

*Source:* Nautiyal and Nautiyal, 2004.

Medicinal plants' farming is not an easy task as its history reflects. For example in Russia the cultivation is well developed yet about half of the supplies are still gathered from wild populations (Cunningham, 1998). Most of the farmers in trans-Himalayan region of India have replaced the medicinal plants farming by common crops such as pea (*Pisum sativum*), potato (*Solanum tuberosum*) and hop (*Humulus lupulus*) due to the lengthy cultivation cycle of medicinal plants like *Saussurea costus* (C.P. Kuniyal, Personal Communication). In Uttarakhand, many farmers have deep doubts on the economic return from the medicinal plants farming, and thus they drop the idea of medicinal plants farming.

## Constraints in Medicinal Plants Sector

There are many hurdles in developing the medicinal plants sector including poor infrastructure and limited information on marketing system.

One of the major obstacles in marketing medicinal plants of the remote and wilderness areas such as the Himalayan region is a poor road network, and therefore there are long walking distances from market to the place of product availability. The cost of getting a product to market increases with distance, because hiring labor or porters and vehicles for transporting products is expensive. There are middlemen who buy medicinal plants from harvesters and collectors and transport them to markets but reliability of transportation through middlemen decreases with distance. If the medicinal plants farming and harvesting areas are far from markets, then medicinal plant may spoil before ever reaching markets due to absence of cold storage facility. If somehow the markets are reached with viable products, the income earned may be too low to offset the costs of transportation. These important issues if sorted out may play a key role in developing the medicinal plants sector. Overcoming obstacles to market access (distance to market) can boost rural incomes, but may lead to intensification of forest management and destructive harvesting (Hall and Bawa, 1993).

Generally, in medicinal plants sector there is a top down approach and even many actors at the bottom are not aware of the rising demand of their product and the availability of its market. It was noticed that in some parts of Uttarakhand state of India some valuable medicinal plant product was gone wasted due to lack of their market. In some villages of Chamoli district of Uttarakhand the farmers had cultivated Kut (*Saussurea costus*) and Dolu (*Rheum emodi*) but they could not make out to sell them. On the other hand, most of the trade in medicinal plants is routed through illegal channels. The medicinal plant collectors are generally the marginal farmers and laborers. They get cash income to meet their basic requirements for food, health and children education by selling medicinal plants (Kala, 2003). However, they are often unaware about the actual trade channels and real market prices of many medicinal plant species (Kala, 2003; KIT, 2004). Therefore, to improve the medicinal plant sector there should be proper linkages and communications among the different actors of this sector. Besides, I have identified the following constraints in medicinal plants sector based on the fieldwork and literature review.

- ☆ Absences of consolidated dataset for even a single medicinal plant species on the actual availability in wild, production by cultivation, pricing, and trade within India and abroad.

- Continuous addition of species in the Materia Medica but lack of their standardization and correct identification.
- Lack of suitable cultivation technologies.
- Slow production rate, small quantity production and long gestation period of many valuable medicinal plants.
- Unscientific harvesting of medicinal plants from wild.
- Over-harvesting of many medicinal plants from wild due to escalating demand resulting in the loss of their existing populations.
- Over-collection of some valuable medicinal plants due to multiple uses. For instance, *Hemidesmus indicus* is used to cure 34 types of diseases, *Aegle marmelos* in 31, *Phyllanthus emblica* in 29 and *Gloriosa superba* in 28 types of diseases.
- Negative impacts on the supply and livelihoods of the indigenous people living on forest margins due to overexploitation of medicinal plant species.
- Lack of research on the high yielding varieties.
- Inefficient processing techniques of medicinal plants.
- Limited information on market system and poor marketing infrastructure.
- Existing enormous illegal trade.
- Fluctuation in demand and supply round the year.
- Lack of good manufacturers.
- Preference over wild medicinal plants by manufactures in comparison to cultivated ones, as they have a general feeling that wild plant species contain better chemical contents.
- Poor quality control procedures.
- Lack of coordination among different stakeholders.

## Patent Issue

Patenting medicinal plants knowledge is one of the important issues, at present. The approaches for awarding patents on medicinal plants in United States, Europe, Canada and Andean countries are different, and thus illustrative *sui generis* system from United States, Europe and India are contrasted (Koo *et al.*, 2004). In most countries, plants and inventions directed to plants and plant products such as seeds, flowers, gums, resins are not eligible for filing a patent. However, in United States, any living organism derived by human invention, such as by breeding or by laboratory-based manipulation can be filed for awarding patent. Developing countries and many scientists who want to exploit medicinal plants demand more specified rules on the record of nativity of samples and sharing of their benefits between the nations of origin, the inventor and the commercial sponsors. But US Patent authority is not inclined to accept such rules. These conflicts have frustrated many scientists who believe that natural products remain the most promising source of new drugs.

On patent issues, India has chosen a more expansive approach. The Indian Protection of Plant Varieties and Farmers Rights Act 2001 recognizes the contribution of professional plant breeders and farmers who actively participate in breeding programs. This Act contains provisions for benefit sharing whereby local communities are acknowledged as a contributor of plants (Koo *et al.*, 2004). However, globally most of the issues with reference to protect the legal status for indigenous knowledge and to compensate the indigenous herbal practitioners for that knowledge are extremely complicated. There are arguments on the present state of compensation or benefit sharing under the intellectual property rights, which is being considered a new legal form of bio-piracy by one group, whereas others advocate the intellectual property right is a legal tool to protect the rights of knowledge holders (Green *et al.*, 1999).

There is a wide gap between developing and developed nations on patenting the products. For instance, out of 3,125,603 patents filed over 91 countries only 301,177 or 9.6 per cent are registered in developing countries and the rest in industrialized countries. Of these, only 0.2 per cent of the total and 2.3 per cent of those registered in developing countries belong to residents. And 97.7 per cent of the total patents filed so far are on the name of non-residents, who apply only to control export markets in developing countries (Egziabher, 2003). There are reports, which have attracted the attention of developing nations by stating that patent monopolies on plant and plant products threaten to harm the developing nations in three major ways. First, by raising prices; second, by blocking local production when the patent owner so chooses; and third, for agricultural varieties, by unwelcoming farmers to continue breeding them as has been done for thousands of years.

## Policy Issues

Seventy countries across the world have certain national regulations on herbal medicines (Bagozzi, 2003). The Convention of International Trade in Endangered Species (CITES), which has widely taken up across the world, has also drawn certain regulatory policies to check the further overexploitation of threatened medicinal plant species. In the National Five Years Plans of India, medicinal plants are subjected to the integral part of the Indian System of Medicine and Homeopathy since its inception in First Five Year Plan to Eighth Five Year Plans (Ahuja, 2001). In 1983, the National Health Policy recognized that the large stock of manpower in Ayurveda, Sidha, Unani, Homeopathy and Naturopathy has not been adequately utilized therefore steps need to be taken to move towards a meaningful integration of the indigenous and modern systems of medicine (Anonymous, 1983).

The Planning Commission and the National Medicinal Plants Board (NMPB) of the Government of India have prepared policy documents on the promotional and commercial aspects of the medicinal plants sector. In the beginning, NMPB has prioritized 32 medicinal plant species for research and development, and the Planning Commission has enlisted 24 medicinal plant species, which needs priority attention for research and development in order to meet the desired aim of the medicinal plant sector (Table 3.6). NMPB has also revised the list of prioritized species of medicinal plants and added 50 more species in the previous list for cultivation, conservation and commercialization of medicinal plants at large scale. Based on the four-selected prioritized categories, such as endemism, use value, mode of harvesting and rarity status, Kala *et al.* (2004) has identified 17 plant species for priority attention (Table 3.7). The top prioritized group obtains 5 medicinal plants, such as *Aconitum heterophyllum, Arnebia benthamii, Gloriosa superba, Nardostachys grandiflora* and *Podophyllum hexandrum*. Except for *Gloriosa superba*, rest of the top prioritized species are critically endangered. The second group of prioritized species obtains

**Table 3.6: Important Medicinal Plants in Short Supply and Prioritized for the Research and Development**

| Sl.No. | Botanical Name | Local Name | Part Used | No. of Uses[a] | Important Uses | Quantity Required Tonnes/ Annum | Species in Short Supply[b] | Species prioritized for R&D[c] |
|---|---|---|---|---|---|---|---|---|
| 1. | *Acacia catechu* (L. f.) Willd. | Khair | Root, bark | 16 | Asthma, bronchitis | 2.4 | ✓ | – |
| 2. | *Aconitum ferox* Wall. | Vatsnabh | Root | 6 | Rheumatism | – | – | ✓ |
| 3. | *Aconitum heterophyllum* Wall. | Atees | Root | 12 | Fever, cough, piles, stomachache | 0.55 | ✓ | ✓ |
| 4. | *Aegle marmelos* (L.) Correa | Bel | Fruit, bark | 31 | Dysentery, diarrhoea, fever | – | – | ✓ |
| 5. | *Alpinia galanga* (L.) Willd. | Kulanjan | Bulb | 2 | Health tonic | 0.22 | ✓ | – |
| 6. | *Andrographis paniculata* (Burm. f.) Wall. | Kalmegh | Whole plant | 22 | Malaria, liver complaints, blood purifier | – | – | ✓ |
| 7. | *Aquillaria malaccensis* Lamk. | Agaru | Leaf, resin | 2 | To remove fish spine from throat | 0.17 | ✓ | – |
| 8. | *Artemisia maritima* L. | Kunja | Whole plant | 7 | Antiseptic, blood purifier | 0.33 | ✓ | – |
| 9. | – | Ashtavarga | – | – | – | 0.095 | ✓ | – |
| 10. | *Asparagus racemosus* Willd. | Shatavari | Root | 22 | Dysentery, cough, cut and wounds | – | – | ✓ |
| 11. | *Bacopa monnieri* (L.) Penn. | Brahmi | Whole plant | 20 | Brain tonic, blood purifier, fever | – | – | ✓ |
| 12. | *Berberis aristata* DC. | Kingora | Root, stem | 4 | Eye diseases | – | – | ✓ |
| 13. | *Cassia angustifolia* Vahl | Senna | Root | 3 | Rheumatism | – | – | ✓ |
| 14. | *Chlorophytum tuberosum* Bak. | Safed musli | Tuber | 4 | Leucorrhoea, sexual tonic | – | – | ✓ |

Contd...

**Table 3.6–Contd...**

| Sl No. | Botanical Name | Local Name | Part Used | No. of Uses[a] | Important Uses | Quantity Required Tonnes/ Annum | Species in Short Supply[b] | Species prioritized for R&D[c] |
|---|---|---|---|---|---|---|---|---|
| 15. | *Coleus barbatus* Benth. | Patharchur | Root | 3 | Tonic, blood pressure | – | – | ✓ |
| 16. | *Commiphora wightii* (Arn.) Bhandari | Guggul | Resin, bark | 9 | Asthma, typhoid | 2.3 | ✓ | ✓ |
| 17. | *Crocus sativus* L. | Kesar | Flower | – | – | – | – | ✓ |
| 18. | *Curculigo orchioides* Gaerten. | Kali musli | Root | 26 | Asthma, dysentery, tonic | 2.25 | ✓ | – |
| 19. | *Curcuma zedoaria* (Christ) Rosc. | Kachora | Rhizome | 4 | Jaundice, blood pressure | 0.225 | ✓ | – |
| 20. | *Embelia ribes* Burm. f. | Jheum | Seed, fruit | 4 | Skin diseases, leprosy | – | – | ✓ |
| 21. | *Garcinia indica* Choisy | Kokam | Fruit | 2 | Skin diseases | – | – | ✓ |
| 22. | *Gloriosa superba* L. | Kalihari | Rhizome | 28 | Snake bite, leprosy, tonic | – | – | ✓ |
| 23. | *Glycyrrhiza glabra* | Mulethi | – | – | – | – | – | ✓ |
| 24. | *Gymnema sylvestre* (Retz.) R. Br. | Gudmar | Root, leaf | 8 | Gastric disorders, eye diseases | – | – | ✓ |
| 25. | *Hemidesmus indicus* (L.) Br. | Anantmul | Root | 34 | Cough, hypertension, dysentery | 1.2 | ✓ | – |
| 26. | *Mallotus philippensis* Muell.–Arg. | Kamela | Fruit | 16 | Constipation, skin diseases, ulcer | 0.155 | ✓ | – |
| 27. | *Myrica esculenta* Ham. ex Don | Kaphal | Bark, fruit | 12 | Asthma, fever, cough | 0.225 | ✓ | – |
| 28. | *Myristica fragrans* Hoult. | Jaiphal | – | – | – | 0.33 | ✓ | – |

Contd...

**Table 3.6–Contd...**

| Sl.No. | Botanical Name | Local Name | Part Used | No. of Uses[a] | Important Uses | Quantity Required Tonnes/ Annum | Species in Short Supply[b] | Species prioritized for R&D[c] |
|---|---|---|---|---|---|---|---|---|
| 29. | *Nardostachys jatamansi* (Don) DC. | Jatamansi | Rhizome | 18 | Bronchitis, blood purifier, hysteria | 0.66 | ✓ | ✓ |
| 30. | *Nelumbo nucifera* Gaertn. | Kamalphool | Fruit, seed | 4 | Cholera, diarrhoea, tonic | 0.31 | ✓ | – |
| 31. | *Ocimum sanctum* L. | Tulsi | Seed, leaf | 18 | Fever, vomiting, liver complaints, blood purifier | – | – | ✓ |
| 32. | *Phyllanthus amarus* Schum. and Thonn. | Bhui amla | Whole | 3 | Jaundice, aphrodisiac, dysentery | – | – | ✓ |
| 33. | *Phyllanthus emblica* L. | Amla | Fruit | 29 | Constipation, diabetes, tonic | – | – | ✓ |
| 34. | *Picrorhiza kurrooa* Benth. | Katuki | Rhizome | 13 | Headache, fever, dysentery, anemia, asthma | 1.55 | ✓ | ✓ |
| 35. | *Piper cubeba* L. f. | Kabab chini | Fruit | 7 | Cholera, fever, cough | 0.335 | ✓ | – |
| 36. | *Piper longum* L. | Pippal | Root | 16 | Indigestion, child birth, dysentery | – | – | ✓ |
| 37. | *Pistacia chinensis* Bunge | Kakadshingi | Fruit | 3 | Scorpion bite, dysentery | 0.45 | ✓ | |
| 38. | *Plantago major* L. | Isabgol | Whole | 7 | Wounds, weakness, constipation | – | – | ✓ |
| 39. | *Rauvolfia serpentina* (L.) Benth. ex Kurz. | Sarpagandha | Root | 14 | Malarial fever, snake bite | – | – | ✓ |
| 40. | *Santalum album* L. | Chandan | Wood | 7 | Dysentery, skin diseases | – | – | ✓ |
| 41. | *Saraca asoca* (Roxb.) De Wilde | Ashok | Bark, leaf | 4 | Heart disorder, tonic | 6.8 | ✓ | ✓ |

*Contd...*

**Table 3.6–Contd...**

| Sl.No. | Botanical Name | Local Name | Part Used | No. of Uses[a] | Important Uses | Quantity Required Tonnes/ Annum | Species in Short Supply[b] | Species prioritized for R&D[c] |
|---|---|---|---|---|---|---|---|---|
| 42. | *Saussurea costus* (Falc.) Lipsch. | Kut | Root | 7 | Dysentery, asthma, ulcer | 0.43 | ✓ | ✓ |
| 43. | *Smilex* sp | Chopchini | Root | 12 | Menstrual complaints, small pox | 0.55 | ✓ | – |
| 44. | *Solanum nigrum* L. | Makoy | Fruit | 27 | Jaundice, piles, skin diseases | – | – | ✓ |
| 45. | *Swertia chirayita* (Roxb. ex Flem.) Karsten. | Chirata | Whole plant | 16 | Malarial fever, blood purifier | 2.5 | ✓ | ✓ |
| 46. | *Tinospora cordifolia* (L.) Merr. | Giloe | Whole plant | 22 | Jaundice, tonic, bone fracture | – | – | ✓ |
| 47. | *Valeriana jatamansi* Jones | Tagar | Root, leaf | 4 | Epilepsy, urinary complaints | 0.275 | ✓ | – |
| 48. | *Withania somnifera* (L.) Dunal | Ashwagandha | Root, leaf | 14 | Eye complaints, asthma, cough | – | – | ✓ |
| 49. | *Wrightia tinctoria* Br. | Indrajava | Bark, latex | 14 | Toothache, piles, dysentery | 0.418 | ✓ | – |

a: Based on Jain, 1991.

b: Medicinal plants in short supply according to the Planning Commission, Government of India.

c : Prioritized species of medicinal plants for research and development according to National Medicinal Plants Board, Government of India.

–: Not known.

6 medicinal plant species such as *Aconitum balfourii, Angelica glauca, Dactylorhiza hatagirea, Fritillaria roylei, Meconopsis aculeata* and *Saussurea costus.* The third group of priority species also obtains 6 medicinal plant species, such as, *Aconitum falconeri, Artemisia maritima, Delphinium cashmerianum, Picrorhiza kurrooa, Thymus linearis* and *Acorus calamus.*

**Table 3.7: Priority List of Medicinal Plant Species Based on Endemism, Use Value, Mode of Harvesting and Rarity Status**

| *Prioritized Species* | *Endemism* | *Use Value* | *Mode of Harvesting* | *CAMP Status* |
|---|---|---|---|---|
| | **Top priority** | | | |
| *Aconitum heterophyllum* Wall. | Endemic | 12 | Rt | CR-EN |
| *Arnebia benthamii* (Wall. Ex G. Don) Johnston | Endemic | 11 | Rh | CR-EN |
| *Gloriosa superba* L. | - | 25 | Sh+Rt | EN |
| *Nardostachys grandiflora* DC. | - | 18 | Rh | CR-EN |
| *Podophyllum hexandrum* Royle | - | 11 | Rh+Fr | CR-EN |
| | **IInd priority** | | | |
| *Aconitum balfourii* Stapf | Endemic | 6 | Rt | CR-EN |
| *Angelica glauca* Edgew. | Endemic | 6 | Rt | CR-EN |
| *Dactylorhiza hatagirea* (D. Don) Soo | Endemic | 7 | Tuber | CR-EN |
| *Fritillaria roylei* Hook. | Endemic | 6 | Rt | CR-EN |
| *Meconopsis aculeate* Royle | Endemic | 4 | Rt+Sh | CR-EN |
| *Saussurea costus* (Falc.) Lipsch. | Endemic | 7 | Rt | CR-EN |
| | **IIIrd priority** | | | |
| *Aconitum falconeri* Stapf | Endemic | 3 | Rt | CR-EN |
| *Acorus calamus* L. | - | 25 | Rh | VU |
| *Artemisia maritima* L. | - | 6 | Rt+Sh | EN |
| *Delphinium cashmerianum* Royle | Endemic | 11 | Rt+Sh | R |
| *Picrorhiza kurrooa* Benth. | - | 13 | Rh | EN |
| *Thymus linearis* Benth. | - | 5 | Rt+Sh | CR-EN |

Codes: 1. Mode of harvesting: Rt–Root; Sh–Shoot; Rh–Rhizome.

2. CAMP status: CR-EN–Critically Endangered; En–Endangered; VU–Vulnerable; R–Rare

*Source*: Kala *et al.*, 2004.

Being a part of tradition, there are many other social issues attached with the medicinal plants sector. While preparing policies one has to take the perceptions of local people in improving the sector, as the use of medicinal plant species is a centuries old tradition of the local people and they have fair amount of knowledge right from harvesting of medicinal plants to preparing medicine and methods of storage. Gathering perceptions of local people for evaluation of medicinal plant sector may also inform the societal decision mechanism in working out the ways of allocating scarce resources among competing demand. The user group willingness to pay for the medicinal plants and the producer willingness to accept should also be studied for the development of better market infrastructure.

## Recommendations

For the successful establishment of medicinal plants sector I have identified the following points on the basis of observations and existing literature. There is a need to:

- ☆ Establish linkages among various stakeholders.
- ☆ Involve the agricultural support agencies in the sector for viable farming.
- ☆ Develop the networks of medicinal plants conservation areas across the country on a priority basis.
- ☆ Encourage the traditional herbal healers and practitioners of Ayurveda.
- ☆ Conserve the indigenous knowledge on medicinal plants and their uses through documentation, implementing policies and legal reforms.
- ☆ Document the traditional uses of low profile and less known medicinal plants also in order to disseminate their therapeutic efficacy by preparing well acceptable medicines and also to reduce the pressure on over exploited species.
- ☆ Renew the available herbal formulations by standardizing their efficacy.
- ☆ Bring into laboratory the folklores on medicinal plants along with formulation developed by using them.

- ✰ Monitor and evaluate the status of medicinal plants regularly and to conserve the critical habitats of rare medicinal plants with collaboration of local communities.
- ✰ Consider the traditional rights of local people on the use of medicinal plants.
- ✰ Share benefits accruing from the sector with local communities in order to generate alternative income opportunities for indigenous communities
- ✰ Establish a Social Capital Trust for herbal healers in order to promote the research and development.
- ✰ Develop viable agro-technology for valuable medicinal plant species.
- ✰ Conduct regular research and training on scientific harvesting and processing techniques.
- ✰ Study the infected medicinal plants and causal factors in order to develop the healthy farming.
- ✰ Analyze the market policies.
- ✰ Set-up a community-based management of medicinal plants farming and marketing.
- ✰ Disseminate any available scientific knowledge on the medicinal plants through network structure of communication.
- ✰ Discourage any attempt of adulteration of herbal medicine through certification of raw materials for quality control by using the modern tools such as high performance thin layer and liquid chromatography, gas and column chromatography, volumetric analysis and gravimetric determinations.
- ✰ Ascertain certain policies for collection of planting material, especially of rare and endangered medicinal plants from natural habitats for various experimental purposes.

Apart from these aspects, it has been observed that a major part of documentation and research on indigenous uses of medicinal plants is focused on the human aspect. Animal husbandry is a backbone of economy in majorities of indigenous societies and maintaining their healthy population will obviously benefit these communities. In North East

Himalaya, possessing the high numbers of domestic animals is an indication of prosperity of their respective owners. Although, the history of using plants as a veterinary medicine traces back to pre-Vedic times, and it has been also stated that veterinary medicine paved the way to the advancement of human medicine, with due course of time this important aspect of medicinal plants was overlooked by subsequent researchers and user groups. In rural areas, about 85 per cent of the domestic animals are still cured by indigenous techniques and medicinal plants (Ghotge, 2004). Since there are many medicinal plant species used in curing various animal related disorders and diseases, the research work should also be carried out and emphasized on the documentation and identification of medicinal plants for curing livestock diseases.

One of the major tasks is to create opportunities for sharing of knowledge by encouraging the real knowledge holders. Conservationists and policy makers should come forward to bridge the gaps they themselves have with the indigenous knowledge holders. If they do so, then they may find themselves sometimes in positions of trust. There are strong reasons for indigenous communities to guard their knowledge. The local knowledgeable persons on many occasions do not reveal the localities of valuable medicinal plants realizing that they will be neglected once such localities are known by others and the same will be used by competitors to their disadvantage. According to Convention of Biological Diversity, benefits for conservation of biodiversity should accrue from its process, however there are often difficulties for communities, researchers and policy makers to agree what exactly they should be (Hamilton, 2004). Such policies of benefits sharing should be framed in a holistic manner bearing the significance of such knowledge keepers and caretaker of such knowledge and knowledge related resources for centuries.

## Institution's Role and Networking

In India, many government and non-government organizations have had the focused attention for improving the medicinal plants sector (Table 3.8). Opportunities for funding have created to assist the people whoever are willing to work and to build capacity of the medicinal plants sector. According to the mandate of National Medicinal Plants Board (NMPB), a nodal agency for medicinal plants research and development in India,

**Table 3.8: Major Institutions Involved in Funding Projects to the Medicinal Plants Research in India**

| *Institutions* | *Funding for Major Areas in Medicinal Plants Research* |
|---|---|
| University Grant Commission, UGC | Ecology, biochemistry, survey, documentation |
| Department of Science and Technology, DST | Taxonomy, ecology, pathology, survey, propagation, documentation, cultivation, conservation |
| Department of Atomic Energy, DAE | Pathology, value addition |
| Indian Council of Medical Research, ICMR | Breeding, value addition |
| All India Council for Technical Education, AICTE | Management technology |
| Council for Scientific and Industrial Research, CSIR | Ecology, taxonomy, biochemistry, survey, documentation, cultivation, genetics, agro-technology, conservation |
| Defense Research and Development Organization, DRDO | Agro-technology, survey, documentation, conservation |
| Department of Biotechnology, DBT | Agro-technology, molecular biology, Biochemistry, rural bio-technology |
| Indian Council of Agricultural Research, ICAR | Breeding, pathology, molecular biology |
| Ministry of Environment and Forest, MoEF | Survey, documentation, conservation, management, ecological impact assessment, cultivation |
| National Medicinal Plants Board, NMPB | Survey, documentation, cultivation, marketing, conservation |
| Herbal Research and Development Institute, HRDI | Survey, documentation, nursery development |
| G.B. Pant Institute of Himalayan Environment and Development, GBPIHED | Survey, documentation, cultivation, conservation |

the research projects can be submitted for funding within two major schemes *viz.*, promotional scheme and commercial scheme. The major thrust areas for research within promotional scheme are (*i*) survey and inventory of medicinal plants, (*ii*) *in-situ* conservation and *ex-situ* cultivation of selected medicinal plants, (*iii*) production of quality planting material, (*iv*) diffusion of knowledge through education and communication, (*v*) promotion of global and domestic market system and (*vi*) strengthening research, development and man power. Within commercial scheme, the major objectives are (*i*) bulk production of medicinal plants and ensuring supply of quality planting material, (*ii*) expansion of selected medicinal plants farming areas, (*iii*) value addition in harvesting, processing and marketing of medicinal plants, and (*iv*) developing innovative marketing mechanism.

Apart from this, the role of NMPB is to co-ordinate with different ministries, departments, organizations, state and union territory Governments in order to develop and strengthen the medicinal plant sector. To make contacts and building networks with national and international organizations devoted to similar mandates and goals is one of the major roles of NMPB. A total 31 State Medicinal Plants Boards have also been set up for smooth functioning of the medicinal plants sector. NMPB has also sanctioned more than 1000 projects worth Rs 45 crores on the medicinal plants research and development during past two financial years all over the country. For the large-scale farming of commercially important medicinal plants, about 25,000 acres of land has been selected and brought under cultivation under the supervision of NMPB. One of the schemes of NMPB is a contractual farming in which any group, institution or person that possesses at least 3 years of experience in medicinal plant sector is eligible to receive at least 30 per cent financial assistance of the total project cost (Rawat and Uniyal, 2004).

Before setting up NMPB, about a decade ago (during 1992-93 financial years), of the total 1420 projects sanctioned by some major organizations about 170 research projects were allocated to medical sciences in which a single project was allocated to study the medicinal plants of the Himalayan region (Jain and Kumar, 1994). During past one decade, there has been a considerable expansion in the Himalayan medicinal plants research as it is evident by the fact that during the period many projects have been launched exclusively on the medicinal plants. Apart from major funding organizations, being a prime institution solely devoted to the research and development across the Indian Himalaya, the G.B. Pant Institute of Himalayan Environment and Development has sanctioned the highest number of research proposals on the medicinal plants under the supervision of Integrated Eco-development Research Programs.

National Bank for Agriculture and Rural Development (NABARD) has taken up a policy with a view to develop a suitable environment for financial institutions by providing bankable models of some 50 medicinal and aromatic crops with the unit cost and scale of finance at the state level. These 50 medicinal plant species have chosen on the bases of drawing crops suitability index. Besides, NABARD helps in supporting the capacity building of prospective entrepreneurs through Rural Entrepreneurs Development Programs by providing 100 per cent refinance (Anonymous, 2004; Kumar, 2004). NABARD has also close linkages with NMPB and different State Medicinal Plants Boards. Attempts have been made by different organizations at various levels to establish and promote the medicinal plant sector, notwithstanding there are still many gaps in the medicinal plant research, and institutions should identify these gaps and build up capacity in improving the medicinal plants sector. There are many other organizations having similar mandate, and there should be a proper networking with such organizations for handling various issues related to the medicinal plants sector.

Fortunately, in Uttarakhand attempts are being made by the Forest Department to develop certain areas for the medicinal plants conservation. According to Chandola (2004) about 1.02-lakh hectares of Reserve Forests, falls in 189 compartments of 134 Forest Ranges that is distributed over 28 territorial Forest Divisions, have been identified for medicinal plants conservation within the state. To develop the adjacent forest areas, as a production of targeted medicinal plants around these conservation compartments, is also in the Forest Department's policy. Forest Department also claims for developing 473 nurseries in Uttarakhand, which have distributed more than 57.30 lakhs saplings of medicinal plant species to the state farmers. Besides, the Forest Department has identified 12.22-lakh hectare area for the medicinal plants harvesting in the state.

Generally, the success of medicinal plants sector may depend on the awareness and interest of the farmers as well as its other stakeholders, supportive government policies, availability of assured markets, profitable price levels, and assess to simple and appropriate technology. The successful establishment of medicinal plants sector may help in raising rural employment in the developing countries, boost commerce around the world, and contribute to the health of millions. In the modern era of globalization, the human populations are increasingly exercising free choices and movements. Today, if any epidemic disease outbursts at any corner of the world, the probability of its spread to any other community is much higher than the past when most of the indigenous communities were intact and restricted to certain geographical area. The spreading of swine flue disease across the world is one of the examples of rapid spread of diseases. Keeping these views in mind, to validate the efficacy of medicinal plants and to prepare standardized herbal drugs is an important tool to decline the increasing risk of spreading any disease.

## References

Ahuja, A.K. (2001). Need for a comprehensive approach to medicinal plants. In: *Himalayan Medicinal Plants: Potential and Prospects*, (Eds. S.S. Samant, U. Dhar and L.M.S. Palni), Gyanodaya Prakashan, Nainital, India, pp. 1-21.

Anonymous (1983). National Health Policy. Ministry of Health and Family Welfare, Government of India, New Delhi, India.

Anonymous (2003). *Conservation Assessment and Management Prioritization for the Medicinal Plants of Jammu-Kashmir, Himachal Pradesh and Uttarakhand*. Foundation for Revitalization of Local Health Traditions, Bangalore, India.

Anonymous (2004). *Herbals in India: Opportunities, Challenges and Initiatives by NABARD*. National Bank for Agriculture and Rural Development, India.

Awasthi, A. and S.K. Uniyal (2003). Meadow to market. *Sanctuary Asia*, XXIII: 28-31.

Bagozzi, D. (2003). *Traditional Medicine*. World Health Organization. http://www.who.int/mediacentre/factsheets/fs134/en/

Barany, M., A.L. Hammett, A. Sene and B. Amichev (2001). Non timber forest benefits and HIV/AIDS in sub-Saharan Africa. *Journal of Forestry*, 99: 36-41.

Borthakur, S.K., K. Nath and T.R. Sharma (2001). Inquire into old lead: ethnoveterinary medicine for treatment of elephant in Assam. In: *Plant Diversity of the Himalaya* (Eds. P.C. Pande and S.S. Samant). Gyanodaya Prakasan, Nainital. pp. 573-582.

Chandola, S. (2004). MAP sector in Uttarakhand and role of the Forest Department. *Financing Agriculture*, 36 (3): 27-32.

Cunningham, A.B. (1998). Medicinal plants and sustainable trade. In: *Medicinal Plants: A Global Heritage*. Proceedings of the International conference on medicinal plants for survival. International Development Research Center, New Delhi, India, pp. 109-121.

Dhyani, P.P. (2000). Common plant species have potential for economic upliftment of rural populace–Bantulsi a case in point. *Hima-Paryavaran*, 12: 11-13.

Dhyani, P.P. and C.P. Kala (2005). Current research on medicinal plants: Five lesser known but valuable aspects. *Current Science*, 88 (3): 335.

Egziabher, T.B.G. (2003). Africa proposes. *Down To Earth*, 12: 55.

Farooquee, N.A., B.S. Majila and C.P. Kala (2004). Indigenous knowledge systems and sustainable management of natural resources in a high altitude society in Kumaun Himalaya, India. *Journal of Human Ecology*, 16: 33-42.

Ghotge, N.S. (2004). Plants in veterinary medicine. *Financing Agriculture*, 36 (3): 54-57.

Green, E.C., K.J. Goodman and M. Hare (1999). Ethnobotany, IPR and benefit sharing: the forest people fund in Suriname. *Indigenous Knowledge and Development Monitor*, 7: 8-11.

Hall, P. and K.S. Bawa (1993). Methods to access the impact of extraction of non-timber tropical forest products on plant populations. *Economic Botany*, 47: 234-247.

Hamilton, A.C. (2004). Medicinal plants, conservation and livelihoods. *Biodiversity and Conservation*, 13: 1477-1517.

Jablonski, D. (2004). Extinction: past and present. *Nature*, 427: 589.

Jain, A.P. and H. Kumar (1994). R and D funding in Himalayan region in India: A comparison. *Hima-Paryavaran*, 6: 10-11.

Jain, S.K. (1991). *Dictionary of Indian folk medicine and ethnobotany*. Deep Publications, New Delhi.

Joshi, K., P. Chavan, D. Warude and B. Patwardhan (2004). Molecular markers in herbal drug technology. *Current Science*, 87: 159-165.

Kala, C.P. (1998). *Ethnobotanical Survey and Propagation of Rare Medicinal Herbs in the Buffer Zone of the Valley of Flowers National Park, Garhwal Himalaya*. International Center for Integrated Mountain Development, Kathmandu, Nepal.

Kala, C.P. (2000). Status and conservation of rare and endangered medicinal plant in the Indian trans-Himalaya. *Biological Conservation*, 93: 371-379.

Kala, C.P. (2002). *Medicinal Plant of Indian Trans-Himalaya*. Bishen Singh Mahendra Pal Singh, Dehradun, India.

Kala, C.P. (2003). Commercial exploitation and conservation status of high value medicinal plants across the borderline of India and Nepal in Pithoragarh. *The Indian Forester*, 129: 80-84.

Kala, C.P. (2004a). *Studies on the Indigenous Knowledge, Practices and Traditional Uses of Forest Products by Human Societies in Uttarakhand State of India*. G.B. Pant Institute of Himalayan Environment and Development, Almora, India.

Kala, C.P. (2004b). Revitalizing traditional herbal therapy by exploring medicinal plants: A case study of Uttarakhand State in India. In: *Indigenous Knowledges: Transforming the Academy*, Proceedings of an International Conference, Pennsylvania State University, Pennsylvania, USA. pp. 15-21.

Kala, C.P. (2004c). *The Valley of Flowers: Myth and Reality*. International Book Distributors, Dehradun, India.

Kala, C.P. (2004d). Assessment of species rarity. *Current Science*, 86: 1058-1059.

Kala, C.P. (2005). Indigenous uses, population density, and conservation of threatened medicinal plants in the protected areas of the Himalayas. *Conservation Biology*, 19 (2): 368-378.

Kala, C.P., N.A. Farooquee and U. Dhar (2004). Prioritization of medicinal plants on the basis of available knowledge, existing practices and use value status in Uttarakhand, India. *Biodiversity and Conservation,* 13: 453-469.

Kala, C.P. and V.B. Mathur (2002). Patterns of plant species distribution in the trans-Himalayan region of Ladakh, India. *Journal of Vegetation Science,* 13: 751-754.

KIT (2003). *Cultivating a Healthy Enterprise.* Bulletin 350, Royal Tropical Institute, Amsterdam, The Netherlands.

KIT (2004). *Searching Synergy.* Bulletin 359, Royal Tropical Institute, Amsterdam, The Netherlands.

Koo, B., C. Nottenberg and P.G. Pardey (2004). Plants and intellectual property: An international appraisal. *Science,* 306: 1295-1297.

Kumar, R. (2004). Medicinal, aromatic and herbal crops. *Financing Agriculture,* 36 (3): 3-6.

Lacuna-Richman, C. (2002). The socio-economic significance of subsistence non-wood forest products in Leyte, Philippines. *Environmental Conservation,* 29: 253-262.

Myers, N. (1991). The world's forests and human population: the environmental interconnections. *Population and Development Review,* 16: 1-15.

Nadkarni, K.M. and A.K. Nadkarni (1908). *Indian Materia Medica.* Popular Prakashan, Bombay, India.

Nautiyal, M.C. and B.P. Nautiyal (2004). *Agrotechniques for High Altitude Medicinal and Aromatic Plants.* Bishen Singh Mahendra Pal Singh, Dehradun, India.

Nautiyal, S., K.S. Rao, R.K. Maikhuri, K.S. Negi and C.P. Kala (2002). Status of medicinal plants on way to Vashuki Tal in Mandakini Valley, Garhwal, Uttarakhand. *Journal of Non-Timber Forest Products,* 9: 124-131.

Nayar, M.P. and A.R.K. Sastry (1987). *Red Data Book of Indian Plants.* Botanical Survey of India, India.

Pearson, H. (2004). First 'black drug' nears approval. Nature. Published online. http://www.nature.com/news/2004/040719/full/040719-16.html

Prahalathan, S. (2004). Export potential of Indian medicinal plants and products. *Financing Agriculture,* 36: 33-36.

Prajapati, N.D., S.S. Purohit, A.K. Sharma and T. Kumar (2003). *A Handbook of Medicinal Plants.* Agrobios, Jodhpur, India.

Samal, P.K., A. Shah, S.C. Tiwari and D.K. Agrawal (2004). Indigenous health care practices and their linkages with bio-resource conservation and socio-economic development in central Himalayan region of India. *Indian Journal of Traditional Knowledge,* 3: 12-26.

Samant, S.S., U. Dhar and L.M.S. Palni (1998). *Medicinal Plants of Indian Himalaya: Diversity Distribution Potential Values.* G.B. Pant Institute of Himalayan Environment and Development, Almora, India.

Samant, S.S., U. Dhar and R.S. Rawal (2001). Diversity and distribution of wild edible plants of the Indian Himalaya. In: *Plant Diversity of the Himalaya,* (Eds. P.C. Pande and S.S. Samant). Gyanodaya Prakashan, Nainital, India. pp. 421-482.

Schippmann, U., D.J. Leaman and A.B. Cunningham (2002). *Impact of Cultivation and Gathering of Medicinal Plants on Biodiversity: Global Trends and Issues.* Inter-Department Working Group on Biology Diversity for Food and Agriculture, FAO, Rome, Italy.

Sharma, A.B. (2004). Global Medicinal Plants Demand May Touch $5 Trillion By 2050. *Indian Express.* Monday, March 29, 2004.

Shiva, V. (1996). *Protecting our Biological and Intellectual Heritage in the Age of Biopiracy.* The Research Foundation for Science, Technology and Natural Resources Policy, New Delhi, India.

Silori, C.S. and R. Badola (2000). Medicinal plants cultivation and sustainable development: A case study in buffer zone of the Nanda Devi Biosphere Reserve, Western Himalaya, India. *Mountain Research and Development,* 20: 272-279.

Singh, D.K. and P.K. Hajra (1996). Floristic diversity. In: *Biodiversity Status in the Himalaya* (Ed. Gujral). British Council, New Delhi, pp. 23-38.

Stein, R. (2004). Alternative remedies gaining popularity. *The Washington Post*, Friday, May 28, 2004.

Rao, M.R., M.C. Palada and B.N. Becker (2004). Medicinal and aromatic plants in agro-forestry systems. *Agroforestry Systems*, 61: 107-122.

Raven, P.H. (1998). Medicinal plants and global sustainability: The canary in the coal mine. In: *Medicinal Plants: A Global Heritage*. Proceedings of the International conference on medicinal plants for survival. International Development Research Center, New Delhi, India. pp. 14-18.

Rawat, R.B.S and R.C. Uniyal (2004). Status of the medicinal and aromatic plants sector in Uttarakhand: initiative taken by the Government of India. *Financing Agriculture*, 36 (3): 7-13.

Plate 1: *Dactylorhiza hatagirea*

Plate 2: *Podophyllum hexandrum*

Plate 3: *Saussurea obvallata*

Plate 4: *Oxyria digyna*

Plate 5: *Picrorhiza kurrooa*

Plate 6: *Megacarpaea polyandra*

Plate 7: *Pleurospermum candolli*

Plate 8: *Aconitum heterophyllum*

Plate 9: *Arisaema jacquamontii*

Plate 10: *Geranium wallichianum*

Plate 11: *Delphinium denudatum*

Plate 12: *Rhododendron arboreum*

Plate 13: *Saussurea simpsoniana*

Plate 14: *Syringa emodi*

Plate 15: *Arnebia benthamii*

Plate 16: *Meconopsis aculeata*

Plate 17: A View of Alpine Meadows (Valley of Flowers) Rich in Medicinal Plants

Plate 18: *Potentilla atrosanguinea*

Plate 19: *Thymus linearis*

Plate 20: *Rheum Moorcroftianum*

# Chapter 4

# People Preferences of Medicinal Plants and Environment Conservation

## Introduction

The sustainable use of medicinal plants through community-based conservation has become one the central points in the modern conservation domain after the Earth Summit held in Rio de Janeiro in 1992, which strongly acknowledged the significance of indigenous knowledge in conservation of biological diversity. The use of natural resources, however, has been regulated in order to check the over-harvesting of such valuable forest produce, which is a cause of conflict between resource management agency and local people. Such dilemma in the conservation of useful plant species exists across the globe wherein global perceptions of plant conservation and scientific understanding of resource management are confronted with local people's knowledge of perceptions and values associated with surrounding forests (Berkes *et al.*, 2000; Ghimire *et al.*, 2005).

The rich biodiversity in Uttarakhand has provided an initial advantage to its inhabitants for observing, and scrutinizing the rich flora and fauna for developing their own traditional knowledge (Kala, 2005a). With the modernization and invasion of outside forces the centuries old knowledge on the utilization of many plant species has diminished several folds as explained in the previous chapters. The modern education system has also added a new dimension in the understanding of social, economical, and biological values which on many occasions do not match with the traditional ones. The indigenous knowledge and practices are considered to have certain affinities with the complex environmental conditions that are manipulated through indigenous traditional knowledge to deal with uncertainties and to cope up with the environmental changes (Berkes *et al.*, 2000). Therefore, it is very important to analyze and understand the indigenous knowledge, practices and perceptions for developing the appropriate management policies for conserving biodiversity and environment that build on both local knowledge and scientific basis.

The dependency of villages situated on and at the edges of mountainous areas is higher on the forest and forest produces than the lowland settlements (Lacuna-Richman, 2002). Uttarakhand being a hilly state and endowed with high diversity of medicinal plants, its inhabitants use plants for curing various ailments. This fact has made Uttarakhand as one of the important states in India for understanding the perceptions of local people with reference to important medicinal plants as well as making scientific analysis for improving the medicinal plants sector. By integrating the local people's knowledge, proper selection of suitable species among the large number of medicinal plant species may be accomplished for designing policies and advancement of the medicinal plants sector. With this idea, a study was conducted in the hilly areas of Uttarakhand realizing the high dependency of local people on various medicinal plant species. The findings of this study are discussed in this chapter, which deals with preferences of local people towards the important medicinal plant species and its implications for environmental conservation.

## Methodology

Three hill districts located of Uttarakhand state namely Pithoragarh, Chamoli and Pauri were selected for present study realizing that mountain people have more dependency on forest and forest produce than the residents of lowland and plains of India, hence they occupy a great deal of knowledge on the use of plant species. Each district selected for this study has different cultural, social, altitudinal, vegetational and environmental set up. Pithoragarh district obtains highest population of two major tribal communities (*e.g.*, Bhotiya and Raji) and Chamoli district obtains Bhotiya tribal community (Table 4.1). There has been a marginal decrease in forest cover after 1974 in these hill districts of Uttarakhand. For example, Chamoli shows 7.33 per cent decrease in forest cover, Pauri shows 5.99 per cent decrease, and Pithoragarh shows 1.94 per cent decrease in the forest cover (Anonymous, 1996). The fallow land has been increasing in the state over past three decades.

**Table 4.1: Characteristics of the Districts Studied in the Uttarakhand State of India**

| *Parameters* | *Pauri* | *Chamoli* | *Pithoragarh* |
|---|---|---|---|
| Total population | 697078 | 370359 | 462289 |
| ✰ Rural | 607203 | 319656 | 402456 |
| ✰ Urban | 89875 | 50703 | 59833 |
| Schedule caste | 106653 | 67539 | 106449 |
| Schedule tribe | 1594 | 10484 | 10279 |
| ✰ Bhotia | 214 | 10192 | 18647 |
| ✰ Boksha | 1202 | 7 | 7 |
| ✰ Tharu | 7 | 9 | 39 |
| ✰ Jaunsari | 83 | 21 | 7 |
| ✰ Raji | 17 | 0 | 364 |
| Altitudinal range (study villages) | 700–1800 m | 1500–2500 m | 1800–3000 m |
| Major vegetation type | Sub-tropical, temperate | Sub-tropical, temperate, alpine | Temperate, alpine |
| Major forest type | Sal forest, Sal-mixed forest, Pine forest, Pine-Oak forest, Oak forest | Pine forest, Pine-Oak forest, Oak forest | Pine forest, Pine-Oak forest, Oak forest |
| Forest cover (per cent) | 59.40 | 61.93 | 51.84 |
| Wasteland (per cent) | 4.50 | 19.60 | 4.22 |
| Pasture land (per cent) | 5.69 | 2.59 | 13.26 |
| Tree crops and groves land (per cent) | 8.09 | 4.20 | 7.18 |

*Contd...*

**Table 4.1–Contd...**

| Parameters | Pauri | Chamoli | Pithoragarh |
|---|---|---|---|
| Fallow land (per cent) | 2.36 | 0.20 | 2.23 |
| Agriculture + agro-forestry land (per cent) | 11.82 | 5.37 | 10.03 |
| Change in forest cover after 1974 (per cent) | –5.99 | –7.33 | –1.94 |
| Change in agriculture + agro-forestry land after 1974 (per cent) | –14.44 | –3.51 | –7.09 |

*Source*: Anonymous, 1996; Census of India, 2001; Kala *et al.*, 2004.

Structured questionnaire surveys were conducted from 2003 to 2005 in the villages of all 3 hill districts. Ten villages in each district were approached and minimum 10 households in each village were surveyed intensively. An attempt was made to interview the male or female head of every household and in case of their absence the elder person of the family was interviewed. The other members of the household were also present, in many cases, during the interview to clarify the points made by the main respondent. Each respondent was asked to select and prioritize 5 important medicinal plant species. In this approach, the informants themselves had valued the significance of plant species.

The respondents were also asked on the plant parts used and the local uses of medicinal plant species selected by them as the priority species. This way the second round of interview was open ended in which the other members of the family had helped in cross checking the data on indigenous uses of medicinal plant species. During the open ended interviews the local people disclosed many environmental and management issues of medicinal plants. In order to verify the identity of plant species mentioned by the respondents, field visits were undertaken with the respondent and in his inability any other person of his family and village who knows the concerned species. The collected plant specimens were again verified from the respondents who had mentioned the species as a preferred one.

## Results and Discussion

### Local Preferences of Medicinal Plants

The preferences of local people on the importance of medicinal plant species were varied across the different hill districts of Uttarakhand surveyed during the present investigations. A total 32 important medicinal plant species were selected by the local people of Uttarakhand, of these 19 species were selected by the local people of Chamoli, 16 species by the local people of Pithoragarh, and 13 species by the local people of Pauri district. Only two species, *Swertia sp.*, and *Ocimum sanctum* were common preferences of the local people in all three districts. *Aconitum heterophyllum* and *Picrorhiza kurrooa* were the most preferred medicinal plant species in Pithoragarh whereas in Chamoli and Pauri *Swertia chiraiyta* and *Phyllanthus emblica* were preferred by maximum number of respondents. Of the total medicinal plants preferred, 8 species were exclusively preferred by the local people of Pauri and 5 species each by the local people of Pithoragarh and Chamoli. In Chamoli, the preferences of local people were more or less uniform on the various medicinal plant species whereas in Pithoragarh the maximum preferences of respondents were restricted to *Aconitum heterophyllum* and *Picrorhiza kurrooa* (Table 4.2)

The medicinal plants preferred by the local people were used in curing various ailments (Table 4.2). Different parts of these species such as leaf, fruit, seed, stem and bark were used as traditional medicine. There were many species of *Swertia* (*e.g. S. angustifolia, S. chiraiyta, S. incana*) inhabited in different localities within the study area and most of them were used in curing malarial fever by the local people. All three species of *Swertia* were known to the local people on a common name 'chirayta'. However, *Swertia chiraiyta* was considered the most potential and effective herbal medicine for malarial fever. The local people were so much confident on the use of *Swertia* sp. that they even did not consult the *Vaidya* (practitioners of Ayurveda) before its use for curing fever. Many locally preferred medicinal plant species were also used as regular spice by the local people. *Zanthoxylum armatum, Curcuma domestica, Cinnamomum tamala, Zingiber officinale, Allium sativum* and *Angelica glauca* were preferred medicinal plant species by the local people, which were used as spice also. Of these 6 spice and medicinal species, 3 were threatened and none of them was cultivated in the study villages and collected from the wild for the domestic and commercial purposes. The distribution of these threatened species is restricted to certain altitudinal range as *Angelica glauca* grows in alpine region whereas *Cinnamomum tamala* and *Zanthoxylum armatum* grow in the middle Himalayan ranges.

**Table 4.2: Indigenous Uses, Plant Part Used, Rarity Status and Preferences of Local People on the Importance of Various Medicinal Plant Species Across Three Hill Districts of Uttarakhand State in India**

| *Local, Latin Name of Medicinal Plant Species* | *Part Used* | *Major Indigenous Uses* | **Rarity Status in Uttarakhand* | *Preferences of Local People (in per cent)* | | |
|---|---|---|---|---|---|---|
| | | | | *Pauri* | *Chamoli* | *Pithoragarh* |
| Chiraita, *Swertia chiraiyta* (Roxb. Ex Fleming) Karsten | Leaf, stem | Malarial fever | EN | 92 | 48 | 42 |
| Awala, *Phyllanthus emblica* L. | Fruit, bark | Blood purifier, throat-ache | – | 92 | 45 | – |
| Katuki, *Picrorhiza kurrooa* Benth. | Stem | Fever, blood purification | CR EN | – | 42 | 80 |
| Ateesh, *Aconitum heterophyllum* Wall. | Root | Tonic, diarrhoea, aphrodisiac | CR EN | – | 41 | 95 |
| Tulsi, *Ocimum sanctum* L. | Leaf | Bronchitis, constipation | – | 58 | 33 | 14 |
| Salampanja, *Dactylorhiza hatagirea* (Don) Soo. | Tuber | Tonic, kidney complaints | CR EN | – | 27 | 50 |
| Timur, *Zanthoxylum armatum* DC. | Fruit | Toothache | VU | – | 25 | 32 |
| Haldi, *Curcuma domestica* Valeton | Rhizome | Blood purifiers, digestive disorder | – | 16 | 22 | – |
| Tejpat, *Cinnamomum tamala* Nees | Bark, leaf | Hearth and throat complaints | VU | – | 22 | – |
| Dolu, *Rheum australe* Don | Root | Internal pain | EN | – | 16 | 20 |
| Lahsun, *Allium sativum* L. | Bulb | Blood and digestive disorders | – | – | 16 | – |
| Kut, *Saussurea costus* (Falc.) Lipsch. | Root | Dysentery, ulcer, stomachache | CR EN | – | 13 | 43 |
| Adrak, *Zingiber officinale* Roscoe | Rhizome | Headache, toothache, cough | – | 8 | 12 | – |
| Choru, *Angelica glauca* Edgew. | Root | Gastric complaints | EN | – | 12 | 15 |

*Contd...*

**Table 4.2–Contd...**

| Local, Latin Name of Medicinal Plant Species | Part Used | Major Indigenous Uses | *Rarity Status in Uttarakhand | Preferences of Local People (in per cent) | | |
|---|---|---|---|---|---|---|
| | | | | Pauri | Chamoli | Pithoragarh |
| Geranium sp. | Leaf | Skin disease | – | – | 11 | – |
| Brahmakamal, *Saussurea obvallata* (DC.) Edgew. | Flower-bud | Reproductive disorder | EN | – | 7 | – |
| Buransh, *Rhododendron arboreum* Smith | Bark | Digestive and respiratory disorders | – | – | 6 | 7 |
| Pashanved, *Bergenia stracheyi* (Hk. f. and Th.) Engler | Root, flower | Blisters | NT | – | 6 | 9 |
| Devdar, *Cedrus deodara* (Roxb.) Loud. | Stem | Ulcer, rheumatic pain | – | – | 2 | – |
| Thuner, *Taxus baccata* L. | Bark | Tumors, cancer | EN | – | – | 18 |
| Bankakdi, *Podophyllum hexandrum* Royle | Fruit | Cough | EN | – | – | 12 |
| Banj, *Quercus leucho-trichophora* A. Camus | Seed | Scabies, urinary disorder | – | – | – | 2 |
| Kharshu, *Quercus semecarpifolia* Smith | Seed | Scabies | – | – | – | 3 |
| Pangar, *Aesculus indica* (Colebr. ex Camb.) Hk. | Root, bark | Rheumatic pain | – | – | – | 6 |
| Kingod, *Berberis asiatica* Roxb. ex DC. | Root | Eye diseases | – | 67 | – | – |
| Karonda, *Carissa opeca* Stapf. | Leaf, root | Fever | – | 67 | – | – |
| Brahmi, *Centella asiatica* (L.) Urban | Leaf | Blood purifier, liver complaints | – | 25 | – | – |

*Contd...*

**Table 4.2–Contd...**

| *Local, Latin Name of Medicinal Plant Species* | *Part Used* | *Major Indigenous Uses* | **Rarity Status in Uttarakhand* | *Preferences of Local People (in per cent)* | | |
|---|---|---|---|---|---|---|
| | | | | *Pauri* | *Chamoli* | *Pithoragarh* |
| Neem, *Azadirachta indica* A.H.L. Juss. | Leaf, bark toothache | Diarrhoea, antibiotic, | – | 25 | – | – |
| Akhrot, *Juglans regia* L. | Bark | Toothache | – | 16 | – | – |
| Daikan, *Melia azedarach* L. | Fruit, leaf | Antiseptic | – | 8 | – | – |
| Hardi, *Terminalia chebula* Retz. | Fruit, seed | Cough, gastritis | – | 8 | – | – |
| Ganna, *Sacharum officinarum* L. | Stem juice | Constipation. | – | 8 | – | – |

*: Abbreviations: CR EN: Critically Endangered; EN: Endangered; VU: Vulnerable; NT: near threatened.

The findings of this study explicitly indicate that the local people of Uttarakhand had number of choices in case of medicinal plant species whereas in other groups of ethnobotanical species they had relatively less number of choices. Except the responses on medicinal plants by the local people of Chamoli district, the first species in each ethnobotanical group was preferred by >90 per cent of the respondents. The homogenous responses of the local people of Chamoli district about the importance of medicinal plants indicate that the knowledge on medicinal plants is more or less uniformly distributed among the local people and it is a common knowledge. The survey regarding preferences on medicinal plants by the inhabitants of Chamoli may therefore need few informants to generate reliable results. Similar observations have been made on the edible plant species used by the villagers of Gourounsi in Burkina Faso (Kristensen and Lykke, 2003). Three endangered species such as *Swertia chiraiyta, Picrorhiza kurrooa* and *Aconitum heterophyllum* were also considered the important medicinal plant species due to their reliable therapeutic efficacy by the local people of Uttarakhand.

Of the total medicinal plant species preferred by the local people of Uttarakhand, 12 species were threatened and one species was near threatened. The pressure on the survival of these threatened species has increased many folds due to their low population size, over collection from the wild (Kala, 2005b) and high preferences of the local people. The pressure has increased on such threatened species with the increase of number of preferences for various ethnobotanical uses. For example, *Taxus baccata* and *Cedrus deodara* were preferred for medicinal as well as for timber. The bark of *Taxus baccata* was also used in local tea by the Bhotiya tribal community of Chamoli and Pithoragarh. *Saussurea obvallata* was one of the preferred medicinal plant species, which was highly exploited from the wild as the offerings to the local deity by the local people of Chamoli and Pithoragarh. Although, there are provisions to check the illicit collection of rare and endangered plant species from the wild, this does not stop the continued illicit harvest of many high value plant species (Kala, 2005b). There are sufficient arguments on the importance of rare and less common species for the proper functioning of any terrestrial ecosystem (Lyons *et al.*, 2005); therefore planting of these threatened and most preferred species of local people is an important task for maintaining the ecosystem and environmental conservation.

## Implications for Conservation

The species selected by local people of Uttarakhand were native to their surrounding village areas. Studies conducted elsewhere have also indicated that in majority of cases the local people prefer the native plant species for growing in the surroundings of their residential areas (Peterson and Martin, 2000). The variations in the preferences of various ethnobotanical species by the local people of different districts of Uttarakhand support the global views that public opinions remain sharply divided on the natural resource utilization patterns and prospects for sustaining the environmental basis of human well-beings (Holl *et al* , 1999). It is argued that the preferences of species may be varied on the basis of respondent's awareness on the indigenous uses of the species and his/her level of knowledge. Such heterogeneity in indigenous knowledge systems within a given area is important for designing localized sustainable management practices (Ghimire *et al.,* 2005).

The dilemma of species selection for cultivation and large scale plantation may be mitigated by involving the local people in the planning process of plantation and designing schemes for conservation. It has been reported that instead of co-operating the plantation projects, the local people deliberately damage the plantations for several reasons, which include (*i*) restrictions on economic benefits from timber to the local people, (*ii*) complete ban on collection of many valuable medicinal plant species, and (*iii*) fear of notification of community land into government forest land (Maikhuri *et al.,* 1997; Rao *et al.,* 2002).

In developing countries, the localized community-based conservation has been projected as the most practical approach for biodiversity conservation (Rai *et al.,* 1994). Since developing countries have low technical and financial resources for relying exclusively on a model of centralized-regulatory control to protect biodiversity from increasing human populations, the community-based conservation scheme that emphasizes the management of biodiversity by, for and with local communities will succeed only if local communities receive sufficient benefits and participation in management (Meffe and Carroll, 1994; Mehta and Kellert, 1998). It has been established that in some cases, local incentives may be more effective than national policy in sustaining the conservation policies and halting over-use of natural resources (Lacuna-Richman, 2002).

Uttarakhand is well-known for its religious sanctity, and local people worship a number of plant species as a symbol of various gods and goddesses. If such religious plant species are also included in the plantations with other preferred species it will help in mitigating the conflicts as the local people are emotionally attached with these species and rarely harm them. Decreasing forest cover and increasing fallow land are the matters of great concern to the state. On the basis of local people's preferences, the restoration programs of medicinal plants can be standardized at village, regional and national levels. It is believed that a clear understanding of most important medicinal plant species is essential for proper allocation of conservation efforts.

There are many reasons of failures of afforestation and cultivation schemes of medicinal plant species such as lack of proper care taking of plantation areas, frequent forest fire, livestock grazing, improper land selection and ignorance of indigenous knowledge systems. The local people preferences should be added in the beginning of such programs for making the successful stories in holistic environmental conservation. If they are averse of any such planting material to grow in their surroundings, attempts should be made to find out its causes. Setting some successful stories may make them aware on the wider implications of such programs. Incorporating indigenous knowledge and practices in the scientific research may open the new avenues and hypothesis for designing research experiment relevant to their management. Moreover, in democratic societies such as India, understanding public concerns on issues of health and livelihood are essential, because public preferences may play a major role in designing and implementing the policy in the context of environmental conservation. This study is a step ahead for resuming the holistic environment around the human settlements and re-vegetation of degraded lands through community involvement in selection of key species and their conservation.

## References

Anonymous (1996). Indian Agricultural Statistics. New Delhi, India: Directorate of Economics and Statistics, Ministry of Agriculture, Government of India.

Berkes, F., Colding, J. and Folke, C. (2000). Rediscovery of traditional ecological knowledge as adaptive management. *Ecological Applications* 10: 1251-1262.

Census of India (2001). Provisional Populations Totals: Uttarakhand. Office of the Registrar General, New Delhi, India.

[Online] URL: http://www.censusindia.net/profiles/utc.html

Ghimire, S.K., McKey, D. and Aumeeruddy-Thomas, Y. (2005). Heterogeneity in ethnoecological knowledge and management of medicinal plants in the Himalayas of Nepal: Implication for conservation. *Ecology and Society* 9 (3): 6. [Online] URL: http://www.ecologyandsociety.org/vol9/iss3/art6/

Holl, K.D., Daily, G.C., Daily, S.C., Ehrlich, P.R. and Bassin, S. (1999). Knowledge of and attitudes toward population growth and the environment: university students in Costa Rica and the United States. *Environmental Conservation* 26 (1): 66-74.

Kala, C.P. (2005a). Ethnomedicinal botany of the Apatani in the Eastern Himalayan region of India. *Journal of Ethnobiology and Ethnomedicine* 1 (11): 1-8. [Online] URL: http://www.ethnobiomed.com/content/pdf/1746-4269-1-11.pdf

Kala, C.P. (2005b). Indigenous uses, population density and conservation of threatened medicinal plants in protected areas of the Indian Himalayas. *Conservation Biology* 19: 368-378.

Kala, C.P., Farooquee, N.A. and Dhar, U. (2004). Prioritization of medicinal plants on the basis of available knowledge, existing practices and use value status in Uttarakhand, India. *Biodiversity and Conservation* 13 (2): 453-469.

Lacuna-Richman, C. (2002). The socioeconomic significance of subsistence non-wood forest products in Leyte, Philippines. *Environmental Conservation* 29 (2): 253-262.

Lyons, K.G., Brigham, C.A., Traut, B.H. and Schwartz, M.W. (2005). Rare species and ecosystem functioning. *Conservation Biology* 19 (4): 1019-1024.

Maikhuri, R.K., Semwal, R.L., Rao, K.S. and Saxena, K.G. (1997). Rehabilitation of degraded community lands for sustainable development in Himalaya: a case study in Garhwal Himalaya, India. *International Journal of Sustainable Development and World Ecology* 4: 192-203.

Meffe, G.K. and Carroll, C.R. (1994). *Principles of Conservation Biology*. Sinauer Associates, Sunderland, MA.

Mehta, J.N. and Kellert, S.R. (1998). Local attitudes toward community-based conservation policy and programmes in Nepal: a case study in the Makalu-Barun conservation area. *Environmental Conservation* 25 (4): 320-333.

Peterson, K.A. and Martin, C.A. (2000). Effects of planned residential community covenant, codes and restrictions on urban plant community structure. *Ecological Society of America* 85: 392.

Rai, S.C., Sharma, E. and Sundriyal, R.C. (1994). Conservation in the Sikkim Himalaya: Traditional knowledge and land-use of the Mamley watershed. *Environmental Conservation* 21 (1): 30-34.

Rao, K.S., Semwal, R.L., Maikhuri, R.K., Nautiyal, S., Sen, K.K. and Saxena, K.G. (2002). Traditional natural resource management in Central Himalaya and its relevance to biosphere management. In: *Traditional Ecological Knowledge for Managing Biosphere Reserves in South and Central Asia*, eds. P.S. Ramakrishnan, R.K. Rai, R.P.S. Katwal and S. Mehndiratta, pp. 71-96. New Delhi, India: Oxford and IBH Publishing Co. Pvt. Ltd.

## Chapter 5

# 'Yarsha Gumba'

There is a living creature flourishing in the high altitudes of the Uttarakhand Himalaya, which is just like a worm but the scientists have placed it with the plant family because its aboveground part is a fungus and belowground organ is a worm. This creature is called as caterpillar fungus (*Cordyceps sinensis*) or winter worm-summer herb. In the Munsyari and Dharchula regions of Pithoragarh district of Uttarakhand this interesting creature is known as kira jadi or yarshagumba: yarsha means summer herb and gumba means winter worm. Few people call this creature as yachara gombu. This mysterious medicinal source is fetching tremendous money in the region for its use as a substitute to Viagra. In the rainy season, after the caterpillars died, a large number of people roam in the high altitudes of the Kumaon hills for gathering yarshagumba as it occurs above 3,500 m in the alpine meadows, and also there is no clue how to domesticate and commercially reproduce this fungus.

There was lot of confusion regarding the characteristics of this creature. After years of study, D.N. Pegler and few other mycologists found that yarshagumba is a fruiting body produced by a fungus (*Cordyceps sinensis*) on dead caterpillars of the moth *Hepialus* spp (*e.g. H. humuli, H. lupulinus* and *H. fabricius*). The fungus produces a stalked fruiting body, which produces spores once the caterpillar dies. The spores grow inside the caterpillar filling the caterpillar with hyphae and are responsible for the next generation of the caterpillar. There are few other varieties of genus *Cordyceps* found in the different parts of the world those are used as a substitute of yarshagumba. Notably of them are *C. gracilis, C. glaziowii* and C *subsessilis*. Researchers classified the compounds found in *Cordyceps* as HDP *"Host Defense Potentiators"*. These compounds include: hemicellulose, polysaccharides, polysaccharide-peptides, and few other complex starches. Combinations of these compounds are now believed to target the human immune system as well as hormonal balance. Besides, scientists have got encouraging results in taming and regenerating the mycelium of yarshagumba on malt yeast extract agar.

It is believed that yarshagumba was first discovered by shepherds in the high altitude pastures of Himalayan Mountains of Tibet about 1500 years ago. The shepherds noticed that after nibbling and chewing a small mushroom-like grass, the cattle and sheep became very strong, even old yaks show signs of being younger, and had increased natural vigor. Later on, knowing this fact an amchi (traditional healer) used yarshagumba as medicament to their patients. To his surprise he got encouraging results in curing respiratory and reproductive disorders. The travelogue of M.M. Gabriyal reports that in Pithoragarh, the borderline district of India, yarshagumba was probably first discovered in 1992, when the trade was reopened and local people came in contact with the Tibetans and Nepalese.

According to the reports of D.C. Steinkraus and J.B. Whitfield, the use of yarshagumba was relatively unknown even in China until it was credited for the success of Chinese women athletes at the National Games in Beijing, in 1993. Three Chinese track runners set new world records during the Games at three different distances and their coach, Ma Zunren, attributed the runner's success to intensive training as well as a stress-relieving tonic prepared from the yarshagumba.

Today, yarshagumba is a top quality nutraceutical product for people health and many pharmaceutical companies are making drugs out of it. In United Kingdom, KALA Health Inc. is making capsules, which are considered safe even with very high dosages. In Chinese and Tibetan Medical System yarshagumba has multiple uses. Besides a good energy tonic, it increases endurance and prevents allergies, depression, and colds and flu by enhancing adrenal and lung energy. It is also recommended for people who feel short of breath, achy, or depressed from overwork, pollution, and bad dietary habits. It is believed to cure circulatory disorders, respiratory disorders, sexual dysfunction and other health hazards. Its major use as a general health tonic is mainly due to its capability to improve energy, stamina, appetite and endurance. A study of Georges Halpern demonstrates that yarshagumba helps in lowering the bad cholesterol concentrations and its dietary supplements do not cause any significant side effects.

In animals, yarshagumba shows bronchodilatory, sedative and hypnotic actions as mentioned in the CHINESE MATERIA MEDICA. Zhang investigated that the sedative action of yarshagumba is due to the amino acids, tyrosine and L-tryptophan. Further scientists have discovered that yarshagumba acts as an antiasthmatic and anticancer agent, which causes smooth muscle relaxation and can potentiate the effects of epinephrine. A study reveals, that rodents and logomorph of high altitude areas feed yarshagumba, which make them to survive in severe cold climatic conditions and extreme low oxygen environment. The diverse uses of yarshagumba mentioned here have been compiled from numerous studies, research papers, journals and web sites. I must suggest that readers should not use the information contained here for diagnosing or treating a health problem or disease, or prescribing any medication without consulting the medical practitioners.

Few medicinal dishes are also made up of yarshagumba in China such as roasted duck with yarshagumba and chicken soup with yarshagumba. Inspite of the several uses of yarshagumba, except few veteran Bhotiya shepherds, the local people of Pithoragarh district rarely know the medicinal properties of yarshagumba and they collect it only for the purpose of sale. Few veteran Bhotiya people admit that in past they used to feed the yarshagumba to their cattle and especially to the yaks while going for long trek and trade to Tibet.

China has the largest market for yarshagumba and major part of yarshagumba collected from Pithoragarh is traded to China. The cost of yarshagumba at Munsyari is about US$ 1000 per kg. At Dharchula, the cost of yarshagumba enhances from US$ 1300 to 1700 per kg. This sudden increase in the cost of yarshagumba at Dharchula is due to its location at borderline. Yarshagumba now has also been traded to Delhi and the cost at Delhi is about US$ 3000 per kg. The natural population of yarshagumba is restricted to limited places and within China it is mostly restricted to the southwestern part. The small population size, narrow range of distribution, low production amount, high demand in markets and availability in tough geographical terrain with harsh environmental conditions are the few causes for expensive rates of wild yarshagumba that goes upto US$ 1000 for 100 gm in China. Yarshagumba is also used as a gift, and a gift box costs about US$ 400. The contractors from Pithoragarh involved in the illegal trade are minting money by selling it at Talakot, in Tibet, the biggest international market of medicinal herbs, mentioned Deep Joshi. In 2001, yarshagumba of worth Rs 1 crore was extracted from the Sobla area of Pithoragarh district alone, a report said. Thus, yarshagumba could be the next ginseng due to its reported effects on increasing energy levels, sex drive and income generation. Nonetheless, the Food and Drug Administration have not evaluated the dietary supplements of yarshagumba provided by various sources.

Since there are some regulations on the collection of yarshagumba in Nepal and it is free for all in Munsyari region, the people from Nepal are also coming to Munsiyari for the collection of yarshagumba. Therefore, conservationists feel that the population of yarshagumba is declining rapidly due to over collection in the limited areas. Jawahar Singh Nabiyal, ex-town area chairman of Dharchula, reiterates that collection does not impose any threat to yarshagumba, as it is a fungus and will be wasted if not used. However, there is a need to regulate the trade in yarshagumba as a large number of outsiders are tricking in the high altitude areas for gathering it at a large-scale. The Forest Department should develop a mechanism to regulate the trade and take the entry fee from the person going for its collection. The local village communities are seriously thinking to interfere if outsiders are making the collection from their panchayat area. One of the remote villages in Munsyari named Ralam has started taking royalty from the outside collectors.

Besides hundreds of local people, a large number of Nepali labors are busy in its collection those have been hired by local contractors to collect it. The collected material is being sold at spot as contractors also reach at the places yarshagumba occurs. In few remote villages, where to obtain ration (rice, wheat and pulses) is very hard, the contractors are providing ration on behalf of yarshagumba. The business is flourishing such an extent that in 2002, a few trained people came from Nepal to train the local people how to identify, explore, collect and preserve this precious medicinal resource.

The valid scientific information and true family history of yarshagumba will help target the search for other nature-based pharmaceuticals and for potentially useful compounds. Thomas Eisner, a biologist at Cornell University mentioned that an estimated 90 per cent or more of the world's fungi have yet to be identified, scientifically cataloged and examined. The discovery of yarshagumba has given an ample opportunity to prepare the medicine for drastic diseases. Therefore, scientists should continue to visit and survey the potential areas in the Himalaya for invention of new drug sources.

# Bibliography


Aggarwal, D. and K.S. Barna (2004). Tissue culture propagation of elite plant of *Aloe vera* Linn. *Journal of Plant Biochemistry and Biotechnology*, 13 (1): 77-79.

Ahluwalia, K.S. (1965). Medicinal plants of Har-Ki-Dun, Tons division, Uttar Pradesh. *Nagarjun*, 8: 135-139.

Airi, S.K., A. Tiwari, P.P. Dhyani and U. Dhar (1993). Diploknema butyracea H.J. Lam (Chiura): potential priorities and application. *Hima Paryavaran*, 5 (2):10-11.

Airi, S.K., R.S. Rawal, U. Dhar and A.N. Purohit (1997). *Podophyllum hexandrum* Royle–A dwindling valuable plant resource of the Himalaya. *Plant Genetic Resource Newsletter*, 110: 29-34.

Airi, S., R.S. Rawal, U. Dhar and A.N. Purohit (2000). Assessment of availability and habitat preference of Jatamansi–a critically endangered medicinal plant of west Himalaya. *Current Science*, 79 (10): 1467-1471.

Alam, G. and J. Belt (2004). Medicinal plants sector in Uttaranchal: finding of a recent study. In: *Searching Synergy*. Bulletin 359, Royal Tropical Institute, Amsterdam, The Netherlands. pp. 13-20.

Anonymous (1970-1988). *The Wealth of India: Raw Materials*. Council of Scientific and Industrial Research, New Delhi, India (Reprinted). Vol-1-6.

Anonymous (2003). *Conservation Assessment and Management Prioritization for the Medicinal Plants of Jammu-Kashmir, Himachal Pradesh and Uttaranchal*. Foundation for Revitalization of Local Health Traditions, Bangalore, India.

Arya, K.R., P.C. Pande and V.P. Tiwari (1999). Ethnobotanical study on tribal areas of Almora district. *Ethnobotany*, 11:100-104.

Aswal, B.S. (1992). Less known medicinal uses of three plants from Kumaun Himalaya, India. *Indian Journal of Forestry*, 15(1): 76-77.

Aswal, B.S. (1996). Conservation of ethnomedicinal plants diversity of Garhwal Himalaya in India. In: *Ethnobiology of Human Welfare* (Ed. S.K. Jain). Deep Publications, New Delhi. pp: 133-135.

Atkinson, E.T. (1882). *The Himalayan Gazetteer*. Reprinted by Cosmo Publications, India (1973), Vol-I, Part-II.

Awasthi A. and S.K. Uniyal (2003). Meadow to market. *Sanctuary Asia*, XXIII: 28-31.

Badoni, A.K. (1986). Some aspects of the ethnobotany of the hill tribes of Uttarkashi district. *Proceedings of Indian Botanical Conference*, 65: 57-58.

Badoni, A.K. (1987-1988). Ethnobotany of hill tribes of Uttarkashi, plants used in rituals and psychomedicinal practices. *Journal of Himalayan Studies and regional Development*, 11&12: 103-115.

Badoni, A.K. (1995). *Garhwal Himalaya Mein Jaivik Vividhata Avam Satat Vikas Hetu Jari Booti Udhyog*. Society of Himalayan Environmental and Development, Vikasnagar, Dehradun.

Badoni, A.K. (1989-1990). Remark on the high altitudinal medicinal plants of Garhwal Himalaya. *Journal of Himalayan Studies and regional Development*, 13&14: 37-45.

Badoni, A.K. (1990). An ethnobotanical study of Pinswari community: A preliminary survey. *Bulletin of Botanical Survey of India*, 32: 103-115.

Badoni, A. and K. Badoni (2001). Ethnobotanical heritage. In: *Garhwal Himalaya: Nature, Culture and Society* (Eds. O.P. Kandari and O.P. Gusain.). Transmedia, Media House, Srinagar, Garhwal. pp: 127-147.

Bhadula, S.K., A. Singh, H. Lata, C.P. Kuniyal and A.N. Purohit (1996). Genetic resources of *Podophyllum hexandrum* Royle, an endangered medicinal species from Garhwal Himalaya, India. *Plant Genetic Resource Newsletter*, 108: 26-29.

Bhadula, S.K., A. Singh, H. Lata, C.P. Kuniyal and A.N. Purohit (2000). Distribution pattern, population diversity and propagation of some high altitude medicinal herbs from Garhwal Himalaya: problems and prospects for conservation. In: *High Altitude of the Himalaya-II (Biodiversity, Ecology and Environment)* (Ed. Y.P.S. Pangtey), Gyanodaya Prakasan, Nainital, 2: 389-413.

Bhargava, K.S. (1959). Unusual and supplementary food plants of Kumaun. *Journal of Bombay Natural History Society*, 56: 26-31.

Bhatt, A., C.M. Sharma and V.P. Khanduri (2002). Growing stock variations in different *Cedrus deodara* forests of Garhwal Himalaya. *The Indian Forester*, 218 (8): 903-916.

Bhatt, A., R. Rawal, and U. Dhar (2006). Ecological features of a critically rare medicinal plant, *Swertia chirayita*, in Himalaya. *Plant Species Biology*, 21 (1): 49-52.

Bhatt, B.P., M. Kumar and N.P. Todaria (1997). Studies on the allelopathic effects of *Terminalia* species of Garhwal Himalaya. *Journal of Sustainable Agriculture*, 11 (1): 71-84.

Bhatt, I.D. and U. Dhar (2000). Micropropagation of Indian wild strawberry (*Fragaria indica* Andr.). *Plant Cell Tissue and Organ Culture*, 60: 83-88.

Bhatt, I.D. and U. Dhar (2000). Combined effect of cytokinins on multiple shoot production from cotyledonary node explants of *Bauhinia vahlii*. *Plant Cell Tissue and Organ Culture*, 62: 79-83.

Bhatt, I.D. and U. Dhar (2004). Factors controlling micropropagation of *Myrica esculenta* Buch.-Ham. ex D. Don: a high value wild edible of Kumaon Himalaya. *African Journal of Biotechnology*, 3 (10): 534-540.

Bhatt, I.D., R.S. Rawal and U. Dhar (2000). Improvement in seed germination of *Myrica esculenta* Buch.-Ham. ex D. Don–a high value tree species of Kumaun Himalaya, India. *Seed Science and Technology*, 28: 597-605.

Bhatt, I.D., R.S. Rawal and U. Dhar (2000). The availability, fruit yield and harvest of *Myrica esculenta* Buch.-Ham ex D. Don in Kumaun (West Himalaya), India. *Mountain Research and Development*, 20: 146-153.

Bhatt, K.C. and R.D. Gaur (1992). A contribution to ethnobotany of Rajis in Pithoragarh district. *Acta Botanica Indica*, 20: 76-83.

Bhatt, K.C., M.K. Bist and R.D. Gaur (1987-89). Folk-medicines of Byans valley in Pithoragarh. *JOHSARD*, 11 (12): 117-123.

Bhatt, V.P. (1999). Ethnobiology of high altitude Himalayan communities in district Chamoli: A conservation perspective. *Zoos Print*, 24 (11): 137-146.

Bisht, A.K., S. Manjkhola and M. Joshi (2003). Comparative account of two high value species of Himalaya: *Angelica glauca* and *Angelica archangelica*. *The Indian Forester*, 129: 1241-1248.

Bisht, C. and A. Badoni (2009). Medicinal strength of some alpine and sub-alpine zones of western Himalaya, India. *New York Science Journal*, 2 (5): 41-46.

Bist, M.K. and A.K. Badoni (1990). Araceae in the folk life of tribal populace in Garhwal Himalaya. *J. Eco. Bot. Phytochem.*, 1: 21-24.

Bist, M.K., K.C. Bhatt and R.D. Gaur (1988). Folk medicine of Arakot valley in district Uttarkashi: An ethnobotanical study. In: *Indigenous Medicinal Plants* (Ed. P. Kaushik). Today and Tomorrow Printers and Publishers, New Delhi. pp: 157-166.

Biswas, S. (1988). Rare and threatened taxa in the forest flora of Tehri Garhwal Himalaya and the strategy for their conservation. *Indian Journal of Forestry*, 11: 233-237.

Chandola, S. (2004). MAP sector in Uttaranchal and role of the forest department. *Financing Agriculture*, 36 (3): 27-32.

Chandra, B., L.M.S. Palni and S.K. Nandi (2003). Foliar application of inhibitors of GA biosynthesis improves tuber size and biomass in seedlings of *Aconitum violaceum* Jacq. ex Stapf.: a critically rare medicinal herb of Himalayan alpines. *Science Letters*, 26: 203-207.

Chandra, K and H.C. Pande (1983). Collection of plants around Agora-Dodital in Uttar Kashi district of Uttar Pradesh, with medicinal values and folklore. *International Journal of Crude Drugs Research,* 21: 21-28.

Chauhan, R.S. and M.C. Nautiyal (2005). Commercial viability of cultivation of an endangered medicinal herb Nardostachys jatamansi at three different agroclimatic zones. *Current Science,* 89 (9): 1481-1488.

Datt, B and B. Lal (1993). Less known medicinal uses of some plants from Pithoragarh district of Kumaun Himalaya, U.P. *Aryavaidyan,* 6: 242-246.

Dhar, U., J. Upreti and I.D. Bhatt (2000). Micropropagation of *Pittosporum nepaulensis* (DC.) Rehder and Wilson–a rare and endemic Himalayan medicinal tree. *Plant Cell Tissue and Organ Culture,* 63: 231-235.

Dhar, U., S. Manjkhola, M. Joshi, A. Bhatt, A.K. Bisht and M. Joshi (2002). Current status and future strategy for development of medicinal plants sector in Uttaranchal, India. *Current Science,* 83 (8): 956-964.

Dhobal, P., S. Sawan and N. Sharma (2007). Studies of medicinal plants of two villages of Chakrata forest division (Uttarakhand). *Annals of Forestry,* 15 (2): 351-357.

Dhyani P.P. (2000). Common plant species have potential for economic upliftment of rural populace–Bantulsi a case in point. *Hima-Paryavaran,* 12: 11-13.

Dhyani, P.P. and C.P. Kala (2005). Current research on medicinal plants: Five lesser known but valuable aspects. *Current Science,* 88 (3): 335.

Dhyani, P.P. and M.P. Khali (1993). Fruit yield and economics of jelly and jam production from fruits of some promising *Ficus* fig tree crops. *Ecology of Food and Nutrition,* 30: 169-178.

Dhyani P.P. and U. Dhar (1994). Myrica esculenta *Box myrtle Kaphal: A promising underexploited tree crop of the Himalaya.* G.B. Pant Institute of Himalayan Environment and Development, Almora, India.

Farooquee, N.A. and K.G. Saxena (1996). Conservation and utilisation of medicinal plants in high hills of the central Himalayas. *Environmental conservation,* 23 (1): 75-80.

Garbyal, S.S., K.K. Aggarwal and C.R. Babu (2004). Impact of *Cordyceps sinensis* in the rural economy of interior villages of Dharchula sub-division of Kumaun Himalaya and its implications in the society. *Indian Journal of Traditional Knowledge,* 3 (2): 182-186.

Gaur, R.D. 1999. *Flora of the district Garhwal northwest Himalaya (with ethnobotanical notes).* TransMedia, Srinagar Garhwal, India.

Gaur, R.D. and J.K. Semwal (1983). Some little known wild edible of Garhwal Himalaya. *Man and Environment,* 7: 161-165.

Gaur, R.D. and J.K. Tiwari (1987). Some little known medicinal plants of Garhwal Himalaya: An ethnobotanical study. In: *Medicinal and Poisonous Plants of the Tropics* (Ed. Leewenberg). Netherlands. pp: 139-192.

Gaur, R.D. (1987). A contribution to the flora of Srinagar Garhwal. *Journal of Economic and Taxonomic Botany,* 9 (31): 63.

Gaur, R.D., J.K. Semwal and J.K. Tiwari (1984). A survey of high altitude medicinal plants of Garhwal Himalaya. *Bull. Med. Ethnobot. Res.,* 4 (3-4): 102-116.

Gaur, R.D., J.K. Semwal and M.P. Sharma (1980). Ethnotoxic plants of Garhwal hills. *The Eastern Anthropologist,* 33: 159-163.

Gaur, R.D., K.C. Bhatt and J.K. Tiwari (1992). An ethnobotanical study of Uttar Pradesh Himalaya in relation to veterinary medicines. *J. Indian Bot. Soc.,* 72: 139-144.

Gaur, R.D., M.K. Bisht and K.C. Bhatt (1988). A note on medicinal and other uses of some animal in Garhwal Himalaya: An ethnozoological perspective. *Man in India,* 68 (2&3): 292-297.

Gaur, R.D., V.P. Purohit and R.A. Silas (1986). *Eunymus tingens* Wall. (Celastraceae) –A tree of multieconomic folk utility in Raath region (Garhwal Himalaya). *Bulletin of Botanical Survey of India,* 28: 146-148.

Gupta, B.L. (1928). *Forest Flora of Chakrata Dehradun and Saharanpur Forest Division.* United Provinces, Calcutta.

Gupta, R.K. (1960). Some useful and medicinal plants of Garhwal Himalaya: An ethnobotanical study. In: *Medicinal and Poisonous Plants of the Tropics* (Ed. Leewenberg). Netherlands. pp: 139-142.

Gupta, R.K. (1960). Some useful and medicinal plants of Nainital district in the Kumaun Himalaya. *The Indian Forester,* 57: 309-324.

Gupta, R.K. (1960). Some useful and medicinal plants of Nainital in Kumaun Himalaya. *Journal of Bombay Natural History Society,* 68 (3): 791-803.

Indrayan, A.K., S. Sharma, D. Durgapal, N. Kumar and M. Kumar (2005). Determination of nutritive value and analysis of mineral elements for some medicinally valued plants from Uttaranchal. *Current Science,* 89 (7): 1252-1255.

Jain, S.K. and A.R.K. Sastry (1980). Plant resources in the Himalayas. In: Proc. National Seminar on *Resources, Development and Environment in The Himalaya Region.* Department of Science and Technology, Government of India, New Delhi. pp: 98-107.

Jain, S.K. (1991). *Dictionary of Indian Folk Medicine and Ethnobotany.* Deep Publications, New Delhi.

Jalal, J.S and G.S. Rawat (2009). Habitat studies for conservation of medicinal orchids of Uttrakhand, Western Himalaya. *African J. of Plant Sciences,* 3 (9): 200-204.

Joshi, P. and P.C. Pande (1997). Ethnobotany of Bhotia tribe of Kumaun Himalaya. In: *Studies on Kumaun Himalaya* (Eds. S.K. Sharma and N.C. Dhauondiyal). Indus Publishing Co., New Delhi. pp: 63-89.

Joshi, D.N., B.C.L. Shah and R.K. Suri (1982). Some medicinal plants of Rudranath Bugyal (Dist. Chamoli), U.P. *Bull. Med. Ethnobot. Res.,* 3: 27-42.

Joshi, H.C., S.C. Arya and S.S. Samant (1999). Diversity, distribution and indigenous uses of medicinal and edible plants in a part of Nanda Devi Biosphere Reserve. *Himalayan Biosphere Reserve,* 1: 49-65.

Joshi, H.C., S.C. Arya and S.S. Samant (2001). Diversity, distribution and indigenous uses of plant species in Pindari area of Nanda Devi Biosphere Reserve. *Indian Journal of Forestry,* 24 (4): 514-536.

Joshi, G.C. (1989). New or little known plants from Kumoun Himalaya. *Journal of Economic and Taxonomic Botany,* 13 (2): 347-348.

Joshi, G.C. (1993). Notes on the vegetation types of inner Himalayan ranges of Kumaun Himalaya with special reference to herbal resources. *Journal of Economic and Taxonomic Botany*, 17 (2): 367-371.

Joshi, G.C. and K.C. Tewari. (1985). Suggestion for medicinal plants cultivation. *Himalayan Research and Development*, 4 (2): 43-46.

Joshi, G.C., K.C. Tewari, R.N. and M.R. Uniyal (1991). Conservation and large-scale cultivation strategy of Indian ginseng – *Panax pseudoginseng* Wall. *The Indian Forester*, 117 (2): 131-134.

Joshi, G.C., K.C. Tewari, R.N. Tewari, N.K. Pandey and G. Pandey (1993). Resource survey of the pharmaceutically important plants of U.P. Himalaya. In: *Himalayan Biodiversity Conservation Strategies* (Ed. U. Dhar.). Gyanodya Prakashan, Nainital. pp: 279-291.

Joshi, G.C., N.K. Pandey and M.R. Uniyal (1993). Inventory of disappearing angiosperms of Kumaun and Garhwal Himalaya: causes and suggestions. *Journal of Economic and Taxonomic Botany*, 17 (2): 421-432.

Joshi, G.C., N.K. Tewari and D.N. Tewari (1987). Depleting plant resources – a case study from Kumaun Himalaya. *Journal of Economic and Taxonomic Botany*, 1 (2): 13-16.

Joshi, M. and U. Dhar (2002). Effect of various presowing treatment on seed germination of *Heracleum candicans* Wall. ex DC: a high value medicinal plant. *Seed Science and Technology*, 31 (3): 737-743.

Joshi, M. and U. Dhar (2003). In-vitro propagation of *Saussurea obvallata* (DC.) Edgew. – An endangered ethnoreligious medicinal herb of Himalaya. *Plant Cell Report*, 21: 933-939.

Juyal, S.P. and M.R. Uniyal (1960). Medicinal plants of commercial and traditional importance in Bhillangana valley of Tehri Garhwal. *Nagarjun*, 10: 26-36.

Kala, C.P. (1998). A palm herbal medicine: *Dactylorhiza hatagirea*. *Amruth*, 2 (6): 8-9.

Kala, C.P. (1998). *Ethnobotanical survey and propagation of rare medicinal herbs in the buffer zone of the Valley of Flowers National Park, Garhwal Himalaya*. International Center for Integrated Mountain Development, Kathmandu, Nepal.

Kala, C.P. (2002). Indigenous knowledge of Bhotiya tribal community on wool dyeing and its present status in the Garhwal Himalaya, India. *Current Science*, 83 (7): 814-817.

Kala, C.P. (2002). *Medicinal Plants of Indian Trans-Himalaya*. Bishen Singh Mahendra Pal Singh, Dehradun, India.

Kala, C.P. (2003). Indigenous uses of plants as health tonic in Uttaranchal Himalaya, India. *Annals of Forestry*, 11 (2): 249-254.

Kala, C.P. (2003). An ethnobotanical survey of the propagation of rare medicinal herbs by small farmers in the buffer zone of the Valley of Flowers National Park, Garhwal Himalaya, India. In: *Applied Ethnobotany: Case Studies from the Himalayan Region*. (Eds. Y. Aumeeruddy-Thomas and P. Shengji) People and Plants Working Paper 12. WWF, Godalming, UK. pp 29-31.

Kala, C.P. (2003). Commercial exploitation and conservation status of high value medicinal plants across the borderline of India and Nepal in Pithoragarh. *The Indian Forester*, 129 (1): 80-84.

Kala, C.P. (2004). Revitalizing traditional herbal therapy by exploring medicinal plants: A case study of Uttaranchal State in India. In: *Indigenous Knowledges: Transforming the Academy*. (Eds. B.L. Farmer, A. Maretzki, and L. Semali), Pennsylvania State University, Pennsylvania, USA. pp 15-21.

Kala, C.P. (2004). *The Valley of Flowers: Myth and Reality*. International Book Distributors, Dehradun, India.

Kala, C.P. (2004). Indigenous uses and structure of chir pine forest in Uttaranchal Himalaya, India. *International Journal of Sustainable Development and World Ecology*, 11 (2): 205-210.

Kala, C.P. (2004). Assessment of species rarity. *Current Science*, 86 (8): 1058-1059.

Kala, C.P. (2004). Pithoragarh kee kira jari–Yarsha Gumba. *Yugwani*, 9: p 39.

Kala, C.P. (2004). Jadi-bootiyon ke gyan aewam sanrakchhan me paramparagat vaidyon kee bhoomika. *ENVIS Bulletin: Himalayan Ecology and Development*, 11 (2): 92-93.

Kala, C.P. (2004). Aconites in danger in paradise. *ENVIS Newsletter on Himalayan Ecology*, 1: p 5.

Kala, C.P. (2004). *Studies on the Indigenous Knowledge, Practices and Traditional Uses of Forest Products by Human Societies in Uttaranchal State of India.* G.B. Pant Institute of Himalayan Environment and Development, Almora, India.

Kala, C.P. (2005). Indigenous uses, population density, and conservation of threatened medicinal plants in protected areas of the Indian Himalayas. *Conservation Biology*, 19 (2): 368-378.

Kala, C.P. (2005). Current status of medicinal plants used by traditional *Vaidyas* in Uttaranchal state of India. *Ethnobotany Research and Applications*, 3: 267-278.

Kala, C.P. (2006). Ethnobotany and ethnoconservation of *Aegle marmelos* (L.) Correa. *Indian Journal of Traditional Knowledge*, 5 (4): 537-540.

Kala, C.P. (2006). Preserving Ayurvedic herbal formulations by Vaidyas: The traditional healers of the Uttaranchal Himalaya region in India. *HerbalGram*, 70: 42-50.

Kala, C.P. (2006). Problems and prospects in the conservation and development of the Himalayan medicinal plants sector. *International Journal of Sustainable Development*, 9 (4): 370-389.

Kala, C.P. (2006). Medicinal plants: Potential for economic development in the state of Uttaranchal, India. *International Journal of Sustainable Development and World Ecology*, 13 (6): 492-498.

Kala, C.P. (2006). Medicinal plants of the high altitude cold desert in India: Diversity, distribution and traditional uses. *International Journal of Biodiversity Science and Management*, 2 (1): 43-56.

Kala, C.P. (2007). Local preferences of ethnobotanical species in the Indian Himalaya: Implications for environmental conservation. *Current Science*, 93 (12): 1828-1834.

Kala, C.P. (2009). Medicinal plants conservation and enterprise development. *Medicinal Plants*, 1 (2): 79-95.

Kala, C.P. and B.S. Sajwan (2006). Herbal Gardens in Schools. *Current Science*, 91 (11): 1442-1443.

Kala, C.P. and B.S. Sajwan (2007). Sustainable development of medicinal plant resources in India. *ENVIS Forestry Bulletin,* 7 (2): 1-14.

Kala, C.P. and B.S. Sajwan (2007). Revitalizing Indian systems of herbal medicine by the National Medicinal Plants Board through institutional networking and capacity building. *Current Science,* 93 (6): 797-806.

Kala, C.P., N.A. Farooquee and B.S. Majila (2005). Indigenous knowledge and medicinal plants used by *Vaidyas* in Uttaranchal, India. *Natural Product Radiance,* 4 (3): 195-204.

Kala, C.P., N.A. Farooquee and U. Dhar (2004). Prioritization of medicinal plants on the basis of available knowledge, existing practices and use value status in Uttaranchal, India. *Biodiversity and Conservation,* 13 (2): 453-469.

Kala, C.P., N.A. Farooquee, and U. Dhar (2005). Traditional uses and conservation of timur (*Zanthoxylum armatum* DC.) through social institutions in Uttaranchal Himalaya, India. *Conservation and Society,* 3 (1): 224-230.

Kala, C.P., P.P. Dhyani, and B.S. Sajwan (2006). Developing the medicinal plants sector in Northern India: challenges and opportunities. *Journal of Ethnobiology and Ethnomedicine,* 2: 1-15. [Online]:

http://www.ethnobiomed.com/content/pdf/1746-4269-2-32.pdf

Kala, C.P. and G.S. Rawat (1998). Conservation status and distribution of rare medicinal herbs in and around the Valley of Flowers National Park, Western Himalaya. In: *Medicinal Plants a Global Heritage.* Proceedings of the International Conference on Medicinal Plants for survival. IDRC-CRDI, New Delhi, India, pp 75-87.

Kala, C.P. and G.S. Rawat. (2001). Human use and conservation status of wild medicinal herbs in the Bhyundar Valley, Western Himalaya. In: *Plant Diversity of the Himalaya* (Eds. P.C. Pande and S.S. Samant). Gyanodaya Prakasan, Nainital. pp: 547-559.

Kala, C.P., G.S. Rawat, and S.K. Mukherjee (2001). Prospects for the *ex-situ* conservation of wild medicinal plants in and around Bhyundar Valley, Garhwal Himalaya. In: *Himalayan Medicinal Plants: Potential and Prospects* (Eds. S.S. Samant, U. Dhar and L.M.S. Palni), Gyanodaya Prakashan Nainital, India, pp 271-284.

Kalakoti, B.S. and Y.P.S. Pangtey. (1988). Ethnomedicine of Bhotiya tribe of Kumaun Himalaya, UA. *Bull. Med. Ethnobot. Res.*, 9:11-20.

Kandari, L.S., K.S. Rao, R.K. Maikhuri and K. Chauhan (2008). Effect of pre-sowing, temperature and light on the seed germination of *Arnebia benthamii* (Wall. ex G. Don): An endangered medicinal plant of Central Himalaya, India. *African Journal of Plant Science*, 2 (1), 5-11.

Kandari OP and Gusain OP (2001). *Garhwal Himalaya: Nature, Culture and Society*. TransMedia, Srinagar Garhwal, India.

KIT 2003. *Cultivating a Healthy Enterprise*. Bulletin 350, Royal Tropical Institute, Amsterdam, The Netherlands.

KIT 2004. *Searching Synergy*. Bulletin 359, Royal Tropical Institute, Amsterdam, The Netherlands.

Khali, M.P., S.C. Joshi and P.P. Dhyani (1996). Rooting response of branch cuttings of two promising sacred *Ficus* tree species of the tropics. *Journal of Tropical Forest Science*, 9 (2): 184-188.

Khali, R.P. and A.K. Sharma (2003). Effect of phytohormones on propagation of Himalayan Yew (*Taxus baccata* L.) through stem cuttings. *The Indian Forester*, 129 (2): 289-294.

Khanuja, S.P.S. and A.K. Singh (2004). Geranium, the enabling crop for rural entrepreneurship: end-to-end mission programme of CIMAP in Uttaranchal. *Financing Agriculture*, 36 (3): 37-39.

Krishnamurthy, T., G.V. Karira, B.K. Sharma and K. Bhotia (1965). Cultivation and exploitation of *Podophyllum hexantrum* Royal (Syn. *P. emiodi* Wall. ex Hook. f. and Thoms). *The Indian Forester*, 91: 470-475.

Kirtikar, K.R. and B.D. Basu 1933. *Indian Medicinal Plants*. Vol: I-IV. Allahabad.

Kumar, A., S.K. Nandi, B. Chandra and M. Pal (2004). Conservation of some Himalayan medicinal plants using biotechnological approaches. *The Indian Forester*, 130 (2): 187-199.

Kumar, V. and G.S. Shamet (2002). Vegetative propagation of Himalayan Yew (*Taxus baccata* Linn.) through branch cuttings. *Journal of Non-Timber Forest Products*, 9 (1&2): 32-36.

Lal, B., H Dasmana and R.K. Nigam (1989). A contribution to the medicinal plants lore of Garhwal region. *Himalayan Research and Development*, 8 (182): 24-30.

Lal, B. and D.K. Upreti. (1995). Ethnobotanical notes on three Indian lichens *Lichenologist*, 27 (1): 77-79.

Maheshwari, J.K. and H. Singh (1990). Herbal remedies of Boxas of Nainital district, U.P. *Ayurvaidan*, 4: 251-259.

Maheshwari, J.K. and J.P. Singh (1984). Contribution to the ethnobotany of Bhoxa tribe of Bijnor and Pauri Garhwal district, U.P. *Journal of Economic and Taxonomic Botany*, 5 (2): 253-259.

Maikhuri, R.K., R.L. Semwal, K.S. Rao, S. Nautiyal and K.G. Saxena (2000). *Cleome viscosa*, Capparidaceae: a weed or a cash crop. *Economic Botany*, 54 (2): 150-154.

Maikhuri, R K, S. Nautiyal, K.S. Rao, and R.L. Semwal (2000). Indigenous knowledge of medicinal plants and wild edibles among three tribal sub-communities of the Central Himalayas, India. *Indigenous Knowledge and Development Monitor*, 8 (2): 7-13.

Maikhuri, R.K., S. Nautiyal, K.S. Rao, and K.G. Saxena (1998). Medicinal plants cultivation and biosphere reserve management: a case study from Nanda Devi Biosphere Reserve, Himalaya. *Current Science*, 74 (2): 157-163.

Maikhuri, R.K., S. Nauityal, K.S. Rao and K.G. Saxena. (1998). Role of medicinal plants in the traditional health care system: a case study from Nanda Devi biosphere reserve. *Current Science*, 75 (2): 152-157.

Maikhuri, R.K., S. Nautiyal and K.S. Rao (1991). *Nanda Devi Jaiv Mandal Aarkshit Chetra (Biosphere Reserve) Mai Auoshdhi Padpo kee Paramparagat Krishi Tachnik*. G.B. Pant Institute of Himalayan Environment and Development, Kosi-Katarmal, Almora.

Maikhuri, R.K., K.S. Rao, L.S. Kandari, R. Joshi and D. Dhyani (2005). Does the outreach programme make an impact? A case study of medicinal and aromatic plant cultivation in Uttaranchal. *Current science*, 88: 1480-1486.

Maikhuri R.K., K.S. Rao, K. Chauhan, L.S. Kandari, P. Prasad and Rajasekaran (2003). Development of marketing of medicinal plants and other forest products–can it be a path way for effective management and conservation ? *The Indian Forester*, 129: 169-178.

Malhotra, C.L. and B. Balodi (1984). Wild medicinal plants in the use of Johari tribals. *Journal of Economic and Taxonomic Botany*, 5 (4): 881-883.

Malhotra, C.L. and D. Bashu (1984). A preliminary survey of plants resources of medicinal and aromatic value from Almora. *Journal of Economic and Taxonomic Botany*, 5: 859-864.

Manjkhola, S. and U. Dhar (2002). Conservation and utilization of *Arnebia benthamii* (Wall. ex G. Don) Johnston–a high value Himalayan medicinal plant. *Current Science*, 83 (4): 484-488.

Mehrotra, B.N. (1979). Survey of medicinal plants around Kedarnath Shrine of Garhwal Himalaya. *The Indian Forester*, 105: 788-801.

Muddaiya, R.K., G.C. Joshi and N.K. Pandey (1995). Status of some valnerable plant species from Ranikhet (Kumoun Himalaya). *Journal of Economic and Taxonomic Botany*, 19 (3): 663-666.

Mumgain, S.K. and R.R. Rao (1990). Some medicinal plants of Pauri Garhwal. *Journal of Economic and Taxonomic Botany*, 14 (30): 633-640.

Nadeem, M., L.M.S. Palni, A.N. Purohit, H. Pandey and S.K. Nandi (2000). Propagation and conservation of *Podophyllum hexandrum* Royle: an important medicinal herb. *Biological Conservation*, 92: 121-129.

Nadeem, M., H.C. Rikhari, A. Kumar, L.M.S. Palni and S.K. Nandi (2002). Taxol content in the bark of Himalayan Yew in relation to tree age and sex. *Phytochemistry*, 60 (6): 627-631.

Nadkarni, K.M. and A.K. Nadkarni (1908). *Indian Materia Medica*. Popular Prakashan, Bombay, India. 1319 pp.

Nautiyal, A.R., M.C. Nautiyal and A.N. Purohit (1997). *Harvesting Herbs-2000, Medicinal and Aromatic Plants – An Action Plan for Uttarakhand*. Bishen Singh Mahendra Pal Singh, Dehradun.

Nautiyal, M.C. (1996). Cultivation of medicinal plants and biosphere reserve management in alpine zone. In: *Conservation and Management of Biological Resources in Himalayas*. (Eds. P.S. Ramakrishnan, A.N. Purohit, K.G. Saxena, K.S. Rao and R.K. Maikhuri). Oxford and IBH Publishing, New Delhi.

Nautiyal, M.C. and B.P. Nautiyal (2004). Collaboration between farmers, research institutions and industry: experiences of *Picrorhiza kurrooa* cultivation at Ghese village in Chamoli district, Uttaranchal. In: *Searching Synergy*. Bulletin 359, Royal Tropical Institute, Amsterdam, The Netherlands. pp. 63-71.

Nautiyal M.C. and B.P. Nautiyal (2004). *Agrotechniques for High Altitude Medicinal and Aromatic Plants*. Bishen Singh Mahendra Pal Singh, Dehradun, India.

Nautiyal, S. (1981). Some medicinal plants of Garhwal hills: a traditional use. *Journal of Scientific Research in Plants and Medicines*, 2: 12-18.

Nautiyal, S., K.S. Rao, R.K. Maikhuri, R.L. Semwal and K.G. Saxena (2000). Traditional knowledge related to medicinal and aromatic plants in tribal societies in a part of Himalaya. *Journal of Medicinal and Aromatic Plant Sciences*, 22/4A and 23/1A, 528-441.

Nautiyal, S., K.S. Rao, R.K. Maikhuri, K.S. Negi, and C.P. Kala (2002). Status of medicinal plants on way to Vashuki Tal in Mandakini Valley, Garhwal, Uttaranchal. *Journal of Non-Timber Forest Products*, 9 (3/4): 124-131.

Nautiyal, S., R.K. Maikhuri, K.S. Rao and K.G. Saxena (2001). Medicinal plant resources in Nanda Devi Biosphere Reserve in the central Himalaya. *Journal of Herbs, Spices and Medicinal Plants*, 8 (4): 47-64.

Nautiyal, S., R.K. Maikhuri, K.S. Rao and K.G. Saxena (2003). Ethnobotany of the Bhotiya tribe of the buffer zone villages of the Nanda Devi Biosphere Reserve. *Journal of Economic and Taxonomic Botany*, 23 (1): 119-141.

Negi, K.S. and K.C. Pant (1992). Less known wild species of *Allium* Linn (Amaryllidaceae) form mountainous region of India. *Economic Botany*, 46 (1): 112-116.

Negi, K.S. and R.D. Gaur (1991). A contribution to the Indian wild edible fruits of U. P. hills. *Bulletin Botanical Survey of India*, 33 (1-4): 233-266.

Negi, K.S. and R.D. Gaur (1991). Little known endemic wild Allium species in the Uttar Pradesh hills. *Mountain Research and Development*, 11 (2): 162-164.

Negi, K.S., J.K. Tiwari, R.D. Gaur and K.C. Pant (1993). Notes on ethnobotany of five districts of Garhwal Himalaya, U.P., India. *Ethnobotany*, 5: 73-81.

Negi, K.S., K.C. Muneem, G. Pandey, H. Manral, V.K. Pant, H.Y. Shukla, A.K. Sharma and D.D. Kushwaha (2001). Status of some economically important under exploited medicinal plant species in the Uttaranchal hills. *Journal of Non-Timber Forest Products*, 8 (1&2): 1-13.

Paliwal, G.S. and A.K. Badoni (1990). Ethnobotany of hill tribes of Uttarkashi, II. Medicinal plants. *Journal of Economic and Taxonomic Botany*, 14: 421-442.

Pande, B.C., B. Datt and P.C. Pande (2000). Notes on the ethnomedicinal aspect of some common Pteridophytes of Almora district of Kumaun Himalaya (Uttaranchal). *Ethnobotany*, 12: 56-59.

Pande, P.C., D.S. Pokharia and J.C. Bhatt (Eds. 1999). *Ethnobotany of Kumaun Himalaya*. Scientific Publishers, Jodhpur.

Pande, P.C. and H.C. Pande (2004). Traditional usage of 'Urd' (*Vigna mungo*) in Kumaon Himalaya, Uttaranchal. *Ethnobotany*, 16: 96-98.

Pandey, A., M. Nadeem and L.M.S. Palni (2002). Improvement in seed germination in Himalayan Yew through simple soil treatments. *Indian Journal of Forestry*, 25 (2): 109-113.

Pandey, B. and P.C. Pande (1999). Ethnobotanical studies on Gymnospermic plants of Kumaun Himalaya. *Journal of Economic and Taxonomic Botany*, 23 (2): 253-255.

Pandey, B. and N. Koranga (2003). Gahat: *Dolichos biflorus* Linn.) the queen of pulses in Uttaranchal. In: *Dimension of Uttaranchal* (Ed. C.M. Agrawal). India Publication Distributor, Delhi. pp. 603-606.

Pandey G. (1995). *Medicinal Plants of Himalaya*. Vol. I-II. Sri Satguru Publications, Delhi, India.

Pandey, H., S.K. Nandi, A. Kumar, U.T. Palni, B. Chandra and L.M.S. Palni (2000). In-vitro propagation of *Aconitum balfourii* Stapf.: an important aconite of the Himalayan alpines. *Journal of Horticultural Science and Biotechnology*, 79 (1): 34-41.

Pandey, H., S.K. Nandi, B. Chandra, M. Nadeem and L.M.S. Palni (2000). $GA_3$ induced flowering in *Podophyllum hexandrum* Royle: a rare alpine medicinal herb. *Acta Physiologiae Plantarum*, 23 (4): 467-474.

Pandey, H., S.K. Nandi, M. Nadeem and L.M.S. Palni (2000). Chemical stimulation of seed germination in *Aconitum heterophyllum* Wall. and *Aconitum balfourii* Stapf.: important Himalayan species for medicinal value. *Seed Science and Technology*, 28: 39-48.

Pangtey, Y.P.S. and G.S. Rawat (1987). A contribution to the ethnobotany of alpine region of Kumaun. *Journal of Economic and Taxonomic Botany*, 11 (1): 139-148.

Pangtey, Y.P.S., S.S. Samant and G.S. Rawat (1989). Ethnobotanical notes on Bhotia tribes of Kumaun Himalaya. *Indian Journal of Forestry*, 12 (2): 191-196.

Pant, G. and S.D. Tiwari (1989). Various human uses of Bryophytes in the Kumaun region of North West Himalaya. *Bryologist*, 92: 120-122.

Purohit, A., R.K. Maikhuri, K.S. Rao and S. Nautiyal (2001). Impact of bark removal on survival of *Taxus baccata* L. in Nanda Devi Biosphere Reserve, Garhwal Himalaya, India. *Current Science*, 81 (5): 586-590.

Purohit, A.N. (1997). Himalayan medicinal plants– Focus on Uttarakhand. In: *Himalayan Biodiversity: Action Plan*. (Ed. U. Dhar), Gyanodaya Prakashan, Nainital. pp: 91-110.

Purohit, A.N. (1997). Medicinal plants–need for upgrading technology for trading the traditions. In: *Harvesting Herbs –2000*. (Eds. A.R. Nautiyal, M.C. Nautiyal, and A.N. Purohit), Bishen Singh and Mahendra Pal Singh, Dehradun, India, pp. 46-76.

Purohit, A.N. (2004). Overview of state policies, plans and interventions to promote the medicinal plants sector in Uttaranchal In: *Searching Synergy*. Bulletin 359, Royal Tropical Institute, Amsterdam, The Netherlands. pp. 21-29.

Purohit, A.N. (2004). Medicinal and aromatic plants sector: potential and possibilities in Uttaranchal. *Financing Agriculture*, 36 (3): 19-26.

Rao, R.R. and P.K. Hajra (1987). Methods of research in ethnobotany. In: *A Manual of Ethnobotany* (Ed. S. K. Jain). Scientific Publisher, Jodhpur. pp: 33-41.

Rawat, G.S. and Y.P.S. Pangtey (1987). A contribution to the ethnobotany of Alpine regions of Kumaun. *Journal of Economic and Taxonomic Botany*, 11: 139-148.

Rawat, R.B.S and R.C. Uniyal (2004). Status of the medicinal and aromatic plants sector in Uttaranchal: initiative taken by the Government of India. *Financing Agriculture*, 36 (3): 7-13.

Rawat, R.S. and V.K. Bhatt (2002). *Nature's Pharmacopoeia, Medicinal Plants Diversity in Doon Valley*. Navdanya, Dehradun, India.

Rikhari, H.C., S. Sharma, M. Nadeem and L.M.S. Palni (2000). The effect of disturbance levels, forest types and associations on the regeneration of *Taxus baccata*: lesions from the Central Himalaya. *Current Science*, 79: 88-90.

Sajwan, B.S. and C.P. Kala, (2007). Conservation of medicinal plants: Conventional and contemporary strategies, regulations and executions. *Indian Forester*, 133 (4): 484-495.

Samal, P.K., A. Shah, S.C. Tiwari, and D.K. Agrawal (2004). Indigenous health care practices and their linkages with bio-resource conservation and socio-economic development in central Himalayan region of India. *Indian Journal of Traditional Knowledge*, 3 (1): 12-26.

Samant, S.S., U. Dhar and L.M.S. Palni (1998). *Medicinal plants of Indian Himalaya: diversity distribution potential values.* G.B. Pant Institute of Himalayan Environment and Development, Almora, India.

Samant, S.S., U. Dhar and R.S. Rawal (1996). Natural resource use by natives within Nanda Devi Biosphere Reserve in western Himalaya. *Ethnobotany*, 8: 40-50.

Shah, N.C. (1982). Herbal folk medicines in Northern India. *Journal of Ethnopharmacology*, 6: 293-301.

Shah, N.C. and L.K. Gupta (1976). Useful medicinal plants of Ranikhet-I. *Indian Drugs*, 14: 47-52.

Shah, N.C. and M.C. Joshi (1971). An ethnobotanical study of Kumaun region of India. *Economic Botany*, 25: 414-422.

Shah, N.C. and S.K. Jain (1980). Ethnomedicobotany of Kumaun Himalaya, India. *Social Pharmacology*, 2: 359-380.

Shiva, V. and V.K. Bhatt (2002). *Nature's Harvest : Rejuvenating Biodiversity in Doon Valley*. Navdanya, Dehradun, India.

Silori, C.S. and R. Badola (2000). Medicinal plant cultivation and sustainable development: a case study in the buffer zone of the Nanda Devi Biosphere Reserve, Western Himalaya, India. *Mountain Research and Development*, 20: 272-279.

Singh, D. and Y.P.S. Pundir (2004). Wild medicinal plants of Jaunsar-Bawar (Western Himalayas) Uttaranchal-I. *The Indian Forester*, 130 (11): 1259-1271.

Singh, H. (1989). Ethnobotanical studies on *Urtica dioica* among the Bhotiyas of Chamoli Garhwal, Uttar Pradesh. *Journal of Economic and Taxonomic Botany*, 13 (8): 719-724.

Singh, H., A. Saklani and B. Lal (1990). Ethnobotanical observations on some Gymnosperms of Garhwal Himalaya, Uttar Pradesh, India. *Economic Botany*, 44: 349-354.

Singh, H. and J.K. Maheshwari (1993). Phytotherapy for Diphtheria by the Bhoxas of Nainital District, Uttar Pradesh, India. *Ethnobotany*, 5: 63-65.

Singh, K.K., S. Saha and J.K. Maheswari (1987). Observation on the ethnobotany of Boxa tribe of Bajpur block of Nainital district, Uttar Pradesh. *Himalayan Research and Development*, 6 (1-2): 25-29.

Singh, S.K. and K.K. Misra (2002). Effect of tree age and season on root distribution pattern of Bael (*Aegle marmelos* (L.) Correa). *Journal of Non-Timber Forest Products*, 9 (1&2): 43-46.

Sundriyal, R.C., S.C. Negi, A.P. Joshi and R. Dhasmana (1985). Some important medicinal trees of Kotdwara, Lansdowne and vicinity. *Himalayan Chem. Pharm. Bull.* 2: 45-48.

Tewari, L. and P.C. Pande (2004). Traditional veterinary practices in southeastern part of Chamoli district, Uttaranchal. *Indian Journal of Traditional Knowledge*, 3 (4): 397-406.

Todaria, N.P., K.P. Saklani and M.S. Sachan (2004). Variation in pod and seed characteristics of *Acacia catechu* (Willd.) in Garhwal Himalayas. *The Indian Forester*, 130 (1): 53-61.

Uniyal, B. and V. Shiva (2005). Traditional knowledge on medicinal plants among rural women of Garhwal Himalaya. *Indian Journal of Traditional Knowledge,* 4 (3): 287-290.

Uniyal, M.R. (1968). Medicinal plants of Bhagirathi valley lying in Uttarkashi Forest Division. *The Indian Forester,* 94: 407-420.

Uniyal, S.K., A. Awasthi and G.S. Rawat (2002). Current status and distribution of commercially exploited medicinal and aromatic plants in upper Gori valley, Kumaon Himalaya, Uttaranchal. *Current Science,* 82 (10): 1246-1252.

Uniyal, S.K., A. Awasthi, and G.S. Rawat (2002). Traditional and ethnobotanical uses of plants in Bhagirathi Valley (Western Himalaya). *Indian Journal of Traditional Knowledge,* 1 (1): 7-19.

Upreti, D.K. and H.R. Negi (1996). Folk use of *Thamnolia vermicularis* (Swartz) Ach. in Schaerer in Lata village of Nanda Devi biosphere reserve. *Ethnobotany,* 8: 83-86.

# Appendix

## Appendix: Check-List of Medicinal Plants of Uttarakhand

| Sl.No. | Species | Family | Local Name | Plant Used | Important Uses | Life Form |
|---|---|---|---|---|---|---|
| 1. | *Abelmoschus esculenta* (L.) Moench. | Malvaceae | Bhindi | Rt | Abortifacient | Herb |
| 2. | *Abies pindrow* Royle | Pinaceae | Raga | Bk | Cough, bronchitis | Tree |
| 3. | *Abies spectabilis* (D. Don) Mirbel | Pinaceae | Raga | Lf, bk | Fever, asthma, bronchitis | Tree |
| 4. | *Abrus precatorius* L. | Fabaceae | Ratti | Sd, rt | Arthritis, dysentery, fever, cough | Wood Cl |
| 5. | *Abutilon indicum* (L.) Sweet | Malvaceae | Kanghe | Lf, rt, fl | Bone fracture, bronchitis, cough, diarrhoea | Un Sh |
| 6. | *Abutilon ramosum* (Cav.) | Malvaceae | Kanghe | Lf | Fever | Herb |
| 7. | *Acacia catechu* (L. f.) Willd. | Mimosaceae | Khair, kaatha | Bk | Dysentery, bronchitis, menstrual disorders | Sh |
| 8. | *Acacia nilotica* (L.) Willd. ex Delile | Mimosaceae | Babul, Kikar | Bk | Bronchitis, asthma, urinary disorder | Sh |
| 9. | *Acalypha indica* L. | Euphorbiaceae | Kuppi | Lf | Cold, cough | Herb |
| 10. | *Acer acuminatum* Wall. ex D. Don | Aceraceae | Rath-kanchula | Sd | Abortifacient | Tree |
| 11. | *Achillea millefolium* L. | Asteraceae | Gandrain | Wp | Tonic, toothache, cough, cold | Herb |
| 12. | *Achyranthes aspera* L. | Amaranthaceae | Lich-kuri | Rt | Child birth, malarial fever | Herb |
| 13. | *Achyranthes bidentata* Bl. | Amaranthaceae | Chicheree | Rt | Child birth, malarial fever | Un Sh |
| 14. | *Aconitum balfourii* Stapf | Ranunculaceae | Meetha | Rt | Sciatica | Herb |
| 15. | *Aconitum falconeri* Stapf | Ranunculaceae | | Rt | Fever, diarrhoea | Herb |
| 16. | *Aconitum heterophyllum* Wall. | Ranunculaceae | Ateesh | Rt | Fever, cough, diarrhoea, digestive disorder | Herb |

Contd...

**Appendix–Contd...**

| Sl.No. | Species | Family | Local Name | Plant Used | Important Uses | Life Form |
|---|---|---|---|---|---|---|
| 17. | *Aconitum rotundifolium* Kar. and Kir. | Ranunculaceae | | Rt | Headache | Herb |
| 18. | *Aconitum violaceum* Jacq. | Ranunculaceae | Dudatees | Rt | Stomachache, renal pain | Herb |
| 19. | *Acorus calamus* L. | Araceae | Bach | Rt | Gastric complaints, jaundice, bronchitis | Herb |
| 20. | *Actaea acuminata* Wall. ex Royle | Ranunculaceae | Maneeru | Sd | Sciatica, blood inflammation | Herb |
| 21. | *Actiniopteris radiata* (Sw.) Link. | Actiniopteridaceae | Morpankhi | Wp | Bronchitis, headache, dysentery | Herb |
| 22. | *Adenostemma lavenia* (L.) Kuntz. | Asteraceae | | Lf | Antiseptic, cuts, wound | Herb |
| 23. | *Adhatoda zeylanica* Medikus | Acanthaceae | Basingu | Lf, fl | Cough, cold, bronchitis, fever | Sh |
| 24. | *Adiantum incisum* Forsk. | Adiantaceae | | Lf | Cough, skin diseases | Herb |
| 25. | *Adiantum venustum* D. Don | Adiantaceae | | Lf | Fever | Herb |
| 26. | *Aegle marmelos* (L.) Correa | Rutaceae | Bel | Lf, fr, rt | Digestive disorder | Tree |
| 27. | *Aerides multiflorum* Roxb. | Orchidaceae | Mana | Lf | Cut, wounds | Herb |
| 28. | *Aesandra butyracea* (Roxb.) Baehni | Sapotaceae | Chiura | Sd | Rheumatic pain | Tree |
| 29. | *Aesculus indica* (Colebr. ex Camb.) Hk. | Hippocastanaceae | Pangar | Fr, bk, rt | Rheumatic pain | Tree |
| 30. | *Ageratum conyzoides* L. | Asteraceae | | Rt, lf | Headache, cuts, diarrhoea, snake bite | Herb |
| 31. | *Ageratum houstonianum* Mill. | Asteraceae | | Wp | Skin ailments, diarrhoea | Herb |
| 32. | *Agrimonia pilosa* Led. | Rosaceae | Velu | Wp | Cough, diarrhoea | Un Sh |
| 33. | *Ainsliaea aptera* DC. | Asteraceae | Kauru | Wp | Fever, painful urination | Herb |
| 34. | *Ainsliaea latifolia* (D. Don) Sch.-Bip. | Asteraceae | Kauru | Rt | Colic | Herb |

*Contd...*

**Appendix–Contd...**

| Sl.No. | Species | Family | Local Name | Plant Used | Important Uses | Life Form |
|---|---|---|---|---|---|---|
| 35. | *Ajuga bracteosa* Wall. ex Benth. | Lamiaceae | Neelkanthi | Wp | Stomachache, tonic, malarial fever | Herb |
| 36. | *Ajuga parviflora* Benth. | Lamiaceae | | Wp | Stomachache, tonic | Herb |
| 37. | *Alangium salviifolium* (L. f.) Wanger. | Alangiaceae | Kuilu | Bk | Fever, skin diseases | Tree |
| 38. | *Albizia lebbeck* (L.) Benth. | Mimosaceae | Siris | Sd, bk, rt | Dysentery, eye complaints, diarrhoea, piles | Tree |
| 39. | *Albizia procera* (Roxb.) Benth. | Mimosaceae | Karahi, safed-siris | Sd | Gonorrhoea | Tree |
| 40. | *Alcea rosea* L. | Malvaceae | | Fl, fr, sd | Skin diseases, jaundice | Herb |
| 41. | *Alectra parasitica* A. Rich. | Scrophulariaceae | Gaiya | Wp | Leprosy, gynacological disorder | Herb |
| 42. | *Allium carolinianum* DC. | Liliaceae | Ladu | Wp | Diuretic | Herb |
| 43. | *Allium cepa* L. | Liliaceae | Pyaz | Bb | Digestive and skin disorders | Herb |
| 44. | *Allium consanguineum* Kunth. | Liliaceae | | Lf | Indigestion | Herb |
| 45. | *Allium humile* Kunth. | Liliaceae | Faran | Bb, lf | Indigestion | Herb |
| 46. | *Allium rubellum* Bieb. | Liliaceae | | Bb | Indigestion | Herb |
| 47. | *Allium sativum* L. | Liliaceae | Lahsun | Bb | Respiratory, digestive, blood disorders | Herb |
| 48. | *Allium victorialis* L. | Liliaceae | | Lf | Cut, wounds | Herb |
| 49. | *Allium wallichii* Kunth | Liliaceae | Doona, Laddu | Bb | Flatulence, bile complaints | Herb |
| 50. | *Aloe vera* (L.) Burm. f. | Liliaceae | Gwar patta | Lf | Purgative, stomachache, wounds | Herb |
| 51. | *Alstonia scholaris* (L.) Br. | Apocynaceae | | Bk, latex | Asthma, snake bite, mouth ulcer, cholera | Tree |

*Contd...*

**Appendix–Contd...**

| Sl.No. | Species | Family | Local Name | Plant Used | Important Uses | Life Form |
|---|---|---|---|---|---|---|
| 52. | *Alternanthera sessilis* (L.) R.Br. ex DC. | Amaranthaceae | | Lf | Bone fracture, malaria, dysentery | Herb |
| 53. | *Amaranthus paniculatus* L. | Amaranthaceae | Marshu | Rt | Eczema, diarrhoea | Herb |
| 54. | *Amaranthus spinosus* L. | Amaranthaceae | Kateli chaulai | Wp | Blood purification, cold, cough, snake bite | Herb |
| 55. | *Ammania baccifera* L. | Lythraceae | | Wp | Skin diseases, fever | Herb |
| 56. | *Amorphophallus paeoniifolius* (Denns.) Nicolson | Araceae | Zami kand | Tuber | Stomachache | Herb |
| 57. | *Ampelocissus latifolia* (Roxb.) Planchon | Vitaceae | Bhinura | St | Aphthae | Climb H |
| 58. | *Ampelocissus rugosa* (Wall.) Planchon | Vitaceae | Chhipari | St, lf | Bone fracture | Climb H |
| 59. | *Anagallis arvensis* L. | Primulaceae | | Wp | Hydrophobia, leprosy | Herb |
| 60. | *Anaphalis adnata* Wall. ex DC. | Asteraceae | Bugla | Lf | Cut, wounds | Herb |
| 61. | *Anaphalis busua* (Buch.-Ham. DC. ex D.Don) | Asteraceae | Buglya | Lf | Wounds, cut | Herb |
| 62. | *Anemone obtusiloba* D. Don | Ranunculaceae | Kanchphool | Rt, sd | Diarrhoea | Herb |
| 63. | *Anemone rivularis* Buch.-Ham. ex DC. | Ranunculaceae | Angeli | Wp | Wounds, earache, cold | Herb |
| 64. | *Anemone vitifolia* Buch.-Ham. ex DC. | Ranunculaceae | Mudeela | Rt, lf | Ringworm infection, eczema | Herb |
| 65. | *Angelica arc-angelica* L. | Apiaceae | | Rt | Child birth, bodyache | Herb |
| 66. | *Angelica glauca* Edgew. | Apiaceae | Choru | Rh | Constipation, bronchitis | Herb |

*Contd...*

**Appendix–Contd...**

| Sl.No. | Species | Family | Local Name | Plant Used | Important Uses | Life Form |
|---|---|---|---|---|---|---|
| 67. | *Anisochilus carnosus* (L.) Wall. ex Benth. | Lamiaceae | Goplya, Panjri | Wp | Cough, cold | Herb |
| 68. | *Anisomeles indica* (L.) Ktze. | Lamiaceae | Ram tulsi | Wp | Snake bite, fever, wounds, muscular pain | Herb |
| 69. | *Anisomeles latiflolia* Bedd. | Lamiaceae | | Gum | Wounds, fever | Herb |
| 70. | *Anisomeles pendula* Edgew. | Lamiaceae | | Sd | Wounds, fever | Herb |
| 71. | *Annona squamosa* L. | Annonaceae | Sitaphal | Bk, sd, rt | Diarrhoea, hysteria, cuts | Herb |
| 72. | *Anogeissus latifolia* Bedd. | Combretaceae | Dhawadi | Bk | Cholera, cough, headache, liver ailments | Tree |
| 73. | *Anthocephalus chinensis* (Lam.) Richard ex Walpers | Rubiaceae | Kadamb | Lf, bk | Fever, skin diseases | Tree |
| 74. | *Anthriscus nemorosa* (Bieb.) Spr. | Apiaceae | | Wp | Rheumatic pain | Herb |
| 75. | *Apium graveolens* L. | Apiaceae | Salari | Rt | Bodyache | Herb |
| 76. | *Arachne cordifolia* (Decne.) Hurusawa | Euphorbiaceae | Bhartoli, Bhatsor | Lf | Snake bite, wounds | Sh |
| 77. | *Arctium lappa* L. | Asteraceae | | Rt | Gastric complaints | Herb |
| 78. | *Argemone mexicana* L. | Papaveraceae | Piii kateli | Wp | Leucorrhoea, psychological problem | Herb |
| 79. | *Argemone ochroleuca* Sweet | Papaveraceae | Katela | Rt | Leucorrhoea | Herb |
| 80. | *Argyreia speciosa* Sw. | Convolvulaceae | | Rt, sd | Snake bite, anticancer, dysentery, headache | Herb |
| 81. | *Arisaema concinnum* Schott | Araceae | Meen | Fr, tuber | Snake bite, vomiting | Herb |

*Contd...*

**Appendix–Contd...**

| Sl.No. | Species | Family | Local Name | Plant Used | Important Uses | Life Form |
|---|---|---|---|---|---|---|
| 82. | *Arisaema flavum* (Forsk.) Schott | Araceae | Meen | Tuber | Eczema, skin diseases | Herb |
| 83. | *Arisaema intermedium* Blume | Araceae | Meen | Fr | Psycological disorder | Herb |
| 84. | *Arisaema jacquemontii* Blume | Araceae | Saperi mausi | Tuber | Snake bite | Herb |
| 85. | *Arisaema tortuosum* (Wall.) Schott | Araceae | Bag-mungri | Rt | Burns | Herb |
| 86. | *Aristolochia indica* L. | Aristolochiaceae | | Rt | Diarrhoea, menstrual complaints, scabies | Herb |
| 87. | *Arnebia benthamii* (Don) John. | Boraginaceae | Balchhadi | Rt | Fever, headache, hair tonic, cut, wounds | Herb |
| 88. | *Arnebia euchroma* (Royle) John. | Boraginaceae | | Wp | Bodyache, brain and hair tonic | Herb |
| 89. | *Artemisia absinthium* L. | Asteraceae | | Lf | Wounds, skin ailments | Herb |
| 90. | *Artemisia capillaries* Thunb. | Asteraceae | | Lf | Earache, purgative | Herb |
| 91. | *Artemisia japonica* Thunb. | Asteraceae | Pamasi | Lf | Skin diseases | Herb |
| 92. | *Artemisia maritima* L. | Asteraceae | | Wp | Antiseptic, blood purification | Herb |
| 93. | *Artemisia nilagirica* (Cl.) Pamp. | Asteraceae | Kunza | Wp | Asthma, skin ailments, antiseptic, headache | Herb |
| 94. | *Artemisia roxburghiana* Wall. ex Besser | Asteraceae | Kunja | Lf, st | Skin allergy, tonic | Un Sh |
| 95. | *Artemisia stricta* Edgew. | Asteraceae | | Lf | Skin ailments | Herb |
| 96. | *Artocarpus heterophyllus* Lamk. | Moraceae | Kathal | Latex | Wounds | Tree |
| 97. | *Artocarpus lacucha* Buch.-Ham. | Moraceae | Barhal | Sd | Conjuctivitis | Tree |
| 98. | *Aruncus dioicus* (Waltr.) Furnald | Rosaceae | | Rt | Wounds | Sh |
| 99. | *Asclepias curassavica* L. | Asclepiadaceae | Lalma | Lf, latex | Cut, wounds, vomiting | Un Sh |

*Contd...*

**Appendix Contd...**

| Sl.No. | Species | Family | Local Name | Plant Used | Important Uses | Life Form |
|---|---|---|---|---|---|---|
| 100. | *Asparagus adscendens* Buch.-Ham. ex Roxb. | Liliaceae | Satawari, Jhirni | Rt | Diabetes, dysentery | Sh |
| 101. | *Asparagus curillus* Buch.-Ham. | Liliaceae | | Rt | Diabetes, dysentery | Un Sh |
| 102. | *Asparagus filicinus* Buch.-Ham. | Liliaceae | Kaunta, Saranoi | Rt | Diabetes, dysentery, diarrhoea | Sh |
| 103. | *Asparagus racemosus* Willd. | Liliaceae | Jhirna, Satawari | Rt | Antiseptic, aphrodisiac | Wood Cl |
| 104. | *Asphodelus tenuifolius* Cav. | Liliaceae | Piazi | Sd | Diuretic, antiseptic, ulcer | Herb |
| 105. | *Aster asteroids* (DC.) O.K. | Asteraceae | | Rt | Cough | Herb |
| 106. | *Aster peduncularis* Wall. ex Nees | Asteraceae | Phulyan | Rt | Stomachache | Un Sh |
| 107. | *Aster thomsonii* Cl. | Asteraceae | Phulari | Lf | Indigestion | Herb |
| 108. | *Astragalus candolleanus* Royle ex Benth. | Fabaceae | Rudravanti | Rt | Blood purification, cough, skin ailments | Sh |
| 109. | *Astragalus chiorostachys* Lindley | Fabaceae | Rudravanti | Rt | Tuberculosis | Sh |
| 110. | *Astragalus himalayanus* Klotz. | Fabaceae | | Sd | Leprosy, tonsil | Sh |
| 111. | *Asystacia neesiana* (Wall.) Nees | Acanthaceae | | Lf | Swelling, wounds | Herb |
| 112. | *Azadiracta indica* A.H.L. Juss. | Meliaceae | Neem | Lf, bk, sd | Antiseptic, skin diseases, diabetes | Tree |
| 113. | *Bacopa monnieri* (L.) Penn. | Scrophulariaceae | Hingot | Wp | Blood purification, stomachache,eczema | Herb |
| 114. | *Baliospermum montanum* Muell.-Aug. | Euphorbiaceae | Banbhatti | Sd, rt | Cuts, asthma, gastric trouble, snake bite | Sh |
| 115. | *Bambusa arundinacea* Ait. | Poaceae | Bans | St, lf | Wounds, cut, abortificient | Herb |

*Contd...*

**Appendix–Contd...**

| Sl.No. | Species | Family | Local Name | Plant Used | Important Uses | Life Form |
|---|---|---|---|---|---|---|
| 116. | *Barleria cristata* L. | Acanthaceae | Kala-bansa | Rt, lf, sd | Pneumonia, wounds, snake bite | Un Sh |
| 117. | *Barleria prionitis* L. | Acanthaceae | Peela-bansa | Rt, bk | Cough, cold | Un Sh |
| 118. | *Barringtonia acutangula* (L.) Gaertn. | Barringtoniaceae | Hijala | Bk | Liver disorder, toothache, cholera | Tree |
| 119. | *Bauhinia purpurea* L. | Caesalpiniaceae | | Bk, fl, lf | Snake bite, wounds, bone fracture, jaundice | Tree |
| 120. | *Bauhinia racemosa* Lamk. | Caesalpiniaceae | | Bk | Diarrhoea, dysentery | Tree |
| 121. | *Bauhinia retusa* Roxb. | Caesalpiniaceae | | Bk, lf, fl | Snake bite, cholera | Tree |
| 122. | *Bauhinia vahlii* (Wt. and Arn.) Benth. | Caesalpiniaceae | | Fr, sd, rt | Aphrodisiac, stomachache, dysentery | Sh |
| 123. | *Bauhinia variegata* L. | Caesalpiniaceae | Kwiral | Bk, fl, lf | Cough, piles, ulcers, indigestion | Tree |
| 124. | *Begonia picta* Smith ex D. Don | Begoniaceae | Patharchatta | Lf | Dyspepsia | Herb |
| 125. | *Benincasa hispida* (Thunb.) Cogniaux | Cucurbitaceae | Bhuijelu | Fr, sd | Gonorrhoea, tonic | Herb |
| 126. | *Berberis affinis* G. Don. | Berberidaceae | | Rt, bk | Eye diseases | Sh |
| 127. | *Berberis aristata* DC. | Berberidaceae | Kingode | Rt, bk | Fever, eye complaints | Sh |
| 128. | *Berberis asiatica* Roxb. ex DC. | Berberidaceae | Kingode | Rt | Eye diseases | Sh |
| 129. | *Berberis chitria* Edwards | Berberidaceae | Kingode | Rt | Eye diseases | Sh |
| 130. | *Berberis jaeschkeana* Sch. | Berberidaceae | | Rt, fr | Blood purification, jaundice, eye diseases | Sh |

*Contd...*

**Appendix–Contd...**

| Sl.No. | Species | Family | Local Name | Plant Used | Important Uses | Life Form |
|---|---|---|---|---|---|---|
| 131. | *Berberis kumaonensis* Sch. | Berberidaceae | Kingode | Rt | Eye diseases, blood purification, jaundice | Sh |
| 132. | *Berberis lycium* Royle | Berberidaceae | Kingode | Bk, rt | Jaundice, eye ailments, menorhoea | Sh |
| 133. | *Berberis petiolaris* Wall. ex G. Don | Berberidaceae | Chotar | Rt | Eye diseases | Sh |
| 134. | *Bergenia ciliata* (Haworth) Sternb. | Saxifragaceae | Silphara | Rh | Tonic, digestive and cutaneous disorders | Herb |
| 135. | *Bergenis stracheyi* (Hk. f. and Th.) Engler | Saxifragaceae | Pasanbhed | Rt | Cut, wounds, tonic, kindney stones | Herb |
| 136. | *Betula alnoides* Buch.-Ham. ex D. Don | Betulaceae | Kath bhoj | Lf, bk | Snake bite | Tree |
| 137. | *Betula utilis* D. Don | Betulaceae | Bhojpatra | Bk, rt | Cut, wounds, hysteria | Tree |
| 138. | *Bidens bipinnata* L. | Asteraceae | Kumra | Lf | Cuts, leprosy | Herb |
| 139. | *Bidens biternata* (Lour.) Merrill and Sherff | Asteraceae | Kumra | Lf | Cough, bronchitis, leaucoderma | Herb |
| 140. | *Biebersteinia odora* Steph. ex Fish. | Biebersteiniaceae | | Wp | Peptic ulcer, wounds | |
| 141. | *Biophytum sensitivum* (L.) DC. | Oxalidaceae | Chuimui | Lf | Giddiness, headache, antiseptic, cramps | Herb |
| 142. | *Bistorta amplexicaulis* (D. Don) Greene | Polygonaceae | Kutrya | Lf | Dysentery, wounds | Herb |
| 143. | *Bistorta vaccinifolia* (Wall. ex Meisn.) Greene | Polygonaceae | Inuri | Rt | Tuberculosis | Un Sh |
| 144. | *Blumea laciniata* (Roxb.) DC. | Asteraceae | | Lf | Eczema, skin disorder | Herb |

*Contd...*

**Appendix–Contd...**

| Sl.No. | Species | Family | Local Name | Plant Used | Important Uses | Life Form |
|---|---|---|---|---|---|---|
| 145. | *Blumea lanceolaria* (Roxb.) Druce | Asteraceae | | Lf | Wounds, bodyache | Sh |
| 146. | *Blumea mollis* (Don) Merr. | Asteraceae | | Lf | Skin ailments | Herb |
| 147. | *Boehmeria rugulosa* Wedd. | Urticaceae | Genthi | Bk | Bone fracture | Tree |
| 148. | *Boenninghausenia albiflora* (Hk.) Reichb. ex Meissn. | Rutaceae | Upniyaghas | Lf, rt | Cut, wounds, vomiting, dysentery, antiseptic | Un Sh |
| 149. | *Bombax ceiba* L. | Bombacaceae | Semel | Rt, bk | Blood dysentery, asthma, dysentery, fever | Tree |
| 150. | *Boswellia serrata* Roxb. ex Colebr. | Burseraceae | Salar | Bk | Skin and digestive disorder | Tree |
| 151. | *Botrychium lunaria* (L.) Sw. | Botrychiaceae | | Wp | Dysentery | Herb |
| 152. | *Botrychium ternatum* (Thunb.) Sw. | Botrychiaceae | | Wp | Dysentery | Herb |
| 153. | *Brassica compestris* L. | Brassicaceae | Sarson | Wp | Migrain, cough, leprosy | Herb |
| 154. | *Brassica rugosa* (Roxb.) Bailey | Brassicaceae | Pahari rai | Sd | Bodyache, skin diseases, cold | Herb |
| 155. | *Breea arvensis* (L.) Less. | Asteraceae | | Rt | Diuretic | Herb |
| 156. | *Breynia squamosa* (Lamk.) Gaertn. | Euphorbiaceae | | Bk, rt, fr | Wounds | Herb |
| 157. | *Buchanania lanzan* Sprengel | Anacardiaceae | Pural, Piyal | Kernal | Cough, skin ailments | Tree |
| 158. | *Bunicum persicum* (Boiss.) Fedt. | Apiaceae | Kala jira | Fr | Indigestion | Herb |
| 159. | *Bupleurum falcatum* L. | Apiaceae | Jangli jeera | Rt | Fever, liver disorder | Herb |
| 160. | *Bupleurum hamiltonii* Balakrishnan | Apiaceae | Jangli jeera | Rt | Liver trouble | Herb |
| 161. | *Bupleurum himalayense* Klotzsch | Apiaceae | Kala ajwain | Rt | Liver disorder, gastritis | Herb |
| 162. | *Bupleurum thomsonii* Cl. | Apiaceae | | Fr | Stomachache | Herb |

Contd...

**Appendix–Contd...**

| Sl.No. | Species | Family | Local Name | Plant Used | Important Uses | Life Form |
|---|---|---|---|---|---|---|
| 163. | *Butea monosperma* (Lam.) Kuntze | Fabaceae | Dhak | Fl, bk, sd | Antiseptic, blood purification, dog bite | Tree |
| 164. | *Butea parviflora* (Lamk.) Taub. | Fabaceae | Dhak | Bk, rt | Stomachache, madness, diarrhoea | Tree |
| 165. | *Caesalpinia bonduc* (L.) Roxb. | Caesalpiniaceae | | Sd, rt | Fever, skin diseases, tonic | Sh |
| 166. | *Caesalpinia decapitata* (Roth.) Alston | Caesalpiniaceae | | Wp | Mouth sores, jaundice | Sh |
| 167. | *Cajanus cajan* (L.) Millsp. | Fabaceae | Tor | Sd, lf, fl | Skin burn, mouth sores | Herb |
| 168. | *Cajanus mollis* (Benth.) Van der Maessen | Fabaceae | Ban-Sem | Lf, fr | Bodyache | Herb |
| 169. | *Calanthe tricarinata* Lindley | Orchidaceae | Syoru | Lf | Eczema, aphrodisiac | Herb |
| 170. | *Callicarpa arborea* Roxb. | Verbenaceae | Ghiwala | Bk | Skin diseases | Tree |
| 171. | *Callicarpa macrophylla* Vahl | Verbenaceae | Daiya, Bhirmoli | Lf | Rheumatic pain | Un Sh |
| 172. | *Calotropis gigantea* (L.) Dryander | Asclepiadaceae | Madar, aak | Bk | Dysentery, bodyache, asthma | Sh |
| 173. | *Calotropis procera* (Aiton) Dryander | Asclepiadaceae | Madar, aak | Fl | Cold, cough, asthma | Sh |
| 174. | *Caltha palustris* L. | Ranunculaceae | | Rt, lf | Urogenital ailments | Herb |
| 175. | *Cannabis sativa* L. | Cannabinaceae | Bhang | Lf, sd | Delirium, eye disorder, epilepsy | Herb |
| 176. | *Canscora decussata* (Roxb.) Schultes | Gentianaceae | Sankhwali | Shoot | Nervine tonic | Herb |
| 177. | *Canscora diffusa* (Vahl) R.Br. | Gentianaceae | | Shoot | Nervine tonic | Herb |
| 178. | *Capparis sepiaria* L. | Capparaceae | Kanthari | Rt | Paralytic attack | Sh |
| 179. | *Capparis zeylanica* L. | Capparaceae | Bauri | Rt bark | Diabetes | Sh |

*Contd...*

**Appendix–Contd...**

| Sl.No. | Species | Family | Local Name | Plant Used | Important Uses | Life Form |
|---|---|---|---|---|---|---|
| 180. | *Capsella bursa-pastoris* (L.) Medic. | Brassicaceae | Botlya | Wp | Cut and wounds, astringent, antiscorbutic | Herb |
| 181. | *Capsicum annum L.* | Solanaceae | | Fr | Dog bite | Herb |
| 182. | *Cardamine impatiens* L. | Brassicaceae | Ban laiyya | Rt, lf | Fever, stimulant, diuretic | Herb |
| 183. | *Cardiocrinum giganteum* (Wall.) Makino | Liliaceae | Giotira | Lf, bb | Wounds, antiseptic | Herb |
| 184. | *Cardiospermum halicacabum* L. | Sapindaceae | Kanphuti | Rt, lf, sd | Fever, indigestion, suppressed menstruation | Climb H |
| 185. | *Carex rotundus* L. | Cyperaceae | | Rt | Cut, wounds | Herb |
| 186. | *Carica papaya* L. | Caricaceae | Papeeta | Latex | Skin ailments | Tree |
| 187. | *Carissa carandus* L. | Apocynaceae | Karunda | Lf, sd, rt | Epilepsy, fever, itching, wounds | Sh |
| 188. | *Carissa opeca* Stapf. | Apocynaceae | Karunda | Lf, rt, bk | Fever, purgative | Sh |
| 189. | *Carpesium abrotanoides* L. | Asteraceae | Kuleo | Rt, lf, Sd | Diuretic, skin ailments | Herb |
| 190. | *Carthamus tinctorius* L. | Asteraceae | | Fl | Indigestion | Herb |
| 191. | *Carum carvi* L. | Apiaceae | Jangli dhaniya | Sd | Cold, cough, fever, dyspepsia, indigesion | Herb |
| 192. | *Caryopteris foetida* (D. Don) Thellung | Verbenaceae | Karvi | Lf | Wounds | Sh |
| 193. | *Caryopteris odorata* (D. Don) Robinson | Verbenaceae | | Lf | Abortifacient | Sh |
| 194. | *Cascabela thevetia* (L.) Lipp. | Apocynaceae | | Sd | Skin diseases | Tree |

*Contd...*

**Appendix–Contd...**

| Sl.No. | Species | Family | Local Name | Plant Used | Important Uses | Life Form |
|---|---|---|---|---|---|---|
| 195. | *Casearia elliptica* Willd. | Flacourtiaceae | Swarnmul | Lf, bk | Blister, wounds, headache, snake bite | Tree |
| 196. | *Cassia absus* L. | Caesalpiniaceae | | Sd, lf | Cough, eye infection | Sh |
| 197. | *Cassia alata* L. | Caesalpiniaceae | | Lf, fr | Skin diseases, eczema | Sh |
| 198. | *Cassia fistula* L. | Caesalpiniaceae | Amaltas | Fr, bk | Snakebite, asthma, bronchitis, antiseptic | Tree |
| 199. | *Cassia occidentalis* L. | Caesalpiniaceae | Chakunda | Fr, rt | Snakebite, dropsy, piles, ringworm | Un Sh |
| 200. | *Cassia sophera* L. | Caesalpiniaceae | | Lf | Piles, scabies | Sh |
| 201. | *Cassia tora* L. | Caesalpiniaceae | Chakunda | Sd, lf | Bone fracture, skin diseases, cut, wounds | Un Sh |
| 202. | *Cassine glauca* (Rottboell) Kuntze | Celastraceae | Dhebri | Lf | Epilepsy, snake bite | Tree |
| 203. | *Cassiope fastigiata* Don. | Ericaceae | | Wp | Itching | Sh |
| 204. | *Catharanthus pusillus* (Murr.) Don | Apocynaceae | | Lf | Fever | Herb |
| 205. | *Catunaregam uliginosa* (Retz.) Sivarajan | Rubiaceae | Rada, Pindru | Sd | Skin ailments | Sh |
| 206. | *Cautleya gracilis* (Smith) Dandy | Zingiberaceae | Ram haldi | Rh | Burns, wounds | Herb |
| 207. | *Cayratia trifolia* (L.) Domin | Vitaceae | Amal-bel | Lf | Boils | Climb H |
| 208. | *Cedrus deodara* (Roxb.) Loud. | Pinaceae | Devdar | St, resin | Ulcer, rheumatic pain | Tree |
| 209. | *Celastrus paniculatus* Willd. | Celastraceae | Kaunya | Sd, rt | Ophthalmic and mental disorders, snake bite | Sh |
| 210. | *Celosia argentea* L. | Amaranthaceae | Gadrya | Sd | Aphrodisiac | Herb |

*Contd...*

**Appendix–Contd...**

| Sl.No. | Species | Family | Local Name | Plant Used | Important Uses | Life Form |
|---|---|---|---|---|---|---|
| 211. | *Celtis australis* L. | Ulmaceae | Khadik | Bk | Leprosy | Tree |
| 212. | *Centauria iberica* Trev. ex Spr. | Asteraceae | | Lf | Eczema | |
| 213. | *Centaurium meyeri* (Bunge) Druce | Gentianaceae | Barik chirayata | Shoot | Malarial fever | Herb |
| 214. | *Centella asiatica* (L.) Urban | Apiaceae | Brahmi buti | Fr, lf, rt | Brain tonic, mental disorder, blood purifier | Herb |
| 215. | *Centipeda minima* (L.) Braun and Ascherson | Asteraceae | Nakh-chhikni | Lf | Headache | Herb |
| 216. | *Cerastium cerastoides* (L.) Britt. | Caryophyllaceae | | Wp | Bodyache, headache, renal pain, cough | Herb |
| 217. | *Cerastium fontanum* Baumg. | Caryophyllaceae | | Wp | Fever | Herb |
| 218. | *Ceriscoides turgida* (Roxb.) Tirveng. | Rubiaceae | Thanela, Thanera | Rt | Dyspepsia | Tree |
| 219. | *Cestrum nocturnum* L. | Solanaceae | Rat ki Rani | Lf | Epilepsy | Sh |
| 220. | *Chenopodium album* L. | Chenopodiaceae | Bathua | Sd, lf | Skin diseases, urinary trouble | Herb |
| 221. | *Chenopodium botrys* L. | Chenopodiaceae | | Wp | Liver complaints, stomach trouble | Herb |
| 222. | *Chlorophytum tuberosum* Baker | Liliaceae | Safed musli | Tuber | Fever, leucorohea | Herb |
| 223. | *Chonemorpha fragrans* (Moon) Alston | Apocynaceae | Moorva | Lf | Bone injuries | Sh |
| 224. | *Cicer arietinum* L. | Fabaceae | Channa | Wp | Tonic, jaundice | Herb |
| 225. | *Cicerbita macrorhiza* (Royle) Beauv. | Asteraceae | | Lf | Wounds | Herb |
| 226. | *Cichorium intybus* L. | Asteraceae | Kasni | Rt | Bodyache | Herb |
| 227. | *Cinnamomum tamala* Nees | Lauraceae | Tejpat | Bk, lf | Heart and throat complaints | Tree |

*Contd...*

**Appendix–Contd...**

| Sl.No. | Species | Family | Local Name | Plant Used | Important Uses | Life Form |
|---|---|---|---|---|---|---|
| 228. | *Cinnamomum zeylanicum* Nees | Lauraceae | Dalchini | Lf, st, bk | Cough, vomiting, diorrhoea | Tree |
| 229. | *Cirsium verutinum* (Don) Spr. | Asteraceae | Kandaru | Rt | Tonic, wounds | Herb |
| 230. | *Cissampelos pareira* L. | Menispermaceae | Parha | Lf, rt | Dog bite, bodyache, child birth | Climb H |
| 231. | *Cissus quadrangula* L. | Vitaceae | | Lf, st, rt | Wounds, cut, bone fracture, dysentery | Sh |
| 232. | *Cissus repanda* Vahl | Vitaceae | Bhel-chapru | St | Wounds | Wood Cl |
| 233. | *Citrullus colocynthis* (L.) Schrader | Cucurbitaceae | Chota tarbooj | Rt | Jaundice | Herb |
| 234. | *Citrus grandis* (L.) Osbeck | Rutaceae | Chakotra | Fr | Dysentery | Sh |
| 235. | *Citrus latipes* (Sw.) Tanaka | Rutaceae | | Fr | Pimples | Tree |
| 236. | *Citrus limon* (L.) Burm. f. | Rutaceae | | Fr | Indigestion, pimples | Tree |
| 237. | *Citrus medica* L. | Rutaceae | Nimboo | Bk, rt | Pimples, jaundice, kidney disorder | Tree |
| 238. | *Clausena pentaphylla* (Roxb.) DC. | Rutaceae | Ratanjot | Lf, rt | Cold, cough, fever, ulcer | Tree |
| 239. | *Cleistocalyx operculatus* (Roxb.) Merrill and Perry | Myrtaceae | Rai-jamun | Fr, bk | Diabetes | Tree |
| 240. | *Clematis barbellata* Edgew. | Ranunculaceae | Kanrya | Lf | Scabies | Wood Cl |
| 241. | *Clematis buchananiana* DC. | Ranunculaceae | Kanguli | Lf | Skin diseases | Wood Cl |
| 242. | *Clematis montana* Buch.-Ham. ex DC. | Ranunculaceae | Kujju | Rt | Diabetes, urinary trouble | Wood Cl |
| 243. | *Clematis nepaulensis* DC. | Ranunculaceae | Marchya lagulu | Lf | Skin diseases | Wood Cl |

*Contd...*

**Appendix–Contd...**

| *Sl.No.* | *Species* | *Family* | *Local Name* | *Plant Used* | *Important Uses* | *Life Form* |
|---|---|---|---|---|---|---|
| 244. | *Cleome gynandra* L. | Cleomaceae | Safed hulmul | Lf | Headache, rheumatism, neuralgia | Herb |
| 245. | *Cleome viscosa* L. | Cleomaceae | Jakkya | Sd, lf | Rheumatic arthritis, wounds | Herb |
| 246. | *Clerodendrum indicum* (L.) Kuntze | Verbenaceae | Chingori | Rt, lf | Cholera, bronchitis | Un Sh |
| 247. | *Clerodendrum phlomides* L. | Verbenaceae | Urui | Rt | Gonorrhoeal disorder | Sh |
| 248. | *Clerodendrum serratum* (L.) Moon | Verbenaceae | Ban bakri | Rt, lf | Bronchitis, snake bite | Sh |
| 249. | *Clerodendrum viscosum* Ventenat | Verbenaceae | Bhanua, Bhant | Lf | Skin diseases | Sh |
| 250. | *Clinopodium umbrosum* (Bieb.) Koch. | Lamiaceae | Birchee | Wp | Blood purifier, gastric trouble | Herb |
| 251. | *Clinopodium vulgare* L. | Lamiaceae | | Wp | Heart tonic | Herb |
| 252. | *Clitoria ternatea* L. | Fabaceae | | Rt | Snake bite, stomachache | Herb |
| 253. | *Coccinia grandis* (L.) Voigt. | Cucurbitaceae | Kaduri, Kandaroi | Lf, Rt | Diabetes, antiseptic, gonorrhoea | Herb |
| 254. | *Cocculus hirsutus* (L.) Diels | Menispermaceae | Jaljamni | Lf | Joint pain, wounds, body swelling | Wood Cl |
| 255. | *Cochlospermum religiosum* (L.) Alston | Cochlospermaceae | Gaddi, Gehru | Bk | Digestive disorder | Tree |
| 256. | *Codonopsis clematidea* (Schr.) Cl. | Campanulaceae | | Wp | Rheumatic pain | Wood Cl |
| 257. | *Codonopsis ovata* Benth. | Campanulaceae | | Rt | Swelling | Climb H |
| 258. | *Coelogyne cristata* Lindley | Orchidaceae | Gondya | Bb | Constipation, aphrodisiac | Herb |
| 259. | *Coelogyne ovalis* Lindl. | Orchidaceae | | Wp | Headache, fever | Herb |
| 260. | *Colebrookia oppositifolia* Smith. | Lamiaceae | Binda | Lf | Wounds | Sh |

*Contd...*

**Appendix–Contd...**

| Sl.No. | Species | Family | Local Name | Plant Used | Important Uses | Life Form |
|---|---|---|---|---|---|---|
| 201. | *Coleus forskohlii* (Willd.) Sm. | Lamiaceae | | Rt | Tonic, constipation | Herb |
| 262. | *Colocasia esculenta* (L.) Schott | Araceae | Pindalu | Tuber | Indigestion | Herb |
| 263. | *Commelina benghalensis* L. | Commelinaceae | Kanjula | Shoot | Dysentery, bodyache, liver complaints | Herb |
| 264. | *Commelina maculata* Edgew. | Commelinaceae | Kapla | Rt | Fever | Herb |
| 265. | *Convolvulus arvensis* L. | Convolvulaceae | Heyranpatu | Wp | Burns, purgative | Herb |
| 266. | *Corallodiscus lanuginosus* (Wall. ex DC.) Burtt. | Gesneriaceae | Shila-pushpa | Lf | Kindney stones | Herb |
| 267. | *Corchorus aestuans* L. | Tiliaceae | | Lf | Fever, stomachache | Sh |
| 268. | *Cordia dichotoma* Forst. f. | Cordiaceae | | Sd, lf | Lung disorder, cold, constipation | Tree |
| 269. | *Coriandrum sativum* L. | Apiaceae | Dhaniya | Fr | Digestive disorder | Herb |
| 270. | *Cortia depressa* (Don) Norm. | Apiaceae | | Wp | Stomachache, rheumatic pain | Herb |
| 271. | *Corydalis cornuta* Royle | Fumariaceae | Indra jatta | Rt | Body swelling, fever | Herb |
| 272. | *Corydalis govaniana* Wall. | Fumariaceae | | Wp | Antipyretic, gastric pain, liver disorder | Herb |
| 273. | *Corydalis meifolia* Wall. | Fumariaceae | | Wp | Headache, liver and stomach pain | Herb |
| 274. | *Corydalis vaginans* Royle | Fumariaceae | | Fl | Eye disorder | Herb |
| 275. | *Corylus jacquemontii* Decne. | Betulaceae | Kabasi | Fr, sd | Tonic | Tree |
| 276. | *Costus speciosus* (Koenig ex Retz.) Smith | Costaceae | Keun | Rt | Snake bite | Herb |

*Contd...*

**Appendix–Contd...**

| Sl.No. | Species | Family | Local Name | Plant Used | Important Uses | Life Form |
|---|---|---|---|---|---|---|
| 277. | *Cotoneaster adpressus* Boiss. | Rosaceae | | Lf | Skin diseases | Sh |
| 278. | *Cotoneater bacillaris* Wall. | Rosaceae | Ruins | Lf | Scabies, rheumatic arthritis | Tree |
| 279. | *Cotoneater microphyllus* Wall. ex Lindley | Rosaceae | Bugrchilla, wanni | Rh, fr | Cut and wounds, diarrhoea, astringent | Sh |
| 280. | *Crataeva adansonii* DC. | Capparaceae | Berne | Lf, bk | Bronchitis, urinary disorder, skin diseases | Tree |
| 281. | *Crateva magna* (Lour.) DC. | Capparaceae | | Bk | Fever, hydrocele, stomachache, tonic | Tree |
| 282. | *Crateva religiosa* Frost .f. | Capparaceae | | Lf, bk | Stomachache | Tree |
| 283. | *Crinum asiaticum* L. | Amaryllidaceae | Kanwal | Bb | Emetic | Herb |
| 284. | *Crinum defixum* Ker-Gawler | Amaryllidaceae | | Bb | Earache | Herb |
| 285. | *Crotalaria albida* Heyne ex Roth | Fabaceae | Ban methi | Sd, rt | Blood purifier, constipation | Herb |
| 286. | *Crotalaria juncia* L. | Fabaceae | Sunn | Sd | Blood purifier | Un Sh |
| 287. | *Crotolaria spectabilis* Roth. | Fabaceae | | Wp | Scabies | Herb |
| 288. | *Cryptolepis buchanani* Roem. and Schult. | Periplocaceae | | Rt | Dysentery, bodyache, cuts, snake bite | Sh |
| 289. | *Cucumis hardwickii* Royle | Cucurbitaceae | Elaroo | Rt bark | Fever | Herb |
| 290. | *Cucumis melo* L. | Cucurbitaceae | Kharbooja | Sd | Cooling | Herb |
| 291. | *Cucurbita maxima* Duch. ex Lam. | Cucurbitaceae | Kaddu | Sd, fr | Intestinal worms | Herb |
| 292. | *Cuminum cyminum* L. | Apiaceae | Zeera | Fr | Cough, cold, throat pain | Herb |
| 293. | *Curculigo orchioides* Gaertner | Hypoxidaceae | Kali-musi | Rh | Gonorrhoea, jaundice, diarrhoea, aphrodisiac | Herb |

Contd...

**Appendix–Contd...**

| Sl.No. | Species | Family | Local Name | Plant Used | Important Uses | Life Form |
|---|---|---|---|---|---|---|
| 294. | *Curcuma angustifolia* Roxb. | Zingiberaceae | Tikhur | Rh | Tonic | Herb |
| 295. | *Curcuma domestica* Valeton | Zingiberaceae | Haldi | Rh | Skin and digestive disorder, blood purification | Herb |
| 296. | *Cuscuta capitata* Roxb. | Convolvulaceae | | Wp | Fever, antiseptic, ulcer, wounds | Herb |
| 297. | *Cuscuta reflexa* Roxb. | Convolvulaceae | Akash laguli | Wp | Rheumatic pain, skin ailments | Climb H |
| 298. | *Cyamopsis tetragonaloba* (L.) Taub. | Fabaceae | Gawar | Fr | Sprain, swelling | Herb |
| 299. | *Cyananthus integer* Wall. | Campanulaceae | | Wp | Cut, wounds | Herb |
| 300. | *Cyananthus lobatus* Wall. ex Benth. | Campanulaceae | | Rt, fl, lf | Wounds | Herb |
| 301. | *Cyanodon dactylon* (L.) Persoon | Poaceae | Doob, Dublya | Rt, lf | Snake bite, fever, blood purification | Herb |
| 302. | *Cyanoglossum glochidiatum* Wall. ex Benth. | Boraginaceae | | Rt | Vomiting of infants, digestive disorder, dyspepsia | Herb |
| 303. | *Cyanoglossum lanceolatum* Forsk. | Boraginaceae | Lichkura | Wp | Cough, cold | Herb |
| 304. | *Cyanoglossum zeylanicum* (Vahl ex Hornem.) Thunb. ex Lehmann | Boraginaceae | Andhahuli | Lf, rt | Asthma, bronchitis | Herb |
| 305. | *Cyathocline purpurea* (Don) Ktze. | Asteraceae | | Lf, st, rt | Stomachache, headache, fever | Herb |
| 306. | *Cyathula capitata* Moq. | Amaranthaceae | Arsilla | Fr | Abortifacient | Un Sh |
| 307. | *Cyathula tomentosa* (Roth) Moq. | Amaranthaceae | Lichkura | Lf | Snake bite | Un Sh |
| 308. | *Cyclanthera pedata* Schrader | Cucurbitaceae | Meetha karela | Fr | Liver complaints | Climb H |
| 309. | *Cymbopogon martinii* (Roxb.) Wats. | Poaceae | Pirya ghas | Lf | Cold | Herb |

*Contd...*

**Appendix–Contd...**

| Sl.No. | Species | Family | Local Name | Plant Used | Important Uses | Life Form |
|---|---|---|---|---|---|---|
| 310. | *Dactylorhiza hatagirea* (Don.) Soo | Orchidaceae | Hathajadi | Tuber | Bone fracture, aphrodisiac, tonic, wounds | Herb |
| 311. | *Dalbergia indica* (L.) Benn. | Fabaceae | | Sd | Skin diseases | Tree |
| 312. | *Dalbergia sissoo* Roxb. | Fabaceae | Sheesam | Lf, st | Dysentery, skin diseases | Tree |
| 313. | *Daphne papyracea* Wall. ex Steudel | Thymeleaceae | Banchoi | Lf | Eczema | Sh |
| 314. | *Datisca cannabina* L. | Datiscaceae | Bajar bhang | Rt, Lf | Fever, rheumatic pain | Herb |
| 315. | *Datura innoxia* Mill. | Solanaceae | Datura | Lf, sd | Asthma, rheumatism | Herb |
| 316. | *Datura metel* L. | Solanaceae | Kala-datura | Wp | Blister, headache, piles, skin diseases | Herb |
| 317. | *Datura stramonium* L. | Solanaceae | Dhatura | Lf, rt | Asthma, joint pain, stomachache | Sh |
| 318. | *Daucus carota* L. | Apiaceae | Gajar | Rt | Brain tonic | Herb |
| 319. | *Debregeasia longifolia* (Burm. f.) Wedd. | Urticaceae | Tusara | Bk | Bone fracture | Sh |
| 320. | *Debregeasia salicifolia* (D. Don) Rendle | Urticaceae | Syanru | Bk | Bone fracture | Tree |
| 321. | *Deeringia amaranthoides* (Lamk.) Merr. | Amaranthaceae | | Lf | Sores | Un Sh |
| 322. | *Delphinium brunonianum* Royle | Ranunculaceae | | Rt | Wounds | Herb |
| 323. | *Delphinium cashmerianum* Royle | Ranunculaceae | | Wp | Headache, cuts, stomachache | Herb |
| 324. | *Delphinium denudatum* Wall. ex Hk. f. and Th. | Ranunculaceae | Nirbishi | Rt | Snake bite, tonic, stimulant | Herb |

*Contd...*

**Appendix–Contd...**

| Sl.No. | Species | Family | Local Name | Plant Used | Important Uses | Life Form |
|---|---|---|---|---|---|---|
| 325. | *Delphinium vestitum* Wall. ex Royle | Ranunculaceae | Nirbishi | Wp | Snake bite, cuts, wounds, fever | Herb |
| 326. | *Dendrocalamus strictus* Nees | Poaceae | Bans | Rt, bk | Tonic, fever | Tree |
| 327. | *Dendrophthoe falcata* (L. f.) Ettings. | Loranthaceae | Vanda | Bk, lf | Bronchitis, menstrual disorder | Un Sh |
| 328. | *Dendrophthoe pentandra* (L.) Miq. | Loranthaceae | | Lf | Skin eruption, sores | Sh |
| 329. | *Descurania sophia* (L.) Webb. ex Pranti | Brassicaceae | | Sd | Skin ailments | Herb |
| 330. | *Desmodium elegans* DC. | Fabaceae | Chamlai | Rt | Epilepsy | Sh |
| 331. | *Desmodium gangeticum* (L.) DC. | Fabaceae | Salpalnu | Rt | Fever, dysentery | Un Sh |
| 332. | *Desmodium heterocarpon* (L.) DC. | Fabaceae | | Lf | Cough | Un Sh |
| 333. | *Desmodium triflorum* (L.) DC. | Fabaceae | Lichkura | Wp | Bodyache, breast pain, dysentery, wounds | Herb |
| 334. | *Desmodium triquetrum* (L.) DC. | Fabaceae | | Wp | Cold, cough, fever, snake bite | Herb |
| 335. | *Desmostachya bipinnata* (L.) Stapf. | Poaceae | Kusha | Wp | Dysentery | Herb |
| 336. | *Deutzia corymbosa* R. Br. ex G. Don | Hydrangeaceae | Mhujvar | Lf | Diuretic | Sh |
| 337. | *Deutzia staminea* R. Br. ex Wall. | Hydrangeaceae | Bhat kukri | Lf | Diuretic | Sh |
| 338. | *Dichrocephala integrifolia* (L. f.) Ktze. | Asteraceae | | St, bk | Gonorrhoea | Herb |
| 339. | *Dicliptera bupleuroides* Nees | Acanthaceae | Kuthhi | Lf | Gastric disorder, cough | Un Sh |
| 340. | *Dicranopteris linearis* (Burm. f.) . Underw | Dicranopteridaceae | | Wp | Asthma, epilepsy | Fn |

*Contd...*

**Appendix–Contd...**

| Sl.No. | Species | Family | Local Name | Plant Used | Important Uses | Life Form |
|---|---|---|---|---|---|---|
| 341. | *Dictamus albus* L. | Rutaceae | | Rt | Wounds | Tree |
| 342. | *Didymocarpus pedicellatus* R. Br. | Gesneriaceae | Pahar phori | Lf | Kindney stones | Herb |
| 343. | *Dillenia indica* L. | Delleniaceae | Chaltha | Fr | Bronchitis, dyspepsia, fever | Tree |
| 344. | *Dioscorea belophylla* (Prain) Voigt ex Haines | Dioscoreaceae | Taidu | Tuber | Indigestion | Herb |
| 345. | *Dioscorea bulbifera* L. | Dioscoreaceae | Gainthi | Tuber | Antiseptic, burns, wounds | Herb |
| 346. | *Dioscorea deltoidea* Wall. ex Grisebach | Dioscoreaceae | Harbish | Tuber | Abdominal pain, dysentery, urogenital disorder | Herb |
| 347. | *Diospyros malabarica* (Desr.) Kostel. | Ebenaceae | Kala-tendu | Fr, bk | Diarrhoea, dyspepsia | Tree |
| 348. | *Diplocyclos palmatus* (L.) Jeffrey | Cucurbitaceae | Put laguli | Sd | Diabetes | Climb H |
| 349. | *Dipsacus inermis* Wall. ex Roxb. | Dipsacaceae | Phulee | Rt | Leucorrhoea | Herb |
| 350. | *Dodonaea viscosa* (L.) Jacq. | Sapindaceae | | Fr, lf | Cold, cut, wounds | Sh |
| 351. | *Doronicum roylei* DC. | Asteraceae | | Rt | Cough, headache | Herb |
| 352. | *Dregea volubilis* (L. f.) Benth. ex Hk. f. | Asclepiadaceae | Nak-shikni | Lf, rt | Antiseptic, emetic | Wood Cl |
| 353. | *Drimia indica* (Roxb.) Jessop | Liliaceae | Ban pyaz | Lf, bb | Epilepsy, diabetes | Herb |
| 354. | *Drymaria cordata* (L.) Willd. ex Roemer and Schultes | Caryophyllaceae | Pithpapra | Shoot | Bile complaints | Herb |
| 355. | *Dryopteris cochleata* (Don) Chr. | Dryopteridaceae | Hathajodi | Rh | Cholera | Fn |
| 356. | *Drypetes roxburghii* (Wall.) Hurusawa | Euphorbiaceae | Juti | Fr | Fever, skin allergy | Tree |
| 357. | *Duchesnea indica* (Andrews) Focke | Rosaceae | Bhiyn-kaphal | Lf | Diarrhoea, leucorrhoea | Herb |

*Contd...*

**Appendix–Contd...**

| Sl.No | Species | Family | Local Name | Plant Used | Important Uses | Life Form |
|---|---|---|---|---|---|---|
| 358. | *Echinops cornigerus* DC. | Asteraceae | Kantela | Rt | Fever, urinary disorder | Herb |
| 359. | *Eclipta prostrata* (L.) L. | Asteraceae | Bhangru | Lf, st | Fever, constipation, asthma | Herb |
| 360. | *Elaeagnus parviflora* Wall. ex Royle | Elaeagnaceae | Kankal | Lf, sd, fr | Cough, bronchitis, expectorant | Sh |
| 361. | *Elephantopus scaber* L. | Asteraceae | Adhomukh | Rt, lf | Fever, vomiting | Herb |
| 362. | *Elsholtzia ciliata* (Thunb.) Hyland. | Lamiaceae | | Fl | Skin disease | Herb |
| 363. | *Elsholtzia densa* Benth. | Lamiaceae | | Sd | Burns, cuts | Herb |
| 364. | *Elsholtzia fruticosa* (D. Don) Rehder | Lamiaceae | Pothi, Puthoj | Sd | Sciatica | Sh |
| 365. | *Elsholtzia strobilifera* (Benth.) Benth. | Lamiaceae | Pothi | Lf | Wounds | Herb |
| 366. | *Elusine coracana (L.) Gaertn.* | Poaceae | Koda | Sd | Skin eruption, pneumonia | Herb |
| 367. | *Embelia ribes* Burm. f. | Myrsinaceae | | Sd, fr | Skin disease, stomach complaints | Sh |
| 368. | *Embelia robusta* Roxb. | Myrsinaceae | Baya birang | Bk, lf, fr | Cholera, fever, itching, tonic, child birth | Sh |
| 369. | *Emilia sonchifolia* (L.) DC. | Asteraceae | Dudhi | Lf | Night blindness | Herb |
| 370. | *Engelhardtia spicata* Leschenault ex Blume | Juglandaceae | Gath mahua | Bk | Diarrhoea | Tree |
| 371. | *Ephedra gerardiana* Wall. | Ephedraceae | | Rt, st | Blood purification, headache, asthma | Sh |
| 372. | *Epilobium angustifolium* L. | Onagraceae | | Shoot | Abdominal pain, intestinal complaints | Herb |
| 373. | *Epilobium royleanum* Haussk. | Onagraceae | Meelu | Lf, rt | Ringworm infection | Herb |

*Contd...*

**Appendix–Contd...**

| Sl.No. | Species | Family | Local Name | Plant Used | Important Uses | Life Form |
|---|---|---|---|---|---|---|
| 374. | *Epipactis helleborine* (L.) Crantz | Orchidaceae | Trindrya | Lf | Fever, aphrodisiac | Herb |
| 375. | *Erigeron multiradiatus* (Lindley ex DC.) Cl. | Asteraceae | | Wp | Brain tonic, stomachache | Herb |
| 376. | *Eritricum cannum* (Benth.) Kitamara | Boraginaceae | | Lf | Child birth | Herb |
| 377. | *Erythrina arborescens* Roxb. | Fabaceae | Dhauldhak | Bk, lf | Skin diseases, intestinal worms | Tree |
| 378. | *Erythrina suberosa* Roxb. | Fabaceae | | Bk, lf | Dysentery | Tree |
| 379. | *Erythrina variegata* L. | Fabaceae | Madar | Bk | Snake bite, anthelmintic | Tree |
| 380. | *Eulophia dabia* (D. Don) Hochreutiner | Orchidaceae | Salam mishri | Tuber | Cough, cold, tonic, blood purification | Herb |
| 381. | *Eulophia herbacea* Lindl. | Orchidaceae | | Tuber | Tonic | Herb |
| 382. | *Euonymus tingens* Wall. | Celastraceae | Bhambeli | Bk | Eye diseases | Tree |
| 383. | *Eupatorium adenophorum* Sprengel | Asteraceae | Bakura, Kharna | Lf | Wounds | Sh |
| 384. | *Euphorbia chamaesyce L.* | Euphorbiaceae | Dudhi | Shoot, | Dysentery, constipation | Herb |
| 385. | *Euphorbia fusiformis Don* | Euphorbiaceae | | Rt | Fever, dysentery | Herb |
| 386. | *Euphorbia hirta L.* | Euphorbiaceae | Dudhi | Wp | Asthma, bronchitis, snake bite, scabies | Herb |
| 387. | *Euphorbia hispida Boiss.* | Euphorbiaceae | | Wp | Wounds | Herb |
| 388. | *Euphorbia ligularia Roxb.* | Euphorbiaceae | | Lf, st | Snake bite, asthma, jaundice | Sh |
| 389. | *Euphorbia maddeni Boiss.* | Euphorbiaceae | | Lf | Scabies | Herb |
| 390. | *Euphorbia pilosa L.* | Euphorbiaceae | Chuplya | Rt | Constipation | Herb |
| 391. | *Euphorbia prostrata L.* | Euphorbiaceae | | Latex | Wounds | Herb |
| 392. | *Euphorbia royleana* Boissier | Euphorbiaceae | Sullu | Latex | Antiseptic | Sh |

Contd...

**Appendix–Contd...**

| Sl.No. | Species | Family | Local Name | Plant Used | Important Uses | Life Form |
|---|---|---|---|---|---|---|
| 393. | *Euphorbia stracheyi Boiss.* | Euphorbiaceae | Dudhibish | Latex | Rheumatic pain | Herb |
| 394. | *Euphorbia thymifolia L.* | Euphorbiaceae | | Wp | Blood dysentery, eye diseases | Herb |
| 395. | *Euphorbia tibetica Boiss.* | Euphorbiaceae | | Latex | Purgative | Herb |
| 396. | *Euphrasia himalaica Wettst.* | Scrophulariaceae | | Lf | Eye diseases | Herb |
| 397. | *Euphrasia platyphylla* Pennel. | Scrophulariaceae | | Wp | Eye diseases | Herb |
| 398. | *Evolvulus alsinoides*(L.) L. | Convolvulaceae | Sankhpushpi | Shoot | Tonic, cough, cold, brain tonic, bronchitis | Herb |
| 399. | *Excoecaria acerifolia* F. Didrichsen | Euphorbiaceae | Dudhila | Latex | Skin disease, wounds | Sh |
| 400. | *Fagara oxyphylla (Edgew.)* Engler | Rutaceae | Ban-timur | St, bk | Toothache, dyspepsia, indigestion | Sh |
| 401. | *Fagopyron esculantum* (L.) Moench. | Polygonaceae | Phapher | Wp | Lung disorder, urinary complaints | Herb |
| 402. | *Fagopyron tataricum* Gaertn. | Polygonaceae | Phapher | Sd | Tonic | Herb |
| 403. | *Ferula jaeschkeana* Vat. | Apiaceae | | Rt | Wounds, toothache, rheumatic pain | Herb |
| 404. | *Ficus auriculata* Lour. | Moraceae | Timla | Fr | Digestive disorder | Tree |
| 405. | *Ficus benghalensis* L. | Moraceae | Bod | Latex | Dysentery, scabies, tonic, toothache, cholera | Tree |
| 406. | *Ficus palmata* Forsk. | Moraceae | Bedu | Fr | Digestive disorder | Tree |
| 407. | *Ficus racemosa* L. | Moraceae | Gular | Bk, fr | Bronchitis, dysentery, leprosy, scabies | Tree |

*Contd...*

**Appendix–Contd...**

| Sl.No. | Species | Family | Local Name | Plant Used | Important Uses | Life Form |
|---|---|---|---|---|---|---|
| 408. | *Ficus religiosa* L. | Moraceae | Peepal | Lf, bk, fr | Dysentery, cholera, skin diseases | Tree |
| 409. | *Ficus semicordata* Buch.-Ham. | Moraceae ex Smith | Khaina | Fr | Digestive disorder | Tree |
| 410. | *Flacourtia indica* (Burm. f.) Merrill | Flacourtiaceae | Kandai | Fr | Hepatitis, fever, diarrhoea, wounds | Tree |
| 411. | *Flacourtia jangomas* (Lour.) Raeuschel | Flacourtiaceae | Pachnala | Fr, bk | Fever, urinary disorder | Tree |
| 412. | *Flemingia fruticulosa* Wall. ex Benth | Fabaceae | Churan | Rt | Irregular menstruation | Un Sh |
| 413. | *Flemingia macrophylla* (Willd.) Prain ex Merrill | Fabaceae | | Rt | External swelling and ulcer | Un Sh |
| 414. | *Flemingia strobilifera* (L.) Ait. | Fabaceae | Kanphuta | Rt | Bodyache, fever, hysteria | Herb |
| 415. | *Foeniculum vulgare* Mill. | Apiaceae | Sonf | Sd | Cough, cold, skin diseases, tonic, wounds | Herb |
| 416. | *Fragaria nubicola* Lindl. ex Lac. | Rosaceae | Gar-kaphal | Lf | Tooth trouble, earache | Herb |
| 417. | *Fraxinus micrantha* Lingel | Oleaceae | Angu, Angar | Bk | Fever, blood dysentery | Tree |
| 418. | *Fritillaria roylei* Hk. | Liliaceae | | Bb | Asthma, bronchitis, tonic, stomach disorder | Herb |
| 419. | *Fumaria indica* (Haussknecht) Pugsley | Fumariaceae | Pit papra | Lf | Wounds, suppressed urination | Herb |
| 420. | *Gagea reticulata (Palla) Schultes f.* | Liliaceae | Lasnya | Lf, rt | Indigestion, burns | Herb |
| 421. | *Galium acutum* Edgew. | Rubiaceae | Kura, Kutub | Wp | Urinary disorder | Herb |

*Contd...*

**Appendix–Contd...**

| Sl.No. | Species | Family | Local Name | Plant Used | Important Uses | Life Form |
|---|---|---|---|---|---|---|
| 422. | *Galium aparine* L. | Rubiaceae | Khuskhusa | Lf | Aperient, diuretic antiscorbutic, skin diseases | Herb |
| 423. | *Galium asperifolium* Wall. | Rubiaceae | Leswakuri | Wp | Skin ailments | Herb |
| 424. | *Galium elegans* Wall. | Rubiaceae | Manjeethee | Shoot | Jaundice, dyspepsia, colic | Herb |
| 425. | *Garuga pinnata* Roxb. | Burseraceae | | Lf, bk, fr, rt | Asthma, dysentery, wounds | Tree |
| 426. | *Gaultheria nummularioides* D. Don. | Ericaceae | Bheunla | Lf, fr | Antiseptic | Sh |
| 427. | *Geam elatum* Wall. ex G. Don | Rosaceae | | Wp | Toothache | Herb |
| 428. | *Gentiana aprica* Decne. | Gentianaceae | Chirotu | Shoot | Fever, headache | Herb |
| 429. | *Gentiana decumbens* L.f. | Gentianaceae | | Fl | Fever | Herb |
| 430. | *Gentiana stipitata Edgew.* | Gentianaceae | Neelkanthi | Fl | Appetizer | Herb |
| 431. | *Gentianella moorcroftiana* (Wall. Ex Griseb.) Airy-shaw | Gentianaceae | | Wp | Blood purification, fever, headache, cough | Herb |
| 432. | *Geranium himalayense* Klot. | Geraniaceae | | Rt | Stomachache | Herb |
| 433. | *Geranium nepalense* Sweet | Geraniaceae | Phori, syunli | Rt | Fever, eczema, itching, | Herb |
| 434. | *Geranium ocellatum* Cambess. | Geraniaceae | Kaphlya | Rt | Liver trouble, fever, antiseptic | Herb |
| 435. | *Geranium wallichianum* D. Don ex Sweet | Geraniaceae | Ratanjot, laljari | Rt | Ophthalmia | Herb |
| 436. | *Gerbera gossypina* (Royle) Beauv. | Asteraceae | Kapasee | Lf | Cut, wounds, bone fracture | Herb |
| 437. | *Girardinia diversifolia* (Link) Friis | Urticaceae | Bhaisu kandali | Lf | Gonorrhoea | Un Sh |
| 438. | *Gloriosa superba* L. | Liliaceae | Langli, Lakya | Rt, rh, lf | Fever, suppressed urination, asthma, cholera | Herb |

*Contd...*

**Appendix–Contd...**

| Sl.No. | Species | Family | Local Name | Plant Used | Important Uses | Life Form |
|---|---|---|---|---|---|---|
| 439. | *Glycine max* (L.) Merr. | Fabaceae | Bhatt | Sd | Cough, cold | Herb |
| 440. | *Gmelina arborea* Roxb. | Verbenaceae | Gumbhar | Lf, fl, rt | Antiseptic, blood purification, tonic | Tree |
| 441. | *Gnaphalium hypoleucum* DC. | Asteraceae | Buglya | Shoot | Cut, wounds | Herb |
| 442. | *Gonatanthus pumilus (D. Don)* Engler and Krause | Araceae | Ban-pindalu | Tuber | Burns, wounds | Herb |
| 443. | *Gonostegia hirta* (Blume) Miq. | Urticaceae | Atainya | Rt | Bone fracture | Herb |
| 444. | *Goodyera repens* (L.) R.Br. | Orchidaceae | Girwara | Shoot | Syphilis, blood purification | Herb |
| 445. | *Grevia optiva* Dumm. ex Burret. | Tiliaceae | Bhimal | Lf, fr, st | Bone fracture, child birth, fever | Tree |
| 446. | *Grewia hirsuta* Vahl | Tiliaceae | Ghatui | Rt, bk | Blister, dysentery, cuts | Tree |
| 447. | *Gymnadenia orchidis* Lindl. | Orchidaceae | | Rt | Gastric, urinary disorder, tonic | Herb |
| 448. | *Gymnema sylvestre* (Retz.) R.Br. | Asclepiadaceae | | Lf | Diabetes, gastric trouble, snake bite | Sh |
| 449. | *Gypsophila cerastioides* D. Don | Caryophyllaceae | Bakarchee | Lf | Wounds | Herb |
| 450. | *Habenaria intermedia* D. Don | Orchidaceae | Ridhi-bidhi | Tuber | Tonic | Herb |
| 451. | *Habenaria marginata* Colebr. | Orchidaceae | Haldya jari | Shoot | Flatulence | Herb |
| 452. | *Haldinia cordifolia* (Roxb.) Ridsdale | Rubiaceae | Haldu | Bk, rt | Dysentery, diabetes | Tree |
| 453. | *Halenia elliptica* D. Don | Gentianaceae | Hasela | Sd | Fever | Herb |
| 454. | *Hedera nepalensis* K. Koch | Araliaceae | Mithiari | Lf, fr | Ulcer, dyspepsia | Climb H |

Contd...

**Appendix–Contd...**

| Sl.No. | Species | Family | Local Name | Plant Used | Important Uses | Life Form |
|---|---|---|---|---|---|---|
| 455. | *Hedychium spicatum* Ham. ex Smith | Zingiberaceae | Ban-haldi | Rh | Stomachache, carminative, tonic, stimulant, asthma | Herb |
| 456. | *Hedyotis corymbosa* (L.) Lam. | Rubiaceae | | Shoot | Liver disorder | Herb |
| 457. | *Helianthus annuus* L. | Asteraceae | Surajmukhi | Rt | Bone fracture, snake bite, nose bleeding | Herb |
| 458. | *Helicteres isora L.* | Sterculiaceae | Murra | Fr, rt | Asthma, bodyache, fever, snake bite | Sh |
| 459. | *Heliotropium strigosum* Willd | Boraginaceae | Safed bhangra | Shoot | Skin diseases | Herb |
| 460. | *Helminthostachys zeylanica* (L.) Hk. f. | Helminthos-tachyaceae | Kamraj | Lf, rt | Jaundice, blisters | Fn |
| 461. | *Hemidesmus indicus* (L.) R. Br. | Periplocaceae | | Rt | Diarrhoea, menstrual complaints, hypertension | Sh |
| 462. | *Heracleum canescens* Lindley | Apiaceae | Kakrya, arva | Rt | Eczema, ring worm | Herb |
| 463. | *Heracleum lanatum* Michaux | Apiaceae | Kakrya, arva | Rt | Eczema, skin diseases, itching | Herb |
| 464. | *Herminium lanceum* (Thunb. ex Swartz.) Vuijk | Orchidaceae | Jalya | Shoot | Suppressed urination | Herb |
| 465. | *Herminium monophyllum* (Don) Hunt. and Summerh. | Orchidaceae | | Rt | Suppressed urination | Herb |
| 466. | *Heterostemma alatum* Wight and Arn. | Asclepiadaceae | | Lf | Antiseptic | Sh |
| 467. | *Hibiscus rosa-sinensis* L. | Malvaceae | | Fl, rt | Cough, fever, kidney disorder | Sh |
| 468. | *Hippophae rhamnoides* L. | Elaeagnaceae | Amosh | Sd, fr | Aphrodisiac, lung disorder | Sh |
| 469. | *Hippophae salicifolia* D. Don | Elaeagnaceae | | Bk, fr | Dandruff, cuts, ulcer, wounds | Sh |

*Contd...*

**Appendix–Contd...**

| Sl.No. | Species | Family | Local Name | Plant Used | Important Uses | Life Form |
|---|---|---|---|---|---|---|
| 470. | *Hiptage benghalensis* (L.) Kurz | Malpighiaceae | Aita lagula | Lf | Skin diseases | Wood Cl |
| 471. | *Holarrhena pubescens* (Buch.-Ham.) Wall. ex G. Don | Apocynaceae | Kura, kuri | Bk | Dysentery | Sh |
| 472. | *Holmskioldia sanguinea* Retz. | Verbenaceae | Katuri ka phool | Lf | Body swelling | Sh |
| 473. | *Holoptelea integrifolia* (Roxb.) Planchon | Ulmaceae | Papri | Bk | Rheumatic pain | Tree |
| 474. | *Hoppea dichotoma* Hayne ex Willd. | Gentianaceae | | Shoot | Snake bite | Herb |
| 475. | *Hordeum vulgare* L. | Poaceae | Jau | Sd | Pimples, urinary complaints | Herb |
| 476. | *Hoya longilofia* Wall. ex Wt. | Asclepiadaceae | | Lf | Wounds | Herb |
| 477. | *Humulus lupulus L.* | Urticaceae | | Fl | Tonic, improve appetite | Herb |
| 478. | *Hydrocotyle nepalensis* Hk. | Apiaceae | Choti-brahmi | Lf | Eczema, scabies | Herb |
| 479. | *Hymenodictyon excelsum* (Roxb.) Wall. | Rubiaceae | | Rt, bk | Diarrhoea, fever, liver complaints | Tree |
| 480. | *Hypericum oblongifolium* Choisy. | Hypericaceae | | Fl | Wounds, boils | Sh |
| 481. | *Hypericum perforatum L.* | Hypericaceae | | Lf | Cut, wounds, bleeding | Un Sh |
| 482. | *Hypoxis aurea* Lour. | Hypoxidaceae | Golkya | Rt | Aphrodisiac | Herb |
| 483. | *Hyptis suaveolens* (L.) Poit. | Lamiaceae | | Wp | Headache, wounds, fever, toothache | Herb |
| 484. | *Ichnocarpus frutescens* (L.) Br. | Apocynaceae | | Wp | Asthma, dysentery, delirium, bronchitis | Sh |
| 485. | *Impatiens racemosa* DC. | Balsaminaceae | Chunchuni | Sd | Cold, cough | Herb |
| 486. | *Impatiens sulcata* Wall. | Balsaminaceae | Kwal, Chaul | Lf, st | Pimples, eczema, itching | Herb |

*Contd...*

**Appendix–Contd...**

| Sl.No | Species | Family | Local Name | Plant Used | Important Uses | Life Form |
|---|---|---|---|---|---|---|
| 487. | *Imperata cylindrica* (L.) Beauv. | Poaceae | Sirau | Rt | Tonic | Herb |
| 488. | *Indigofera cassioides* Rottler ex DC. | Fabaceae | Saknya | Lf | Malarial fever | Sh |
| 489. | *Indigofera heterantha* Wall. ex Brandis | Fabaceae | Saknya | Lf | Diarrhoea, dysentery, cough | Sh |
| 490. | *Indigofera linifolia* (L. f.) Retz. | Fabaceae | | Wp | Sores, wounds | Herb |
| 491. | *Indigofera prostrata* Willd. | Fabaceae | | Sd | Rheumatism | Herb |
| 492. | *Indigofera tinctoria* L. | Fabaceae | | Lf, rt | Liver disorder, fever, ulcer, wounds | Sh |
| 493. | *Indoneesiella echioides* (L.) Sreemadhavan | Acanthaceae | Kalmegh | Shoot | Scorpion bite, liver tonic | Herb |
| 494. | *Inula cappa* (Buch.-Ham. ex D. Don) DC. | Asteraceae | Athhu | Rt | Suppressed urination | Sh |
| 495. | *Inula cuspidata* (DC.) Cl. | Asteraceae | Jhuri | Rt | Dyspepsia, colic | Sh |
| 496. | *Inula obtusifolia* Kern. | Asteraceae | | Wp | Headache | Herb |
| 497. | *Iphigenia indica* (L.) Gray | Liliaceae | | Rt | Colic | Herb |
| 498. | *Ipomoea alba* L. | Convolvulaceae | Dudhiyakalmi | Bk | Purgative | Herb |
| 499. | *Ipomoea cairica* (L.) Sweet | Convolvulaceae | Neeli bel | Sd | Purgative | Herb |
| 500. | *Ipomoea eriocarpa* R. Br. | Convolvulaceae | | Shoot | Rheumatic pain, wounds | Herb |
| 501. | *Ipomoea muricata* (L.) Jacquin | Convolvulaceae | Michai | Sd | Constipation, fever | Herb |
| 502. | *Ipomoea nil* (L.) Roth | Convolvulaceae | Kaladana | Sd | Fever, constipation | Climb H |
| 503. | *Ipomoea pes-tigridis* L. | Convolvulaceae | Ghiabati | Rt | Snake bite | Herb |
| 504. | *Ipomoea purpurea* (L.) Roth | Convolvulaceae | Kaphlagla | Sd, lf | Purgative | Herb |

*Contd...*

**Appendix–Contd...**

| Sl.No. | Species | Family | Local Name | Plant Used | Important Uses | Life Form |
|---|---|---|---|---|---|---|
| 505. | *Iris kumaonensis* Wall. | Iridaceae | | Sd, rt, lf | Stomachic, scabies, fever | Herb |
| 506. | *Ixora arborea* Roxb. ex Sm. | Rubiaceae | | Rt, fr | Child birth, eczema, spider poison | Sh |
| 507. | *Jasminum arborescens* Roxb. | Oleaceae | Chameli | Lf | Bronchitis | Sh |
| 508. | *Jasminum dispermum* Wall. | Oleaceae | Basilla | Lf | Cut, wounds | Sh |
| 509. | *Jasminum humile* L. | Oleaceae | Pili chameli | Bk, rt | Skin, blood, and heart diseases | Sh |
| 510. | *Jasminum officinale* L. | Oleaceae | Champa | Rt | Ringworm infection | Sh |
| 511. | *Jatropha curcas* L. | Euphorbiaceae | Safed arand | Sd | Rheumatism, skin diseases | Sh |
| 512. | *Juglans regia* L. | Juglandaceae | Akhrot | Bk, lf, fr | Toothache, frost bite | Tree |
| 513. | *Juniperus communis* L. | Cupressaceae | Bedaru | Lf | Kindney trouble | Sh |
| 514. | *Jurinea macrocephala* (Royle) Aswal and Goal | Asteraceae | Dhoop | Rt | Antiseptic, colic, fever | Herb |
| 515. | *Kalanchoe integra* (Medikus) Kuntze | Crassulaceae | Bish-kobra | Lf | Purgative | Herb |
| 516. | *Kickxia ramosissima* (Wall.) Janch. | Scrophulariaceae | | Wp | Diabetes | Herb |
| 517. | *Kydia calycina* Roxb. | Malvaceae | Phuilau | Bk | Body swelling | Tree |
| 518. | *Lablab purpureus* (L.) Sw. | Fabaceae | Sem | Rt, lf | Cough | Herb |
| 519. | *Lagenaria siceraria* Standl. | Cucurbitaceae | Lauki | Fr, lf | Jaundice, cracks | Herb |
| 520. | *Lamium album* L. | Lamiaceae | Tilka | Wp | Gynacological disorder | Herb |
| 521. | *Lannea coromandelica* (Houttuyn) Merrill | Anacardiaceae | Kalmina | Bk | Diarrhoea | Tree |
| 522. | *Lantana camera* L. | Verbenaceae | Kuri | Fr, lf | Skin ailments | Sh |

*Contd...*

**Appendix–Contd...**

| Sl.No. | Species | Family | Local Name | Plant Used | Important Uses | Life Form |
|---|---|---|---|---|---|---|
| 523. | *Launaea acaulis* (Roxb.) Babccock ex Kerr | Asteraceae | Dudhliya | Rt | Diarrhoea | Herb |
| 524. | *Launea acaulis* (Roxb.) Kerr. | Asteraceae | | Rt | Urinary complaints | Herb |
| 525. | *Launea procumbens* (Roxb.) Ram. and Raj. | Asteraceae | | Lf | Fever | Herb |
| 526. | *Lawsonia inermis* L. | Lythraceae | Mehandi | Lf | Cut, wounds | Sh |
| 527. | *Leea asiatica* (L.) Rid. | Leeaceae | | Fl, rt | Urinary complaints, snake bite, wounds | Herb |
| 528. | *Lens esculenta* Moench. | Fabaceae | Masur | Sd | Skin diseases | Herb |
| 529. | *Leonotis nepetaefolia* Br. | Lamiaceae | | Fl, sd | Burns, cramps, cut, eczema | Herb |
| 530. | *Leonurus japonicus* Houtt. | Lamiaceae | | Wp | Tonic | Herb |
| 531. | *Lepidagathis cuspidata* Nees | Acanthaceae | Kandya | Rt | Fever | Sh |
| 532. | *Lepidium apetalum* Willd. | Brassicaceae | | Wp | Skin diseases | Herb |
| 533. | *Lepidium sativum* L. | Brassicaceae | | Wp | Stomachache, urinary disorder, asthma | Herb |
| 534. | *Leptadenia reticulata* (Retz.) Wight and Arn. | Asclepiadaceae | Dori | Lf, rt | Antiseptic, skin diseases | Sh |
| 535. | *Leptodermis lanceolata* Wall. | Rubiaceae | Padera | Fl | Headache | Sh |
| 536. | *Leucas cephalotes* (Roth) Sprengel | Lamiaceae | Gumba, dronpushpi | Wp | Antiseptic, snake bite | Herb |
| 537. | *Leucas indica* (L.) R.Br. ex Vatke | Lamiaceae | Guma | Lf | Wounds, sores | Herb |
| 538. | *Leucas lanata* Benth. | Lamiaceae | Bis-kapra, gumma | Shoot | Cough | Herb |

*Contd...*

**Appendix–Contd...**

| Sl.No. | Species | Family | Local Name | Plant Used | Important Uses | Life Form |
|---|---|---|---|---|---|---|
| 539. | *Leucas plukeneti* (Roth.) Spr. | Lamiaceae | | Lf, rt, sd | Headache, constipation, skin diseases | Herb |
| 540. | *Lilium wallichianum* Schultes | Liliaceae | Findura | Fl | Fever | Herb |
| 541. | *Limnophila rugosa* (Roth.) Merr. | Scrophulariaceae | | Wp | Dysentery | Herb |
| 542. | *Limonia acidissima* L. | Rutaceae | | Rt, bk, fr | Bodyache, itching, tonic | Tree |
| 543. | *Lindenbergia grandiflora* (Buch.-Ham. ex D. Don) Benth. | Scrophulariaceae | Vasanta | Shoot | Skin ailments | Un Sh |
| 544. | *Lindenbergia indica* (L.) Vatke | Scrophulariaceae | Makria jhar | Lf | Cut, wounds, bronchitis | Herb |
| 545. | *Lindera latifolia* Hk.f. | Lauraceae | | Bk | Wounds | Tree |
| 546. | *Linum usitatissimum* L. | Linaceae | Alsi | Sd | Cough, wounds | Herb |
| 547. | *Lippia nodiflora* (L.) A. Rich. | Verbenaceae | | Wp | Bone fracture | Herb |
| 548. | *Litsea glutinosa* (Lour.) Robins. | Lauraceae | Singrau | Bk | Bone fracture, cold, dysentery, sprains | Tree |
| 549. | *Lomatogonium carinthiacum* (Wulf.) Br. | Gentianaceae | | Wp | Antipyretic, blood purification, cough | Herb |
| 550. | *Lonicera myrtillus* Hk. f. and Th. | Caprifoliaceae | | Fr | Constipation | Sh |
| 551. | *Luffa acutangula* (L.) Roxb. | Cucurbitaceae | Turai | Fr | Fever, scabies, snake bite | Herb |
| 552. | *Lyonia ovalifolia* (Wall.) Drude | Ericaceae | Anyar, aiyaar | Wp | Wounds, boils | Tree |
| 553. | *Lysimachia lobelioides* Wall. | Primulaceae | | Lf | Bodyache | Herb |
| 554. | *Macrotyloma uniflorum* (Lam.) Verdc. | Fabaceae | Gaheth | Sd | Leucorrhoea | Herb |
| 555. | *Madhuca longifolia* (Koen.) Mac. | Sapotaceae | Mahua | Bk, fl, lf | Snake bite, cough, diabetes, ulcer | Tree |

Contd...

**Appendix–Contd...**

| Sl.No. | Species | Family | Local Name | Plant Used | Important Uses | Life Form |
|---|---|---|---|---|---|---|
| 556. | *Maharanga emodi* (Wall.) DC. | Boraginaceae | | Wp | Skin diseases, urinary trouble | Herb |
| 557. | *Mahonia nepalensis* DC. | Berberidaceae | | Bk | Eye complaints, fever, skin diseases | Sh |
| 558. | *Maianthemum purpureum* (Wall.) Frankie | Liliaceae | Lamnyat | Lf | Dysmenorrhoea | Herb |
| 559. | *Malaxis acuminata* D. Don | Orchidaceae | Jeevak | Bb | Bronchitis, tonic | Herb |
| 560. | *Malaxis muscifera* (Lindley) Kuntze | Orchidaceae | Jeevak bhed | Bb | Tonic | Herb |
| 561. | *Mallotus philippensis* (Lam.) Muell.-Arg. | Euphorbiaceae | Ruin | Bk | Purgative | Tree |
| 562. | *Malva rotundifolia* L. | Malvaceae | | Wp | Urinary complaints | Herb |
| 563. | *Malva verticillata* L. | Malvaceae | Sochli | Lf, rt | Piles, ulcer, urinary trouble | Herb |
| 564. | *Malvastrum coromendalianum* Garcke | Malvaceae | Suchi | Lf | Wounds, sprain, jaundice, dysentery | Un Sh |
| 565. | *Mangifera indica* L. | Anacardiaceae | Aam | Sd, bk | Diarrhoea, haemorrhage, scabies, tonic | Tree |
| 566. | *Marsdenia roylei* Wt. | Asclepiadaceae | | Rt | Cold, eye complaints | Sh |
| 567. | *Marsdenia tanacissima* Moon | Asclepiadaceae | | Rt | Stomachache, fever, cough, urinary trouble | Sh |
| 568. | *Martynia annua* L. | Martyniaceae | Bichhwa, Bichu | Lf, fr | Epilepsy, cough | Un Sh |
| 569. | *Maytenus royleana* (Lawson) Cufodontis | Celastraceae | Gwaldari | Lf | Dysentery | Sh |
| 570. | *Meconopsis aculeata* Royle | Papaveraceae | | Wp | Backache, colic, tonic | Herb |

Contd...

**Appendix–Contd...**

| *Sl.No.* | *Species* | *Family* | *Local Name* | *Plant Used* | *Important Uses* | *Life Form* |
|---|---|---|---|---|---|---|
| 571. | *Megacarpaea polyandra* Benth. | Brassicaceae | | Wp | Fever, stomach trouble | Herb |
| 572. | *Melia azedarach* L. | Meliaceae | Daikan | Fr, lf | Antiseptic, abortifacient, rheumatic pain | Tree |
| 573. | *Melilotus indica* (L.) Allioni | Fabaceae | Ban-methi | Sd | Diarrhoea, dysentery | Herb |
| 574. | *Mentha arvensis* L. | Lamiaceae | Pudeena | Lf | Indigestion, vomiting | Herb |
| 575. | *Mentha longifolia* (L.) Hudson | Lamiaceae | Pudeena | Wp | Indigestion, vomiting | Herb |
| 576. | *Mentha piperita* L. | Lamiaceae | Pipermint | Lf, lf | Malarial fever, indigestion | Herb |
| 577. | *Micromeria biflora* (Buch.-Ham. ex D. Don) Benth. | Lamiaceae | Ban-ajwain | Lf | Gastric disorder | Herb |
| 578. | *Miliusa velutina* (Dunal) Hk. f. and Th. | Annonaceae | | Lf | Headache | Tree |
| 579. | *Millettia extensa* (Benth.) Baker | Fabaceae | | Rt | Sores, toothache | Sh |
| 580. | *Mimosa himalayana* Gamble | Mimosaceae | Kingrei | Lf | Cold, cough, bronchitis, urinary complaints | Sh |
| 581. | *Mimosa pudica* L. | Mimosaceae | Chui-mui | Rt | Snakebite, digestive trouble | Un Sh |
| 582. | *Mirabilis jalapa* L. | Nyctanginaceae | Gulabans | Tuber | Piles, child birth | Herb |
| 583. | *Mitragyna parvifolia* (Roxb.) Korthals | Rubiaceae | Phaldu | Sd | Purgative | Tree |
| 584. | *Mollugo pentaphylla* L. | Molluginaceae | | Wp | Antiseptic, stomachache | Herb |
| 585. | *Momordica charantia* L. | Cucurbitaceae | Karela | Lf, sd, fr, rt | Diabetes, eczema, malaria | Herb |
| 586. | *Momordica dioica* Roxb. ex Willd. | Cucurbitaceae | Kankora | Wp | Asthma, piles, headache, delirium | Herb |
| 587. | *Monochoria hastata* (L.) Solms-Laubach | Pontederiaceae | Naka | Rh | Bronchitis | Herb |

*Contd...*

**Appendix–Contd...**

| Sl.No. | Species | Famlly | Local Name | Plant Used | Important Uses | Life Form |
|---|---|---|---|---|---|---|
| 588. | *Morina coulteriana* Royle | Morinaceae | | Wp | Wounds | Herb |
| 589. | *Morina longifolia* Wall. ex DC. | Morinaceae | Biskandroo | Rt | Wounds, boils | Herb |
| 590. | *Moringa oleifera* Lam. | Moringaceae | Sunara | Lf, fl, fr | Rheumatism, ascites, circulatory disorder | Tree |
| 591. | *Morus alva* L. | Moraceae | Shahtoot | Fr, bk | Dyspepsia, purgative, sore throat | Tree |
| 592. | *Mucuna pruriens* (L.) DC. | Fabaceae | | Fr, sd | Aphrodisiac, ulcer, madness, snake bite | Sh |
| 593. | *Mukia maderaspatara* (L.) M. Roemer | Cucurbitaceae | Ban kakri | Fr | Malarial fever, vomiting, urinary disorder | Herb |
| 594. | *Murdannia nudiflora* (L.) Brenan | Commelinaceae | Kansura | Shoot | Burns, giddiness, tonic | Herb |
| 595. | *Murraya koenigii* (L.) Spr. | Rutaceae | Gandela | Bk, rt | Diarrhoea, dysentery, malarial fever | Sh |
| 596. | *Murraya paniculata* (L.) Jack | Rutaceae | Machula | Lf | Cough, cold | Sh |
| 597. | *Musa balbisiana* Colla | Musaceae | Kela | Fr | Indigestion | Herb |
| 598. | *Myrica esculenta* Buch.-Ham ex D.Don | Myricaceae | Kaphal | Bk, fr | Asthma, cholera, cough, fever, menorrhoea | Tree |
| 599. | *Myricaria coulteriana* Royle | Tamaricaceae | | Lf | Wounds | Sh |
| 600. | *Myrsine serrata* Wall. | Myrsinaceae | | Fr, sd, bk | Wounds, skin diseases | Sh |
| 601. | *Nardostachys grandiflora* DC. | Valerianaceae | Masi | Rt | Blood purification, cough, diuretic, snake bite | Herb |
| 602. | *Nardostachys jatamansi* (Don) DC. | Valerianaceae | Jatamansi | Rt | Blood purification, cough, diuretic, snake bite | Herb |

*Contd...*

**Appendix–Contd...**

| Sl.No. | Species | Family | Local Name | Plant Used | Important Uses | Life Form |
|---|---|---|---|---|---|---|
| 603. | *Naringi crenulata* (Roxb.) Nicolson | Rutaceae | Kathbel | Fr | Snake bite | Tree |
| 604. | *Nasturtium officinale* R. Br. | Brassicaceae | | Shoot | Constipation, goitre | Herb |
| 605. | *Neolitsea pallens* (D. Don) Momiyama and Hara | Lauraceae | Bilaru | Fr | Scabies, eczema | Tree |
| 606. | *Nepeta ciliaris* Wall. ex Benth. | Lamiaceae | Nueet | Lf, Sd | Fever | Herb |
| 607. | *Nepeta elliptica* Royle ex Benth. | Lamiaceae | Zoofa | Sd | Digestive disorder | Herb |
| 608. | *Nepeta eriostachya* Benth. | Lamiaceae | | Wp | Eye complaints | Herb |
| 609. | *Nepeta glutinosa* Benth. | Lamiaceae | | Wp | Pneumonia, fever | Herb |
| 610. | *Nepeta leucophylla* Benth. | Lamiaceae | Karda | Lf | Malarial fever | Un Sh |
| 611. | *Nepeta royleana* Stew. | Lamiaceae | | Wp | Brain tonic, madness | Herb |
| 612. | *Neptunia triquetra* Benth. | Mimosaceae | | Rt | Dysentery | Herb |
| 613. | *Nerium oleander* L. | Apocynaceae | Kaner | Lf, rt | Skin diseases | Sh |
| 614. | *Nervilia grammieana* (Hk. f.) Schlechter | Orchidaceae | | Rt | Bodyache, wounds | Herb |
| 615. | *Nicotiana plumbaginifolia* Viv. | Solanaceae | Jangli tamakoo | Lf | Skin diseases | Herb |
| 616. | *Nicotiana tabacum* L. | Solanaceae | Tamakoo | Lf, sd | Toothache, wounds, itching | Herb |
| 617. | *Nigella sativa* L. | Ranunculaceae | Kalonji | Sd | Constipation, dysentery, asthma | Herb |
| 618. | *Nyctanthes arbor-tristis* L. | Oleaceae | Kura, Harsingar | Lf | Arthritis | Tree |
| 619. | *Nymphaea stellata* Willd. | Nymphaeaceae | Kamal | Lf, tuber | Child birth | Herb |
| 620. | *Ochna obtusa* DC. | Ochnaceae | | Rt | Dysentery, fever | Tree |

*Contd...*

**Appendix–Contd...**

| Sl.No. | Species | Family | Local Name | Plant Used | Important Uses | Life Form |
|---|---|---|---|---|---|---|
| 621. | *Ocimum americanum* L. | Lamiaceae | Ban tulsi | Lf, rt, sd | Diarrhoea, cough, hysteria, headache | Herb |
| 622. | *Ocimum basilicum* L. | Lamiaceae | Murya | Lf | Fever, cough | Herb |
| 623. | *Ocimum gratissimum* L. | Lamiaceae | Ram-tulsi | Shoot | Tonic, headache, antiseptic, cough | Sh |
| 624. | *Ocimum kilimandscharicum* L. | Lamiaceae | | Lf | Fever, cough | Herb |
| 625. | *Ocimum sanctum* L. | Lamiaceae | Tulsi | Wp | Bronchitis, constipation, headache, vomiting | Herb |
| 626. | *Olea ferruginea* Royle | Oleaceae | | Fr | Toothache | Tree |
| 627. | *Olea glandulifera* Wall. ex G. Don | Oleaceae | Gair, Galdu | Bk | Fever | Tree |
| 628. | *Onosma hispidum* Wall. ex Don | Boraginaceae | Laljari | Wp | Wounds, cut, blood purification | Herb |
| 629. | *Operculina turpethum* (L.) Silva | Convolvulaceae | | Rt | Bodyache | Herb |
| 630. | *Ophioglossum vulgatum* L. | Ophioglossaceae | | Rh | Boils, wounds | Herb |
| 631. | *Origanum vulgare* L. | Lamiaceae | Ban-tulsi | Wp | Diarrhoea, bronchitis | Un Sh |
| 632. | *Oroxylum indicum* (L.) Ventenat | Bignoniaceae | Tantia | Rt | Fever, dysentery, diarrhoea, tonic | Tree |
| 633. | *Osbeckia stellata* Buch.-Ham. ex D. Don | Melastomataceae | Kukur | Lf | Oral aphthae | Sh |
| 634. | *Osyris wightiana* Wall. ex Wight | Santalaceae | Bakroliya | Lf | Blood purification | Sh |
| 635. | *Ougeinia oojeinensis* (Roxb.) Hochr. | Fabaceae | | Bk | Bronchitis, asthma, diarrhoea | Tree |
| 636. | *Oxalis corniculata* L. | Oxalidaceae | Bilmoru | Wp | Conjunctivitis, cataract, indigestion, fever | Herb |

*Contd...*

**Appendix–Contd...**

| *Sl.No.* | *Species* | *Family* | *Local Name* | *Plant Used* | *Important Uses* | *Life Form* |
|---|---|---|---|---|---|---|
| 637. | *Oxyria digyna* (L.) Hill. | Polygonaceae | | Wp | Fever, indigestiion | Herb |
| 638. | *Paeonia emodi* Wall. ex Royle | Paeoniaceae | Chandrayan | Fl | Cuts, ulcers, wounds, dysentery, colic, dropsy, epilepsy, mental disorder | |
| 639. | *Pandanus odoratissimus* L. | Pandanaceae | Keura | Rt | Snake bite, arthritis, skin diseases | Sh |
| 640. | *Papaver somniferum* L. | Papaveraceae | Aphim, post | Latex | Bodyache, dysentery | Herb |
| 641. | *Paris polyphylla* J.E. Smith | Liliaceae | Satwa | Rh | Diarrhoea, fever, anthelmintic | Herb |
| 642. | *Parnassia nubicola* Wall. ex Royle | Parnassaceae | Phutkya | Tuber | Snakebite | Herb |
| 643. | *Parnassia pusilla* Hk. f. | Parnassaceae | | Rt | Wounds | Herb |
| 644. | *Parochaetus communis* Buch.-Ham. ex D. Don | Fabaceae | Tripatri | Wp | Acidity, gastric problem, cut, wounds | Herb |
| 645. | *Paspalum scrobiculatum* L. | Poaceae | Paplya | Rt | Pairiful urination | Herb |
| 646. | *Passiflora foetida* L. | Passifloraceae | Gudsar, Gharibel | Sd, Lf | Tonic, cold and cough | Herb |
| 647. | *Pavetta indica* L. | Rubiaceae | Angari | Rt, lf | Jaundice, dropsy | Sh |
| 648. | *Pecteilis gigantea* (Sm.) Rafin | Orchidaceae | | Rt | Fever, cold | Herb |
| 649. | *Pedicularis pectinata* Wall. ex Benth. | Scrophulariaceae | | Wp | Bodyache | Herb |
| 650. | *Pentapanax parasiticus* Seem (Ham. ex D. Don) | Araliaceae | | | Wounds | Wood Cl |
| 651. | *Pergularia daemia* (Forsk.) Chiovenda | Asclepiadaceae | Utraun, Sagovani | Lf | Snake bite, asthma, bronchitis | Sh |

*Contd...*

**Appendix–Contd...**

| Sl.No. | Species | Family | Local Name | Plant Used | Important Uses | Life Form |
|---|---|---|---|---|---|---|
| 652. | *Perilla frutescens* (L.) Britton | Lamiaceae | Bhangjeera | Lf | Arthritis, bronchitis, cough | Herb |
| 653. | *Periploca calophylla* (Wight) Falconer | Asclepiadaceae | Par | Latex | Tumor, skin eruption | Sh |
| 654. | *Peristrophe paniculata* (Forsk.) Brumitt | Acanthaceae | Kaknadi | Shoot | Wounds | Herb |
| 655. | *Phacelurus speciosus* (Steudel) Hubbard | Poaceae | Ainma | Shoot | Intestinal worms | Herb |
| 656. | *Phalaris minor* Retz. | Poaceae | Phulla | Rt | Wounds | Herb |
| 657. | *Phlomis bracteosa* Royle | Lamiaceae | | Fl | Eye complaints | Herb |
| 658. | *Phoebe lanceolata* (Nees) Nees | Lauraceae | Kaula | Fr | Wounds, sores | Tree |
| 659. | *Phoenix acaulis* Buch.-Ham. ex Roxb. | Arecaceae | Khajuri | Rt | Bronchitis, cough, cold, stomach disorder | Tree |
| 660. | *Phoenix humilis* Royle | Arecaceae | Khajoor | Lf, rt | Sprains | Tree |
| 661. | *Phoenix sylvestris* Roxb. | Arecaceae | Khajoor | St, lf | Toothache, dysentary, diarrhoea | Tree |
| 662. | *Pholidota articulata* Lindley | Orchidaceae | Jeewanti | Wp | Tonic, body pain | Herb |
| 663. | *Phyla nodiflora* (L.) Greene | Verbenaceae | Jal pipali | Shoot | Menstrual complaints | Herb |
| 664. | *Phyllanthus amarus* Schum. and Thonn. | Euphorbiaceae | Jarmala | Shoot | Astringent, diuretic, stomachache | Herb |
| 665. | *Phyllanthus emblica* L. | Euphorbiaceae | Aonla | Fr, Bk | Intestinal disorder, throat ache, blood purifier | Tree |
| 666. | *Phyllanthus virgatus* G. Forster | Euphorbiaceae | Bhiuavate | Sd, fr | Gonorrhoea | Herb |

Contd...

**Appendix–Contd...**

| Sl.No. | Species | Family | Local Name | Plant Used | Important Uses | Life Form |
|---|---|---|---|---|---|---|
| 667. | *Physalis angulata* L. | Solanaceae | | Lf, fr | Gastric disorder, earache | Herb |
| 668. | *Physalis minima* L. | Solanaceae | | Wp | Gastric disorder, earache | Herb |
| 669. | *Physalis peruviana* L. | Solanaceae | Rashbhari | Lf | Stomach disorder | Herb |
| 670. | *Physochlaina prealta* (Decne) Miers. | Solanaceae | | Wp | Liver complaints, ulcer, epilepsy | Herb |
| 671. | *Phytolacca acinosa* Roxb. | Phytolaccaceae | | Wp | Bodyache | Herb |
| 672. | *Picea smithiana* (Wall.) Boiss. | Pinaceae | | Resin | Cuts, bodyache, sores | Tree |
| 673. | *Picrasma quassioides* (D. Don) Bennett | Simaroubaceae | Karui | St | Fever, cough, diarrhoea | Tree |
| 674. | *Picrorhiza kurrooa* Benth. | Scrophulariaceae | Katuki | Rt | Fever, headache, anaemia, jaundice, asthma | Herb |
| 675. | *Pimpinella acuminata* (Edgew.) Cl. | Apiaceae | Raulee | St, Lf | Diarrhoea, dysentery | Herb |
| 676. | *Pimpinella diversifolia* DC. | Apiaceae | Phori | Wp | Cold, cough, digestive disorder | Herb |
| 677. | *Pinus roxburghii* Sarg. | Pinaceae | Kulai, chir | Resin | Bone fracture, cut, wounds | Tree |
| 678. | *Pinus wallichiana* Jacks. | Pinaceae | Kail | Resin, bk | Ulcer, dislocated joints | Tree |
| 679. | *Piper cubeca* L. | Piperaceae | | Fr | Bronchitis, asthma, fever | Herb |
| 680. | *Pistacia integerrima* (Stew.) Rech. f. | Pistaciaceae | | Lf | Snake bite, dysentery | Tree |
| 681. | *Pistacia khinjuk* Stock | Pistaciaceae | Kakra-singi | Lf | Cough, fever | Tree |
| 682. | *Pisum sativum* L. | Fabaceae | Matar | Sd | Diabetes | Herb |
| 683. | *Pithecillobium dulce* (Roxb.) Benth. | Mimosaceae | Jangal jalebi | Lf | Dog bite | Herb |

Contd...

**Appendix–Contd...**

| Sl.No. | Species | Family | Local Namo | Plant Used | Important Uses | Life Form |
|---|---|---|---|---|---|---|
| 684. | *Pittosporum eriocarpum* Royle | Pittosporaceae | Raduthia | Rt, bk | Bronchitis, rheumatic swelling | Tree |
| 685. | *Pittosporum nepaulense* (DC.) Rehder and Wilson | Pittosporaceae | Tumri, Raini | Bk | Bronchitis, skin ailments | Tree |
| 686. | *Plantago depressa* Willd. | Plantaginaceae | Isabgol | Shoot | Digestive troubles, cut and wounds | Herb |
| 687. | *Plantago erosa* Wall. | Plantaginaceae | Isabgol | Sd, rt | Digestive troubles, cut and wounds | Herb |
| 688. | *Plantago himalaica* Pilg. | Plantaginaceae | | Wp | Diarrhoea, dysentery | Herb |
| 689. | *Plantago major* L. | Plantaginaceae | Isabgol | Wp, sd | Burns, cut, wounds, fever, dysentery | Herb |
| 690. | *Pleurospermum angelicoides* (DC.) Cl. | Apiaceae | | Rt | Cough, cold, indigestion | Herb |
| 691. | *Pleurospermum candollii* (DC.) Cl. | Apiaceae | | Fr | Dysentery, stomachache | Herb |
| 692. | *Pluchea lanceolata* (DC.) Cl. | Asteraceae | | Rt | Cold | Herb |
| 693. | *Plumbago zeylanica* L. | Plumbaginaceae | | Lf, rt | Diarrhoea, dysentery, dyspepsia | Herb |
| 694. | *Podophyllum hexandrum* Royle | Podophyllaceae | Bankakdi | Rh, fr | Cancer, fever, gastric ulcer | Herb |
| 695. | *Pogostemon benghalense* (Burm. f.) Kuntze | Lamiaceae | Kala-basingu, Lujrya | Lf | Fever | Sh |
| 696. | *Polycarpaea corymbosa* (L.) Lam. | Caryophyllaceae | Bugyale | Bud | Jaundice, arthritis | Herb |
| 697. | *Polygala arvensis* Willd. | Polygalaceae | Sanjivani | Shoot | Paralysis | Herb |

*Contd...*

**Appendix–Contd...**

| Sl.No. | Species | Family | Local Name | Plant Used | Important Uses | Life Form |
|---|---|---|---|---|---|---|
| 698. | *Polygala crotalarioides* Buch.-Ham ex DC. | Polygalaceae | | Rt, lf | Snake bite, cough and cold | Herb |
| 699. | *Polygala sibirica* L. | Polygalaceae | Mardoi | Rt | Cough and cold | Herb |
| 700. | *Polygonatum cirrhifolium* (Wall.) Royle | Liliaceae | Mahameda | Rt | Aphrodisiac, blood purifier, cuts, wounds | Herb |
| 701. | *Polygonatum multiflorum* (L.) Allioni | Liliaceae | Khaul | Rt | Urinary and genital disorders | Herb |
| 702. | *Polygonatum verticillatum* (L.) All. | Liliaceae | Salam mishri | Rt | Aphrodisiac, nervine tonic, tonic, wound | Herb |
| 703. | *Polygonum nepalense* Meisn. | Polygonaceae | | Wp | Swelling | Herb |
| 704. | *Polygonum rumicifolium* Roy | Polygonaceae | | Lf, rt | Antidote for aconite poison, headache | Herb |
| 705. | *Polygonum viviparum* L. | Polygonaceae | | Wp | Dysentery, ulcer | Herb |
| 706. | *Pongamia pinnata* (L.) Pierre | Fabaceae | | Sd, fr | Bronchitis, cough, eczema, itching, leprosy | Tree |
| 707. | *Populus cilicata* Wall. | Salicaceae | Syan | Bk | Tonic, bone fracture | Tree |
| 708. | *Porana paniculata* Roxb. | Convolvulaceae | | Rt | Cardic trouble | Sh |
| 709. | *Portulaca oleracea* L. | Portulacaceae | | Wp | Headache, fever | Herb |
| 710. | *Potentilla fulgens* Wall ex Hk. | Rosaceae | Bajardanti | Rt | Toothache, stomatitis, aphthae | Herb |
| 711. | *Potentilla sundaica* (Blume) Kuntze | Rosaceae | | Rt, St | Snakebite, itching | Herb |
| 712. | *Potentilla atrosanguinea* Lodd. | Rosaceae | | Lf | Wounds | Herb |
| 713. | *Potentilla fruticosa* L. *var. rigida* (Lehm.) Wolf. | Rosaceae | | Lf | Toothache, wounds | Herb |

*Contd...*

**Appendix–Contd...**

| Sl.No. | Species | Family | Local Name | Plant Used | Important Uses | Life Form |
|---|---|---|---|---|---|---|
| 714. | *Potentilla gerardiana* Lindl. ex Lehm. | Rosaceae | Bajardanti | Rt | Wounds | Horb |
| 715. | *Premna barbata* Wall. ex Schauer | Verbenaceae | Bhakhara | Lf | Rheumatic arthritis | Sh |
| 716. | *Premna latifolia* Roxb. | Verbenaceae | Sitaphal | Bk, rt | Ulcer, gonorhoea | Sh |
| 717. | *Prenanthes brunoniana* Wall. ex DC. | Asteraceae | Nimula | Lf | Wounds | Herb |
| 718. | *Prenanthes violaefolia* Decne. | Asteraceae | Pitlya | Lf | Dysmenorrhoea | Herb |
| 719. | *Principia utilis* Royle | Rosaceae | Bhainkal | Sd, fr, rt | Rheumatic pain, diarrhoea | Sh |
| 720. | *Prunella vulgaris* L. | Lamiaceae | | Wp | Gastric disorder | Herb |
| 721. | *Prunus armeniaca* L. | Rosaceae | Chulu | Sd | Bodyache | Tree |
| 722. | *Prunus cerasoides* D. Don | Rosaceae | Panyyan | Bk | Body swelling | Tree |
| 723. | *Prunus cornuta* (Wall. ex Royle) Steudel | Rosaceae | Jamna | Sd, fr | Neuralgic pains | Tree |
| 724. | *Prunus persica* (L.) Batsch | Rosaceae | Aru | Lf, Bk | Cold and cough, suppressed urination | Tree |
| 725. | *Psidium guajava* L. | Myrtaceae | Amrood | Bk, lf | Throat infection, diarrhoea | Tree |
| 726. | *Pterocarpus marsupium* Roxb. | Fabaceae | | Bk | Bodyache, diabetes, dysentery, skin ailment | Tree |
| 727. | *Pueraria tuberosa* (Willd.) DC. | Fabaceae | | Rt | Bodyache, asthma, cholera, ulcer | Sh |
| 728. | *Punica granatum* L. | Punicaceae | Dalmya, anar | Rt, st, fr | Cough, cold, jaundice, pimples, blood purifier | Tree |
| 729. | *Pupalia lappacea* (L.) Juss. | Amaranthaceae | Nagdamini | Fr | Skin ailments | Un Sh |

*Contd...*

**Appendix–Contd...**

| Sl.No. | Species | Family | Local Name | Plant Used | Important Uses | Life Form |
|---|---|---|---|---|---|---|
| 730. | *Pygmaeopremna herbacea* (Roxb.) Molden. | Verbenaceae | | Wp | Ulcer, rheumatic pain | Sh |
| 731. | *Pyrus pashia* Buch.-Ham. | Rosaceae | Melu | Fr | Digestive disorder | Sh |
| 732. | *Quercus leucho-trichophora* Camus. | Fabaceae | Banj | Sd | Scabies, urinary trouble | Tree |
| 733. | *Rabdosia rugosa* (Wall. ex Benth.) Hara | Lamiaceae | Chhenchneri | Lf | Fever | Sh |
| 734. | *Randia tetrasperma* Lamk. | Rubiaceae | | Fr, rt | Bodyache | Sh |
| 735. | *Ranunculus arvensis* L. | Ranunculaceae | Chambul | Shoot | Fever, asthma, skin ailments | Herb |
| 736. | *Ranunculus hirtellus* Royle | Ranunculaceae | Piryali | Shoot | Wounds | Herb |
| 737. | *Ranunculus sceleratus* L. | Ranunculaceae | | Lf | Eczema | Herb |
| 738. | *Raphanus sativus* L. | Brassicaceae | Muli, mula | Lf, sd | Fever, liver disorder, bronchitis | Herb |
| 739. | *Rauvolfia serpentina* (L.) Benth. ex Kurz | Apocynaceae | Sarpgandha | Rt | Epilepsy, fever, nervous disorders | Un Sh |
| 740. | *Reinwardtia indica* Dumort. | Linaceae | Phyunladi | Lf, fl | Skin ailments | Herb |
| 741. | *Rhamnus purpureus* Edgew | Rhamnaceae | Gaunta | Bk | Digestive disorder | Sh |
| 742. | *Rhamnus virgatus* Roxb. | Rhamnaceae | Choudelu | Bk, fr | Purgative, emetic, eczema | Sh |
| 743. | *Rheum australe* Don | Polygonaceae | Dolu | Rt | Asthma, bronchitis, digestive troubles, piles | Herb |
| 744. | *Rheum webbianum* Royle | Polygonaceae | Archa | Rt | Wounds, purgative, abdominal disorders | Herb |
| 745. | *Rhododendron anthopogon* Don | Ericaceae | | Lf | Cold, cough, bronchitis | Sh |

*Contd...*

**Appendix–Contd...**

| Sl.No. | Species | Family | Local Name | Plant Used | Important Uses | Life Form |
|---|---|---|---|---|---|---|
| 746. | *Rhododendron arboretum* Smith | Ericaceae | Burans | Fl. bk | Digestive and respiratory disorders | Tree |
| 747. | *Rhododendron campanulatum* Don | Ericaceae | Semroo | Rt, lf | Skin diseases, headache, fever, cough | Sh |
| 748. | *Rhus javanica* L. | Anacardiaceae | Damphela | Fr, bk | Cholera, wounds | Tree |
| 749. | *Rhus parviflora* Roxb. | Anacardiaceae | Saunla, Tungla | Lf | Cholera | Sh |
| 750. | *Rhynchostylis retusa* (L.) Bl. | Orchidaceae | | Wp | Wounds | Herb |
| 751. | *Ribes orientale* Desfont. | Grossulariaceae | Askuta | Lf | Diuretic | Sh |
| 752. | *Ricinus communis* L. | Euphorbiaceae | Arandi | Sd, lf | Purgative, cholera, hydrocele, pneumonia | Sh |
| 753. | *Rorippa indica* (L.) Hiern | Brassicaceae | Piria, chamsuru | Lf, rt | Sprains, diarrhoea | Herb |
| 754. | *Rosa brunonii* Lindley | Rosaceae | Kunja | Lf, fl | Wounds, ophthalmia | Sh |
| 755. | *Rosa macrophylla* Lindl. | Rosaceae | Dand-kunja | Fl, fr | Skin ailments | Sh |
| 756. | *Rosa sericea* Lindl. | Rosaceae | Dhurkunja | Rt, fr | Bowel complaints | Sh |
| 757. | *Rosa webbiana* Wall. | Rosaceae | | Fl, st | Hepatitis, jaundice, stomachache | Sh |
| 758. | *Roscoea alpina* Royle | Zingiberaceae | Jilsua | Lf | Tonic | Herb |
| 759. | *Roscoea procera* Wall. | Zingiberaceae | Musli | Rt | Tonic | Herb |
| 760. | *Rosularia rosulata* (Edgew.) Ohba | Crassulaceae | | Wp | Sprains | Herb |
| 761. | *Roylea cinerea* (D. Don) Baillon | Lamiaceae | Karui | Lf | Malarial fever, jaundice | Sh |
| 762. | *Rubia manjith* Roxb. | Rubiaceae | Lichkuru | Rt, st | Snake bite, tonic, dysentery | Climb H |

Contd...

**Appendix–Contd...**

| Sl.No. | Species | Family | Local Name | Plant Used | Important Uses | Life Form |
|---|---|---|---|---|---|---|
| 763. | *Rubus biflorus* Buch.-Ham. | Rosaceae | Hinsaru | Rt | Diarrhoea | Sh |
| 764. | *Rubus ellipticus* Smith | Rosaceae | Hinsalu | Rt, fr | Dysentery, malaria, stomachache | Sh |
| 765. | *Rubus nepalensis* (Hk. f.) Kuntze | Rosaceae | Gangoor | Rt | Burns | Un Sh |
| 766. | *Rumex acetosa* L. | Polygonaceae | | Lf | Stomach disorder | Herb |
| 767. | *Rumex hastatus* Don | Polygonaceae | | Lf | Burns, cuts | Herb |
| 768. | *Rumex nepalensis* Spr. | Polygonaceae | Khukhuinya | Lf | Purgative, colic | Herb |
| 769. | *Saccharum bengalensis* Retz. | Poaceae | Munja | Rt | Wounds | Herb |
| 770. | *Saccharum officinarum* L. | Poaceae | Ganna | St | Constipation | Herb |
| 771. | *Saccharum spontaneum* L. | Poaceae | Munj, Kansh | Lf | Asthma, cholera | Herb |
| 772. | *Sagina saginoides* (L.) Karst. | Caryophyllaceae | | Wp | Headache | Herb |
| 773. | *Salix tetrasperma* Roxb. | Salicaceae | Gad bhains | Bk | Fever | Sh |
| 774. | *Salvia hians* Royle ex Benth. | Lamiaceae | Ghaniya | Lf | Eczema, arthritis | Un Sh |
| 775. | *Salvia lanata* Roxb. | Lamiaceae | Ghaniya | Lf, fl | Diarrhoea, cough | Herb |
| 776. | *Salvia nubicola* Wall. ex Sweet | Lamiaceae | Ghanya | Lf, rt | Cough, wounds | Herb |
| 777. | *Sanicula elata* Buch.-Ham. ex D. Don | Apiaceae | Sinkla | Bud | Leucorrhoea | Herb |
| 778. | *Sapindus mukorossi* Gaertner | Sapindaceae | Reetha | Fr | Food poison | Tree |
| 779. | *Sapium sebiferum* (Michaux) Roxb. | Euphorbiaceae | Pahari shisam | Sd | Purgative | Tree |
| 780. | *Sarcococca saligna* (D. Don) Muell.-Arg. | Buxaceae | Piruli, Geru | Lf | Joint pain | Sh |
| 781. | *Satyrium nepalense* D. Don | Orchidaceae | Salam mishri | Rh | Aphrodisiac, diarrhoea | Herb |

*Contd...*

**Appendix–Contd...**

| Sl.No. | Species | Family | Local Name | Plant Used | Important Uses | Life Form |
|---|---|---|---|---|---|---|
| 782. | *Sauromatum venosum* (Ait.) Kunth | Araceae | | Tuber | Skin diseases, tomors | Herb |
| 783. | *Saussurea albescens* (DC.) Sch.-Bip. | Asteraceae | Pirya | Fl | Bronchitis | Un Sh |
| 784. | *Saussurea auriculata* (DC.) Sch.-Bip. | Asteraceae | | Rt | Indigestion | Herb |
| 785. | *Saussurea costus* (Falc.) Lipsch. | Asteraceae | Kut | Rt | Skin diseases, stomachache, asthma, ulcer | Un Sh |
| 786. | *Saussurea gossypiphora* D. Don | Asteraceae | | Rt | Fever | Herb |
| 787. | *Saussurea heteromalla* (D. Don) Hand.-Mazz. | Asteraceae | Murang | Lf, rt | Fever, wounds | Herb |
| 788. | *Saussurea obvallata* (DC.) Edgew. | Asteraceae | Brahmakamal | Rt | Hydrocele, cuts | Herb |
| 789. | *Saussurea simpsoniana* (Field and Gard.) Lipsch. | Asteraceae | | Fl | Fever, snake bite | Herb |
| 790. | *Schefflera venulosa* (Wt. and Am.) Harms | Araliaceae | | Lf | Skin diseases | Tree |
| 791. | *Schleichera oleosa* (Lour.) Oken. | Sapindaceae | Kusum | Br, sd | Fever, itching, pneumonia, wounds | Tree |
| 792. | *Scilla hyacinthina* (Roth.) Macb. | Liliaceae | | Lf, tuber | Bodyache, swelling | Herb |
| 793. | *Scindapsus officinalis* (Roxb.) Schott | Araceae | Gaj-peepal | Fr | Asthma, bronchitis | Climb H |
| 794. | *Scutellaria scandens* Buch.-Ham. ex D. Don | Lamiaceae | Kappu | Lf, fl | Dysentery, vomiting | Herb |
| 795. | *Securinega virosa* (Roxb. ex Willd.) Baillon | Euphorbiaceae | Rithoul | Rt | Purgative, aphrodisiac | Sh |
| 796. | *Selaginella bryopteris* (L.) Bak. | Selaginellaceae | Patharchatti | Wp | Leucorhorea, dysentery, tonic | Herb |

*Contd...*

**Appendix–Contd...**

| Sl.No. | Species | Family | Local Name | Plant Used | Important Uses | Life Form |
|---|---|---|---|---|---|---|
| 797. | *Selinum candollii* DC. | Apiaceae | Bhutkeshi | Rt | Cough, asthma | Herb |
| 798. | *Selinum vaginatum* (Edgew.) Cl. | Apiaceae | Bhutkeshi | Rt | Hysteria | Herb |
| 799. | *Semecarpus anacardium* L. | Anacardiaceae | Bhilao | Fr | Leprosy, haemorrhoids | Tree |
| 800. | *Senecio graciliflorus* DC. | Asteraceae | Kikret, Luchi | Fl | Ear infection | Herb |
| 801. | *Senecio laetus* Edgew. | Asteraceae | | Lf | Ear infection, sore throat | Herb |
| 802. | *Senecio nudicaulis* Buch.-Ham. ex D. Don | Asteraceae | Neelkanthi, Ratpati | Rt, lf | Skin ailments, fever | Herb |
| 803. | *Sesamum orientale* L. | Pedaliaceae | Til | Sd | Aphrodisiac, bodyache, dysmenorrhoea | Herb |
| 804. | *Sesbania sesban* (L.) Merr. | Fabaceae | | Lf, fl | Ulcer, pneumonia | Tree |
| 805. | *Shorea robusta* Gaertn. f. | Dipterocarpaceae | Sal | Sd, fr | Cramp, hydrocele, chest pain, carbuncle | Tree |
| 806. | *Sida acuta* Burm. f. | Malvaceae | Karenti | Rt | Leucorrhoea, gastric disorder, tonic | Herb |
| 807. | *Sida cordata* (Burm. f.) Borss. | Malvaceae | Bhiyali | Rt | Gonorrhoea, spermatorrhoea, dysentery | Herb |
| 808. | *Sida cordifolia* L. | Malvaceae | Barialas | Sd, rt | Diuretic, tonic, dysentery | Un Sh |
| 809. | *Sida rhombifolia* L. | Malvaceae | Bhiuli | Lf | Joint pain, cuts, child birth, fever, dysentery | Un Sh |
| 810. | *Sida spinosa* L. | Malvaceae | Bhiuli | Rt | Tonic, fever | Un Sh |
| 811. | *Siegesbeckia orientalis* L. | Asteraceae | Liskura | Wp | Diarrhoea, wounds | Herb |
| 812. | *Silene edgeworthii* Bocquet | Caryophyllaceae | Bakroliya | Lf | Eye diseases | Herb |

*Contd...*

**Appendix–Contd...**

| Sl.No. | Species | Family | Local Name | Plant Used | Important Uses | Life Form |
|---|---|---|---|---|---|---|
| 813. | *Silene vulgaris* (Moench) Garcke | Caryophyllaceae | Tomrya | Lf | Bronchitis, asthma | Herb |
| 814. | *Skimmia laureola* (DC.) Zucc. | Rutaceae | Kedarpatta | Lf | Scabies, antiseptic, gastric pain | Sh |
| 815. | *Smilax aspera* L. | Smilaceae | Kukurdar | Rt | Diuretic, arthritis | Wood Cl |
| 816. | *Smilax glaucophylla* Klotzsch | Smilaceae | Kukurdar | Rt | Flatulence, fever | Wood Cl |
| 817. | *Smilax ovalifolia* Roxb. | Smilaceae | Ram dana | Rt | Rheumatic swelling | Wood Cl |
| 818. | *Smilax zeylanica* L. | Smilaceae | Bhitura | Rt | Arthritis, dysentery | Wood Cl |
| 819. | *Solanum anguivi* Lam | Solanaceae | Ban bhatta | Fr | Cough, asthma, fever | Un Sh |
| 820. | *Solanum erianthum* D. Don | Solanaceae | Ban tambaku | Rt, lf, fr | Wounds, urinary and skin troubles | Sh |
| 821. | *Solanum incanum* L. | Solanaceae | Ban bhatuja | Lf | Skin diseases | Sh |
| 822. | *Solanum nigrum* L. | Solanaceae | Kirmoi, makoi | Fr, lf, sd | Fever, diarrhoea, eye disease, hydrophobia | Herb |
| 823. | *Solanum tuberosum* L. | Solanaceae | Aalu | Tuber | Burns, skin irritations | Herb |
| 824. | *Solena amplexicaulis* (Lam.) Gandhi | Cucurbitaceae | Bankakri | Rt | Digestive disorder | Climb H |
| 825. | *Solidago virgaurea* L. | Asteraceae | Pinja-phool | Wp | Asthma, kindney disorder, wounds | Herb |
| 826. | *Sonchus asper* (L.) Hill | Asteraceae | Choplya | Shoot | Blood purification, hepatitis, wounds | Herb |
| 827. | *Sonchus brachyotus* DC. | Asteraceae | Choplya | Rt | Cough, bronchitis | Herb |
| 828. | *Sonchus oleraceus* L. | Asteraceae | Dudiya | Shoot | Liver tonic | Herb |
| 829. | *Sonchus wightianus* DC. | Asteraceae | | Lf | Wounds, fever, jaundice | Herb |

*Contd...*

**Appendix–Contd...**

| *Sl.No.* | *Species* | *Family* | *Local Name* | *Plant Used* | *Important Uses* | *Life Form* |
|---|---|---|---|---|---|---|
| 830. | *Sophora mollis* (Grahm ex Royle) Baker | Fabaceae | | Sd, rt | Burns | Sh |
| 831. | *Sorbaria tomentosa* (Lindl.) Rehder | Rosaceae | Bhiloka, kyans | Fr | Asthma | Sh |
| 832. | *Sorbus aucuparia* L. | Rosaceae | Mohli | Fr | Cough and cold | Sh |
| 833. | *Sorbus cuspidata* (Spach) Hedlund | Rosaceae | Mouli | Bk | Fever | Tree |
| 834. | *Soymida febrifuga* Juss. | Meliaceae | | Bk | Chest pain, fever | Tree |
| 835. | *Spermadictyon sauveolens* Roxb. | Rubiaceae | Padera | Rt | Diarrhoea, cholera | Sh |
| 836. | *Sphaeranthus indicus* L. | Asteraceae | Lamba phool | Fl, lf | Blood purification, hysteria, gastric trouble | Herb |
| 837. | *Sphaeranthus senegalensis* DC. | Asteraceae | Gorkhmundi | Wp | Tonic | Herb |
| 838. | *Spinacea oleracea* L. | Chenopodiaceae | Palak | Lf | Kidney stones | Herb |
| 839. | *Spiraea bella* Sims | Rosaceae | Kuji | Sd | Sores, wounds | Sh |
| 840. | *Spiranthes sinensis* (Persoon) Ames | Orchidaceae | Phirlya | Shoot | Fever, tonic | Herb |
| 841. | *Spondias pinnata* (L. f.) Kurz | Anacardiaceae | Amra | Bk | Bowel complaints, ear problem | Tree |
| 842. | *Sporobolus diander* (Retz.) Beauv. | Poaceae | Sitya | Lf | Burns, pimples | Herb |
| 843. | *Stellaria media* (L.) Villars | Caryophyllaceae | Budyalu | Wp | Wounds, boils, burns | Herb |
| 844. | *Stephania glabra* (Roxb.) Miers | Menispermaceae | Gindaroo | Tuber | Psychomedicine, fever, tuberculosis, asthma | Climb H |
| 845. | *Stephania japonica* (Thunb.) Miers | Menispermaceae | | Tuber | Heart pain, dyspepsia | Climb H |
| 846. | *Sterculia urens* Roxb. | Sterculiaceae | | Rt, bk, gum | Bone fracture, tonic, joint pain | Tree |

*Contd...*

**Appendix–Contd...**

| Sl.No. | Species | Family | Local Name | Plant Used | Important Uses | Life Form |
|---|---|---|---|---|---|---|
| 847. | *Stereospermum chelonoides* (L. f.) DC. | Bignoniaceae | Padeli | Bk, rt | Tonic, nervine disorder | Tree |
| 848. | *Streblus asper* Lour. | Moraceae | Dahia | Lf | Skin diseases | Tree |
| 849. | *Striga asiatica* (L.) Kuntze | Scrophulariaceae | Agia | Shoot | Tonic | Herb |
| 850. | *Swertia alata* (Royle ex D. Don) Cl. | Gentianaceae | Chiratta | Lf, st, fl | Malarial fever | Herb |
| 851. | *Swertia angustifolia* Buch.-Ham. ex D. Don | Gentianaceae | Chiratta | Wp | Malarial fever | Herb |
| 852. | *Swertia chiraiyta* (Roxb. ex Fleming) Karsten | Gentianaceae | Chiratta | Wp | Malarial fever | Herb |
| 853. | *Swertia ciliata* (D. Don ex G. Don) Burtt. | Gentianaceae | Chiratta | Lf | Malarial fever | Herb |
| 854. | *Swertia cordata* (G. Don) Cl. | Gentianaceae | Chiratta | Wp | Malarial fever | Herb |
| 855. | *Swertia lurida* (D. Don ex G. Don) Burtt. | Gentianaceae | | Lf | Fever | Herb |
| 856. | *Swertia paniculata* Wall. | Gentianaceae | Chiratta | Wp | Malarial fever | Herb |
| 857. | *Swertia speciosa* D. Don | Gentianaceae | | Rt | Fever | Herb |
| 858. | *Symplocos chinensis* (Lour.) Druce | Symplocaceae | | Bk | Diarrhoea | Tree |
| 859. | *Symplocos racemosa* Roxb. | Symplocaceae | Lodhra | Bk | Blood purification, cough, bronchitis | Sh |
| 860. | *Synotis alatus* (Wall. ex DC.) Jeffrey and Chen | Asteraceae | Galpatiya | Shoot | Fever | Herb |
| 861. | *Syringa emodi* Wall. ex Royle | Oleaceae | Ghiya, Shafori | Sd, fl | Fever, stomachache | Tree |

*Contd...*

**Appendix–Contd...**

| *Sl.No.* | *Species* | *Family* | *Local Name* | *Plant Used* | *Important Uses* | *Life Form* |
|---|---|---|---|---|---|---|
| 862. | *Syzygium cuminii* (L.) Skeels | Myrtaceae | Jamun | Bk, fr, sd | Diabetes, anaemia, diarrhoea, dysentery | Tree |
| 863. | *Tagetes erecta* L. | Asteraceae | Genda | Fl, lf | Wounds, cut | Herb |
| 864. | *Tagetes patula* L. | Asteraceae | Genda | Lf | Skin ailments | Herb |
| 865. | *Tanacetum dolichophyllum* (Kitamura) Kitamura | Asteraceae | Guggul, Dhoop | Shoot | Headache, bodyache | Herb |
| 866. | *Tanacetum tenuifolium* Jacq. | Asteraceae | | Wp | Bodyache, headache | Herb |
| 867. | *Taraxacum officinale* Weber | Asteraceae | Kanphuliya, karatu | Wp | Migrains, hepatitis, headache | Herb |
| 868. | *Taxus baccata* L. | Taxaceae | Thuner | Lf, fr | Cancer | Tree |
| 869. | *Tecomella undulata* (D. Don) Seen | Bignoniaceae | | Bk | Skin diseases, swelling | Tree |
| 870. | *Tectona grandis* L. | Verbenaceae | Sagaun | Fl, lf | Bronchitis, urinary troubles | Tree |
| 871. | *Tephrosia purpurea* Pers. | Fabaceae | | Rt | Snake bite, blood purification, liver ailments | Herb |
| 872. | *Terminalia alata* Heyne ex Roth | Combretaceae | Asin | Bk | Liver complaints | Tree |
| 873. | *Terminalia arjuna* (Roxb. ex DC.) Wight and Arn. | Combretaceae | Arjun | Bk | Diabetes, heart ailments | Tree |
| 874. | *Terminalia bellirica* (Gaertner) Roxb. | Combretaceae | Bahera | Fr | Cough, cold, constipation, asthma | Tree |
| 875. | *Terminalia chebula* Retz. | Combretaceae | Haira | Fr, sd | Cough, cold, bronchitis, pneumonia | Tree |
| 876. | *Thalictrum foliolosum* DC. | Ranunculaceae | Mameera | Rt | Fever, eye complaints | Herb |
| 877. | *Thalictrum javanicum* Blume | Ranunculaceae | Kirmoli, mameeri | Rt | Ophthalmia, fever | Herb |

*Contd...*

**Appendix Contd...**

| Sl.No. | Species | Family | Local Name | Plant Used | Important Uses | Life Form |
|---|---|---|---|---|---|---|
| 878. | *Thalictrum minus* L. | Ranunculaceae | | Rt | Eye disorder, fever | Herb |
| 879. | *Thalictrum secundum* Edgew. | Ranunculaceae | Peelijari | Rt | Stomach disorder | Herb |
| 880. | *Themeda arundinacea* (Roxb.) Ridley | Poaceae | Kulpura | Rt | Fever | Herb |
| 881. | *Thespesia lampas* (Cav.) Dalzell and Gibson | Malvaceae | Ban kapasi | Rt | Gonorrhoea | Un Sh |
| 882. | *Thlaspi arvense* L. | Brassicaceae | | Wp | Bodyache, wounds, gonorhoea | Herb |
| 883. | *Thymus linearis* Benth. | Lamiaceae | Ban ajwain | Wp | Eye disorder, liver complaints, stomachache | Herb |
| 884. | *Thysanolaena maxima* (Roxb.) Kuntze | Poaceae | Naktura | Sd | Abortifacient | Herb |
| 885. | *Tinospora cordifolia* L. | Menispermaceae | Giloei | Wp | Asthma, aphrodisiac, bone fracture, jaundice | Herb |
| 886. | *Tinospora sinensis* (Lour.) Merr. | Menispermaceae | Giloei | Wh | Eye disorder, urinary complaints | Wood Cl |
| 887. | *Toddalia asiatica* (L.) Lam. | Rutaceae | Chingatti, Kanj | Bk | Malarial fever, bodyache | Tree |
| 888. | *Toona ciliata* Roem. | Meliaceae | Tun | Bk, fr, lf | Antiseptic, bronchitis, fever, dysentery | Tree |
| 889. | *Toona serrata* (Royle) M. Roemer | Meliaceae | Pahari tun | Bk | Ulcer, boils | Tree |
| 890. | *Trachelospermum lucidum* (D. Don) Schumann | Apocynaceae | Dudhi bel | Bk | Fever, dysentery | Wood Cl |
| 891. | *Trachyspermum ammi* (L.) Sprague | Apiaceae | Ajwain | Sd | Digestive disorder | Herb |
| 892. | *Tragopogon gracilis* D. Don | Asteraceae | Gualsi | Latex | Wounds | Herb |
| 893. | *Trianthema portulacastrum* L. | Aizoaceae | Santhi | Rt | Asthma | Herb |
| 894. | *Tribulus terrestris* L. | Zygophyllaceae | Gokhru | Sd | Asthma, cough, skin eruption | Herb |

*Contd...*

**Appendix–Contd...**

| Sl.No. | Species | Family | Local Name | Plant Used | Important Uses | Life Form |
|---|---|---|---|---|---|---|
| 895. | *Trichilia connaroides* (Wight and Arn.) Bentvelzen | Meliaceae | Ban reetha | Bk, lf | Astringent, tonic | Tree |
| 896. | *Trichodesma indicum* (L.) R.Br. | Boraginaceae | Aundhi | Rt, fr | Stomachache, toothache | Herb |
| 897. | *Trichodesma zeylanicum* (Burm.) Br. | Boraginaceae | | Lf | Boils, dysentery | Herb |
| 898. | *Tricholepis glaberrima* DC. | Asteraceae | | Rt | Snake bite, skin diseases | Herb |
| 899. | *Trichosanthes anguina* L. | Cucurbitaceae | Chachinda | Rt | Intestinal worm, diarrhoea | Climb H |
| 900. | *Trichosanthes cucumerina* L. | Cucurbitaceae | Jangli chachinda | Fr | Fever, maleria | Climb H |
| 901. | *Trichosanthes tricuspidata* Lour. | Cucurbitaceae | Lal indrayan | Rt | Bronchitis, asthma, diabetes | Climb H |
| 902. | *Tridax procumbens* L. | Asteraceae | Kumra | Shoot | Wounds | Herb |
| 903. | *Trifolium pratense* L. | Fabaceae | Mithla | Rt, pod | Cough, bronchitis | Herb |
| 904. | *Trigonella corniculata* (L.) L. | Fabaceae | Ban-methi | Wp | Colic pain, diabetes | Herb |
| 905. | *Trigonella emodi* Benth. | Fabaceae | Ban-methi | Wp | Bodyache | Herb |
| 906. | *Trigonella foenum-graecum* L. | Fabaceae | Methi | Wp | Diabetes, dysentery | Herb |
| 907. | *Trillium govanianum* Wall. | Trilliaceae | | Tuber | Dysentery | Herb |
| 908. | *Triumfetta rhomboidea* Jacq. | Tiliaceae | Leswa kura | Rt | Child birth, dysentery, stomachache | Un Sh |
| 909. | *Tulipa clusiana* DC. | Liliaceae | Ghas pyaz | Bb | Snake bite | Herb |
| 910. | *Tylophora hirsuta* (Wall.) Wight and Arn. | Asclepiadaceae | Terni | Lf, rt | Cold, cough | Sh |
| 911. | *Tylophora indica* (Burm. f.) Merr. | Asclepiadaceae | | Wp | Asthma, wounds, backache | Sh |
| 912. | *Typha angustata* Bory and Chaub. | Typhaceae | | Fr | Epilepsy, madness, bleeding | Herb |

*Contd...*

**Appendix–Contd...**

| Sl.No. | Species | Family | Local Name | Plant Used | Important Uses | Life Form |
|---|---|---|---|---|---|---|
| 913. | *Ulmus wallichiana* Planchon | Ulmaceae | Mairu | Bk | Bone fracture | Tree |
| 914. | *Uraria lagopus* DC. | Fabaceae | Pithrain | Lf | Fever, dropsy | Un Sh |
| 915. | *Uraria picta* (Jacq.) Desv. ex DC. | Fabaceae | Dabra | Rt | Gonorrhoea, abdominal pain, bodyache | Un Sh |
| 916. | *Urena lobata* L. | Malvaceae | Chatkura | Rt | Bodyache, rheumatism | Un Sh |
| 917. | *Uritca hyperborea* Jacq. | Urticaceae | | Lf | Rheumatism | Herb |
| 918. | *Urtica ardens* Link. | Urticaceae | Kandali | Sd | Scietica, skin ailments, tonic | Un Sh |
| 919. | *Urtica dioica* L. | Urticaceae | Kandali | Wp | Antiseptic, jaundice, sprain, sciatica | Herb |
| 920. | *Vaccaria pyramidata* Medikus | Caryophyllaceae | Musna | Shoot | Diuretic, liver complaints | Herb |
| 921. | *Valeriana hardwickii* Wall. | Valerianaceae | Shammia | Rt | Joint pain, urinary disorder | Herb |
| 922. | *Valeriana jatamansi* Jones | Valerianaceae | Sumaya | Rh | Aphrodisiac, mental disorder | Herb |
| 923. | *Vallaris solanacea* (Roth) Kuntze | Apocynaceae | Safed bel | Latex | Sores, wounds | Wood Cl |
| 924. | *Vanda cristata* Lindley | Orchidaceae | | St, lf | Tonic | Herb |
| 925. | *Ventilago denticulata* Willd. | Rhamnaceae | Kali-bel, Raidhani | Rt | Paralytic attack | Wood Cl |
| 926. | *Vernonia anthelmintica* (L.) Willd. | Asteraceae | Ghrajiri | Lf, fr | Intestinal disorder, fever | Herb |
| 927. | *Vernonia cinerea* (L.) Lessing | Asteraceae | Kalgira | Lf | Dysentery, cough, cold | Herb |
| 928. | *Veronica revoluta* Buch.-Ham. | Asteraceae | Lampati | Wp | Blisters | Herb |
| 929. | *Vervascum chinense* (L.) Santapau | Scrophulariaceae | Gaderi-tamakhu | Lf | Stop bleeding | Herb |
| 930. | *Vervascum thapsus* L. | Scrophulariaceae | Kakri-tamakhu | Wp | Bronchitis, asthma | Herb |

*Contd...*

**Appendix–Contd...**

| Sl.No. | Species | Family | Local Name | Plant Used | Important Uses | Life Form |
|---|---|---|---|---|---|---|
| 931. | *Vetiveria zizanioides* (L.) Nash | Poaceae | Kash | Rt | Anthelmintic | Herb |
| 932. | *Viburnum cotinifolium* D. Don | Caprifoliaceae | Guya, Matyanu | Bk | Digestive troubles | Sh |
| 933. | *Viburnum grandiflorum* Wall. ex DC. | Caprifoliaceae | Thakla | Bk | Hepatic troubles | Sh |
| 934. | *Viburnum nervosum* D. Don | Caprifoliaceae | Tirnoi, Tileen | Bk | Menorrhagia | Sh |
| 935. | *Vigna mungo* (L.) Hepper | Fabaceae | Urd | Sd | Indigestion | Herb |
| 936. | *Vigna radiata* (L.) Wilcz. | Fabaceae | Moong | Sd | Indigestion | Herb |
| 937. | *Vincetoxicum hirundinaria* Medikus | Asclepiadaceae | Bagmirchi | Rt | Snake bite | Un Sh |
| 938. | *Viola betonicifolia* J. Smith | Violaceae | Vanafsa | Wp | Skin, blood diseases, fever, cough cold | Herb |
| 939. | *Viola bioflora* L. | Violaceae | Vanafsa | Fl, lf | Bronchitis | Herb |
| 940. | *Viola canescens* Wall. | Violaceae | Vanafsa | Lf, fl | Bronchitis, asthma, wounds, malaria | Herb |
| 941. | *Viola pilosa* Blume | Violaceae | Vanafsa | Wp | Jaundice, headache, cough | Herb |
| 942. | *Viscum album* L. | Loranthaceae | | Wp | Bodyache | Sh |
| 943. | *Viscum articulatum* Burm. | Loranthaceae | Budu | Lf | Cut, wounds | Sh |
| 944. | *Vitex negundo* L. | Verbenaceae | Shiwali | St, fl, lf | Arthritis, sprains | Sh |
| 945. | *Vitis vinifera* L. | Vitaceae | Angoor | Shoot, fr | Blood purification, tonic, child dysentery | Wood Cl |
| 946. | *Waldhemia glabra* (Decne) Regel. | Asteraceae | | Rt, lf, | Heart diseases, burns | Herb |
| 947. | *Waldhemia tomentosa* (Decne) Regel. | Asteraceae | | Shoot | Rheumatism | Herb |
| 948. | *Wendlandia heynei* (Roemer and Schultes) Santapau and Merchant | Rubiaceae | Udashu | Fl | Eye diseases | Tree |

Contd...

**Appendix–Contd...**

| Sl.No. | Species | Family | Local Name | Plant Used | Important Uses | Life Form |
|---|---|---|---|---|---|---|
| 949. | *Withania somnifera* (L.) Dunal | Solanaceae | Aswagandha | Lf | Urinary disorder, fever | Un Sh |
| 950. | *Woodfordia fruticosa* (L.) Kurz | Lythraceae | Dhaula | Lf, bk, fl | Tonic | Sh |
| 951. | *Wrightia arborea* (Denn.) Mabber. | Apocynaceae | Darula | Bk | Snake bite | Tree |
| 952. | *Xanthium strumarium* L. | Asteraceae | | Rt, fl, lf | Cancer, wounds, eye diseases, fever | Herb |
| 953. | *Xeromphis spinosa* (Thunb.) Keay | Rubiaceae | | Fr, rt | Malaria, dysentery, wounds | Tree |
| 954. | *Youngia japonica* (L.) DC. | Asteraceae | | Rt | Urinary complaints | Herb |
| 955. | *Yucca gloriosa* L. | Agavaceae | | Rt, lf | Asthma, bronchitis, dysentery | Sh |
| 956. | *Zanthoxylum acanthopodium* DC. | Rutaceae | Timroo, Timur | Sd, fr | Dysentery, headache, stomachache | Sh |
| 957. | *Zanthoxylum armatum* DC. | Rutaceae | Timroo, Timur | Fr, st, bk | Toothache | Sh |
| 958. | *Zingiber officinale* Roscoe | Zingiberaceae | Adu, Adrak | Rh | Headache, toothache, cough, vomiting | Herb |
| 959. | *Ziziphus mauritiana* Lam. | Rhamnaceae | Ber | Fr | Indigestion, headache | Sh |
| 960. | *Ziziphus nummularia* (Burm. f.) Wight and Arn. | Rhamnaceae | | Lf, rt | Tonic, cold, indigestion, dysentery | Sh |
| 961. | *Ziziphus oenoplia* (L.) Miller | Rhamnaceae | | Rt, st, fr | Blood purification, dysentery, indigestion | Sh |
| 962. | *Ziziphus rugosa* Lam. | Rhamnaceae | | Bk, rt, fl | Diarrhoea, dysentery, syphilis | Sh |
| 963. | *Ziziphus xylopyra* (Retz.)Willd. | Rhamnaceae | | Rt, bk | Dysentery | Sh |
| 964. | *Zornia gibbosa* Spanoghe | Fabaceae | Dwipat | Rt | Colic pain, indigestion | Herb |

Abbreviations: Rt: Root; Rh: Rhizome; Bb: Bulb; St: Stem; Fr: Fruit; Fl: Flower; Sd: Seed; Bk: Bark; Wp: Whole plant; Sh: Shrub; Wool Cl: Woody climber; Climb H: Climber herb.

# Index